Christians and the Color Line

Christians and the Color Line

Race and Religion After Divided by Faith

Edited by
J. RUSSELL HAWKINS
AND PHILLIP LUKE SINITIERE

OXFORD
UNIVERSITY PRESS

OXFORD
UNIVERSITY PRESS

Oxford University Press is a department of the University of Oxford.
It furthers the University's objective of excellence in research, scholarship,
and education by publishing worldwide.

Oxford New York
Auckland Cape Town Dar es Salaam Hong Kong Karachi
Kuala Lumpur Madrid Melbourne Mexico City Nairobi
New Delhi Shanghai Taipei Toronto

With offices in
Argentina Austria Brazil Chile Czech Republic France Greece
Guatemala Hungary Italy Japan Poland Portugal Singapore
South Korea Switzerland Thailand Turkey Ukraine Vietnam

Oxford is a registered trade mark of Oxford University Press
in the UK and certain other countries.

Published in the United States of America by
Oxford University Press
198 Madison Avenue, New York, NY 10016

© Oxford University Press 2014

All rights reserved. No part of this publication may be reproduced,
stored in a retrieval system, or transmitted, in any form or by any means,
without the prior permission in writing of Oxford University Press,
or as expressly permitted by law, by license, or under terms agreed with the
appropriate reproduction rights organization. Inquiries concerning reproduction
outside the scope of the above should be sent to the Rights Department,
Oxford University Press, at the address above.

You must not circulate this work in any other form
and you must impose this same condition on any acquirer.

Library of Congress Cataloging-in-Publication Data
Christians and the color line : race and religion after Divided by
faith / edited by J. Russell Hawkins and Phillip Luke Sinitiere.
p. cm.
ISBN 978-0-19-932950-2 (cloth : alk. paper) 1. Racism—Religious aspects—Christianity.
2. Racism—United States. 3. Race relations—Religious aspects—Christianity.
4. United States—Race relations. 5. Reconciliation—Religious aspects—Christianity.
6. Evangelicalism—United States. 7. Emerson, Michael O., 1965- Divided by faith.
I. Hawkins, J. Russell. II. Sinitiere, Phillip Luke.
BT734.2.C47 2013
277.30089—dc23
2013012428
9780199329502

1 3 5 7 9 8 6 4 2
Printed in the United States of America on acid-free paper

for Caleb and Micah,
with the hope that you will one day attend
to the task found in these pages
J. R. H.

for the faculty and staff at the College of Biblical Studies,
as we seek unity in diversity
P. L. S.

for our co-participants in the Power of Race
in American Religion Seminar
J. R. H. & P. L. S.

Contents

Foreword—MICHAEL O. EMERSON — ix

Contributor List — xiii

Acknowledgments — xv

Introduction—J. RUSSELL HAWKINS & PHILLIP LUKE SINITIERE — 1

SECTION ONE: *Looking Back – Failures and Successes in Erasing the Color Line*

1. Neoevangelicalism and the Problem of Race in Postwar America—MILES S. MULLIN, II — 15

2. Healing the Mystical Body: Catholic Attempts to Overcome the Racial Divide in Chicago, 1930–1948—KAREN JOY JOHNSON — 45

3. "Glimmers of Hope": Progressive Evangelicals and Racism, 1965–2000—BRANTLEY W. GASAWAY — 72

4. "Buttcheek to Buttcheek in the Pew": Interracial Relationalism in a Mennonite Congregation, 1957–2010—TOBIN MILLER SHEARER — 100

5. Still Divided by Faith? Evangelical Religion and the Problem of Race in America, 1977–2010—RYON J. COBB — 128

SECTION TWO: *Looking Forward – Possibilities for Overcoming the Color Line*

6. Worshipping to Stay the Same: Avoiding the Local to Maintain Solidarity—MARK T. MULDER   143

7. Beyond Body Counts: Sex, Individualism, and the Segregated Shape of Twentieth-Century Evangelicalism—EDWARD J. BLUM   161

8. Color-Conscious Structure-Blind Assimilation: How Asian American Christians Can Unintentionally Maintain the Racial Divide—JERRY Z. PARK   178

9. Knotted Together: Identity and Community in a Multiracial Church—ERICA RYU WONG   205

10. Much Ado About Nothing? Rethinking the Efficacy of Multiracial Churches for Racial Reconciliation—KORIE L. EDWARDS   231

Theological Afterword: The Call to Blackness in American Christianity—DARRYL SCRIVEN   255

Index   275

Foreword

Michael O. Emerson

I REMEMBER THE first few years of our marriage, while I was still an undergraduate student at Loyola of Chicago, my wife and I attended the historic Moody Church on the near north side of Chicago. Whether we took the EL or drove, we had to walk a few blocks to get to the church. Each week, our path took us directly past an African American church, only a block from Moody Church.

I was naïve about most things then. New to Christianity, I thought it odd that we should walk by one body of believers to worship with another congregation but a block away. I found it even odder that one body of believers was all black and the other, all white. At that time, I had no idea about US church history or even a firm grasp of race relations and inequality. I simply had an uneasy feeling that something seemed far from right.

I also was puzzled that I never heard anyone else in the two churches question such an arrangement. My wife and I would gather with our fellow Moody worshippers, and we would learn of God's love for all people, the God who saw no differences between people, who said we are all equal in the Creator's eyes. I also learned how we are called to love all people. I never had a single conversation with any of the parishioners at the church a block down the street, but I imagined that they were learning the very same realities about God. After our respective services, we would all pour out of our separate churches, while talking with our respective church friends. And away we would go until we returned later in the week, living our racially separate lives.

I couldn't shake the thought that somehow this just wasn't right. The whole pattern seemed to contradict what I was learning in church. But I was new to the faith, and others, much more experienced and mature in their belief, seemed untroubled. So I pushed such thoughts aside, as best as I could.

I did pretty well at pushing such thoughts aside for nearly a decade. I went on to get my Ph.D. in sociology, and took my first position at a university in central Minnesota. My wife and I (and now two young children) lived in what at that time was the whitest metropolitan area in the United States. We bought a little place in a growing suburban area filled with young white families like ours. We found a nice church and made many friends. It was, we thought, the perfect life. Yet, what we didn't realize at the time—and probably wouldn't have been bothered by even if we had—was that our community, church, and neighborhood that made up this "perfect life" were entirely white.

But then our lives got turned around real good. A deacon in our church—my wife's uncle—invited me to attend a Promise Keepers event in Boulder, Colorado. At that time, this all-men's event was becoming popular within the evangelical Christian world. I agreed to attend. While there, my life changed dramatically. Presenters addressed a wide range of spiritual topics at the conference, but I kept hearing messages about race. "I will anger you by that which is not a nation." "Race is a big deal in this nation." "I am calling you to understand what grieves me." "I am calling you to be part of the solution." I thought I was losing my mind. The speakers were not speaking these things. But I was hearing them.

I often liken the experience that began at that Promise Keepers meeting to someone physically picking me up and gluing me to a surf board. Unable to control the direction I was being taken, away I went on a rushing ride. I became consumed with understanding race. I read whatever I could find, including every book on race and religion that I could get my hands on. I remember coming home from Colorado and telling my wife that, although I didn't know how, I was sure that our lives were going to change substantially.

And they did. First, a new position opened up at the college that my wife had attended in the Minneapolis–St. Paul area. In the job description for the advertised position, it listed what the ideal candidate would be able to teach. It just so happened to list each of my specialties. I knew the job was meant for me. At that moment, I also knew *how* our lives were going to change.

I asked my five-month pregnant wife to sit down for the news. "Remember how I said to you a few weeks back that we need to get ready, our lives are going to change somehow?" She nodded yes. "Well, here is what it is. I don't know how I know. I simply can tell you that I know with a certainty that I have never known something before. When I accept that new job and we move, we are to move to a neighborhood where we are the minority, the racial minority. We are to send our children to school where they are the minority. We are to worship in a church where we are the minority. I don't know why, only that we are supposed to do so."

My wife stared at me as the meaning of what I had said for our lives sunk in. Then she burst into tears.

That night she wrote me a long letter, openly wondering if I had lost touch with reality. Had I thought through what I said, what it would mean for our children, for our planned-out lives, for our dreams? If this was really something we were to do, wouldn't she know it too?

I was torn up inside. I knew what we were to do, and I knew that it sounded crazy—I even knew it was incredibly presumptuous of me to expect my wife to go along with such a dramatic life change simply on the faith that I had somehow heard what we were supposed to do.

But I dared not follow through, being certain as I was that we were to do this. I only wished I knew why, other than some vague notion that we shouldn't continue to be part of the separation of people by the human-created category called race.

To make a long story short, through immense trials, marital strains, and miracles, we did make the move to an area of Minneapolis where we were the minority, we did enroll our children in a school where they were the minority, and we did join a church where we were the minority.

We went through culture shock (understatement). Yet over time, our networks of friends changed. Our views of life changed. Our tastes changed. We saw something—racial inequality and discrimination—that we had before been sure no longer existed. We also saw our own prejudices, something we thought for sure we did not have. When we returned for visits to our former white world, we would now experience culture shock in the reverse. Separate worlds these were, that much was starkly clear.

At the same time as these life changing events were occurring, I was working on a research project with several other colleagues, studying evangelical Christians in the United States. As I went around the country interviewing mostly black and white Christians, listening to their stories, I was catapulted back to that block in Chicago—the black church at one end, the white church at the other. Similar spaces, separate worlds. Same faith, divergent perspectives on their faith.

Without the transformations that we were encountering in our personal lives, I would not have grasped the divergences that I was hearing as black and white Christians described their lives to me. I would have dismissed them, pushed them aside, explained them away. But here it was, so clearly different in ways that I now had to wrestle with to understand fully. That wrestling produced *Divided by Faith* and subsequent works including *United by Faith* and *People of the Dream*.

Writing *Divided by Faith* made me physically ill. It felt like the final nail that was breaking us from the world that I had known and trusted. The world of my friends and family and heroes. I didn't want to write the book; but I had to.

I continue to stand in utter amazement that the book has been an ongoing point of discussion, contestation, and use since its publication. At least a few times a month I get an e-mail from someone saying that the book has changed his or her life or his or her church's practices.

When we get these messages, my wife and I often look at each other and simply smile. The smiles are code for what we feel deeply: our lives and the lives of our children have been so enriched, so vastly improved since we made our life changes—changes we continue to live—that to hear such praise for the book seems like an embarrassment of riches.

I am expecting that this volume will be similarly useful. I see it as a starting point for a new generation of scholars and practitioners. The world, we know, changes. Our nation grows more racially and ethnically diverse with each year. How we navigate these changes will go far in shaping the vitality of our future and the legacy we leave behind.

If you allow them to, the chapters that follow will challenge you. Composed by scholars from multiple disciplines, the essays found in *Christians and the Color Line* examine the history of racial division (and occasional unity) within the Church, while analyzing the racial difficulties that American congregations continue to grapple with today. This volume comes at a moment of opportunity to move toward an inclusive, united, multiracial Church . Read it; ponder its claims; discuss it with others. And perhaps in doing so, we can move closer to the day that evangelicals of different races are no longer divided by faith.

Contributor List

EDWARD J. BLUM is an associate professor of history at San Diego State University. His books include (with Paul Harvey) *The Color of Christ: The Son of God and the Saga of Race in America* (2012) and *W. E. B. Du Bois, American Prophet* (2007).

RYON J. COBB is a post-doctoral fellow in the Roybal Institute on Aging at the University of Southern California.

KORIE L. EDWARDS is an associate professor in the Department of Sociology at The Ohio State University. Her work focuses on race and religion in the United States. She has authored several articles and books including *Against All Odds: The Struggle for Racial Integration in Religious Organizations* (2005) and *The Elusive Dream: The Power of Race in Interracial Churches* (2008).

BRANTLEY W. GASAWAY is an assistant professor in the Department of Religion at Bucknell University, where his research and teaching focuses on religion in American public life, politics, and law. He has published articles concerning the political implications of evangelical epistemology, evangelicals and environmentalism, and religious architecture.

J. RUSSELL HAWKINS is an assistant professor of humanities and history in the John Wesley Honors College at Indiana Wesleyan University. His research explores the relationship between evangelical religion and race in recent American history.

KAREN JOY JOHNSON is an assistant professor of history at Wheaton College. Her research is on race, religion, and gender in the urban world.

MARK T. MULDER is an associate professor of sociology and director of the urban studies minor at Calvin College in Grand Rapids, Michigan.

MILES S. MULLIN, II is an assistant professor of Church History at the J. Dalton Havard School for Theological Studies, Southwestern

Seminary's campus in Houston, Texas. Although he maintains broad historical and theological interests, his research focuses on twentieth-century religion and American culture.

DARRYL SCRIVEN was trained in philosophy of religion at Florida A&M University and Purdue University. He has held faculty appointments at Wilberforce University, Southern University, and Tuskegee University and is the author of *A Dealer Of Old Clothes: Philosophical Conversations with David Walker* (2007).

TOBIN MILLER SHEARER is an associate professor of history at the University of Montana where he also directs the African American Studies Program. His most recent book is *Daily Demonstrators: The Civil Rights Movement in Mennonite Homes and Sanctuaries* (2010).

PHILLIP LUKE SINITIERE is professor of history at the College of Biblical Studies, a multiethnic school located in Houston's Mahatma Gandhi District. A scholar of American religion and culture, he is co-author of *Holy Mavericks: Evangelical Innovators and the Spiritual Marketplace* (2009) and co-editor of *Protest and Propaganda: W. E. B. Du Bois,* The Crisis *and American History* (2013).

JERRY Z. PARK is an associate professor of sociology at Baylor University. He has published numerous academic articles on religion, race, Asian Americans, work attitudes, and civic engagement.

ERICA RYU WONG received her Ph.D. in sociology from the University of Michigan. Her research focuses on the intersection and interaction of religious and racial/ethnic identities and diversity in organizations.

Acknowledgments

THE PRODUCTION OF scholarship often takes place in the quiet confines of an office or the stillness of an archive. But occasionally the opportunity comes along to collaborate with accomplished scholars and like-minded colleagues to produce something that far surpasses anything that could have been achieved individually. Such was our experience editing *Christians and the Color Line*. We happily thank the contributors to this volume and are pleased to present their impressive essays and collective reflections to a wider audience. We especially thank Michael O. Emerson. Michael's generous spirit has encouraged many, including us. Not only did we benefit from his wisdom and insight at every stage of this book's development but also from his scholarship beyond *Divided by Faith*, which has continued to shape our work and influence our research.

We also gladly acknowledge both the individuals and the institutions that facilitated the completion of this book. In 2010, the John Wesley Honors College at Indiana Wesleyan University sponsored *Divided by Faith*: A Decade Retrospective, which celebrated the ten-year anniversary of Michael Emerson and Christian Smith's influential book. The majority of the chapters in this anthology were first presented as papers at that conference. While all the faculty and staff of the honors college played significant roles in supporting the *Divided by Faith* conference, a particular note of gratitude is owed to David L. Riggs and Sara Scheunemann. Without David's administrative support and Sara's logistical expertise, the conference—and therefore the volume you are currently reading—would have never transpired. Additional financial support and encouragement for the *Divided by Faith* conference at was generously provided by Henry Smith, David Wright, Darlene Bressler, Wayne Schmidt, and Jerry Pattengale.

When the time came to transform conference papers into book chapters, Donnie and Marcia Sinitiere graciously offered their kitchen table and guest rooms for a collaborative weekend of editing in Houston. Their hospitality (and Marcia's gumbo!) was a welcomed and much appreciated gift.

Cynthia Read at Oxford University Press has been supportive of this volume from its proposal to its completion, and Marcela Maxfield and Smita Gupta's help and guidance in bringing this book to press has been indispensable and invaluable. Cynthia, Marcela, and Smita have made our duties easier at every step in the process.

Our spouses and children also warrant special recognition. Without our families' love, support, and permission to miss occasional weekend activities and bedtime routines, this volume would have never been completed. Jenni, Matthew, Alexander, Madeline, Nathaniel and Elijah; and Kristi, Caleb, and Micah, thank you for making this book possible.

Finally, we would like thank our colleagues and friends from the Power of Race in American Religion Seminar: Tanya Brice, Ryon Cobb, Bruce Fields, Paul Gordiejew, Luke Harlow, Kimberly Hill, Karen Johnson, Rebecca Kim, Mark Mulder, Jerry Park, Julie Park, Regina Shands Stoltzfus, and Erica Wong. Convened at Calvin College and led by Michael Emerson during the summer of 2010, this memorable three-week seminar was the breeding ground for many of the ideas that found their way into the subsequent pages of this book. Joel Carpenter and the Seminars at Calvin staff facilitated and made possible this initial gathering, and we are profoundly grateful to Joel and his staff for making possible a short weekend reunion in mid-2011. The discussions, conversations, meals, and prayers during the course of the seminar challenged and encouraged us all—and continue to inspire.

Christians and the Color Line

Introduction

J. Russell Hawkins & Phillip Luke Sinitiere

AN UNEXPECTED TREND has recently emerged in America's supposedly "post-racial" society: a preponderance of white evangelicals in the United States is suddenly showing interest in embracing racial diversity. Given conservative white Protestants' history regarding matters of race—ranging from apathetic disinterestedness to open hostility—it is surprising to witness a significant number of evangelicals today celebrate and pursue racial inclusiveness. Indeed, a new era of multiethnic and multiracial sensibilities seems to be dawning across the American evangelical landscape, manifesting itself in a myriad of ways. Consider just a few anecdotal examples of this attitudinal sea change that is currently pulsating throughout evangelical communities. Evangelical luminary John Piper—a self-proclaimed "former racist"—pens a book on the need for racial diversity in the Church and offers it to readers at no charge to ensure that none will be hindered from hearing the call to "Christ-exalting ethnic diversity."[1] Bill Hybels, a pioneering advocate for the "homogenous unit principle" that intentionally avoided congregational diversity in order to accelerate church growth, now preaches against white privilege from his Willow Creek pulpit and has committed his mega-church to becoming a multiracial body of believers.[2] John Perkins, a black civil rights activist who was beaten by white supremacists and shunned by white Christians four decades ago in his home state of Mississippi, is today a bona fide evangelical celebrity. Perkins is routinely sought after as a speaker at evangelical colleges and universities—seven of which have bestowed upon him honorary doctorates—and he was the inspiration for a song about love and reconciliation recorded by the popular Christian band Switchfoot (Perkins even had a cameo in the song's music video).[3]

It is not just a group of isolated individual evangelicals who are participating in and celebrating this new wave of cross-racial engagement. In 2012, America's largest Protestant body, the staunchly evangelical Southern Baptist Convention (SBC), elected Fred Luter as the first African American president of that predominately white denomination. A convention created in the nineteenth century in part to preserve slavery now has the descendent of slaves as its president—a situation unimaginable only a few generations ago. In the fanfare accompanying Luter's election, white evangelicals demonstrated further evidence that they are becoming sensitive to the importance of racial diversity. In the nominating speech for Luter's presidency, Baptist minister David Crosby noted that the SBC is "already a convention with great diversity in our membership ranks and our churches. If we are faithful in our work this diversity will continue to grow.... We need Pastor Fred at the head of the table, helping us understand our mission field and our mission. It is time to tap the great resource of his experience, wisdom and passion for this wider purpose."[4]

Christian publishing houses, likewise, have tapped into this growing evangelical interest in racial and cultural diversity, releasing more titles devoted to the topic of racial justice in the past decade than at any time in evangelicalism's history.[5] With so much attention to matters of diversity, it comes as little surprise that in one recent survey nearly 70 percent of American evangelical churches responded that they would like to be racially and culturally diverse.[6] To be sure, the old adage about eleven o'clock Sunday morning being the most segregated hour in the United States remains true. But the proclaimed desire among a sizeable number of American evangelicals to change this reality is growing.

Undoubtedly, some of this newfound evangelical attention to racial diversity is attributable to a small book that had a significant impact in evangelical circles upon its publication in 2000. *Divided by Faith: Evangelical Religion and the Problem of Race in America* (New York: Oxford University Press), written by sociologists and self-professing evangelicals Michael O. Emerson and Christian Smith, questioned the catalytic power of conservative Protestantism for racial unity. Even more provocatively, Emerson and Smith's research argued that evangelical Christianity in America actually exacerbated the country's racial divisions rather than acting to overcome them.[7] The book was instantly recognized by Emerson and Smith's academic peers as groundbreaking and worthy of acclaim; in 2001, the

Society for the Scientific Study of Religion bestowed upon Emerson and Smith's study the Distinguished Book Award, testifying to the scholarship that undergirded Emerson and Smith's work. But award-winning books are published every year without garnering much attention outside the academy. *Divided by Faith*'s unique achievement was that its influence quickly spread beyond the traditional scholarly community and found its way into the evangelical subculture. Indeed, since Emerson and Smith's book graced the cover of *Christianity Today*—the flagship magazine of contemporary American evangelicalism—in the fall of 2000, *Divided by Faith* has been a mainstay of countless church discussion groups across the country. Several evangelical denominations have provided copies of the book to all of their clergy and have made *Divided by Faith* required reading for denominational planning sessions. In a 2010 *Time* magazine article, Bill Hybels even compared reading *Divided by Faith* to having a second conversion experience and credited the book for making him aware for the first time of the problem of race in the evangelical Church.[8] Clearly, *Divided by Faith* was not a typical academic study.

Divided by Faith: Summarizing the Findings

Divided by Faith captivated evangelical readers because of Emerson and Smith's cogent diagnosis of why Sunday morning remains so deeply segregated in evangelical churches. The two sociologists began their study by asserting that American society is "racialized" and defined a racialized society as one "wherein race matters profoundly for differences in life experiences, life opportunities, and social relationships."[9] What Emerson and Smith intended by this definition is that, despite the legislative gains produced by the civil rights movement of the 1960s, race in the United States continues to be a factor—in some cases, a decisive factor—in determining the social rewards or penalties that individuals reap or are assessed. Significantly, Emerson and Smith asserted that racialization is dynamic, fluid, and changes over time. Accordingly, *Divided by Faith* argued that even without explicit state sanction race in the twenty-first century continues to influence such things as where we attend school, where we live, who we marry, what jobs we get, the amount of money those jobs pay, the quality of health care we receive, the type of treatment we are afforded by the criminal justice system, who we are friends with, the type of customer service we get, what music we listen to, what television shows we watch, and where we attend church.[10] In other words, over the past half-century, racialization in the United States has undergone a transformation from blatant, overt displays of discrimination often epitomized by burning crosses and hooded Klansmen to covert and implicit forms of discrimination that exist largely unnoticed within the structures of American society. It is possible, therefore, for individuals to harbor no personal feelings of prejudice toward members of a different race and yet still participate in systems that are inherently discriminatory. And according to Emerson and Smith, this blindness toward the present manifestation of racialization is precisely the position that most white American evangelicals occupy today.

Emerson and Smith arrived at this conclusion by analyzing the results of national surveys that they conducted over the phone with more than 2,500 Americans. Not content to dissect numbers on spreadsheets, however, the two sociologists took to the road to hold additional extensive face-to-face interviews of nearly two hundred evangelicals in twenty-three states. From these interviews in living rooms and coffee shops across the country, Emerson and Smith assembled "a mass of rich, qualitative, contextualized, nationally representative data."[11] They discovered that on the issue of race in the United States, the majority of white evangelicals hold some combination of three predominate views: (i) racial problems are the result of sinful individuals who harbor personal prejudices; (ii) the cause of racial tensions can be traced back to racial groups such as African Americans attempting to make isolated incidents of prejudice between individuals into broader group issues; and (iii) the problem of race in America is simply nonexistent and is a "fabrication" put forward by minority groups, liberals, the media, or the government.[12] Through their surveys and interviews, therefore, Emerson and Smith found that most white evangelicals either did not accept that there was a problem of race in America, or, if they did concede that racism and racialization still existed, they attributed it simply to sinful individuals who needed to repent of their actions and feelings. What is immediately recognizable in these responses is the fact that white evangelicals are apparently unable or unwilling to accept that race continues to profoundly impact the lives of Americans of color through systemic and structural means.

Emerson and Smith proceeded to suggest why white evangelicals are blind to the racialization of American society. In their analysis, the two sociologists argued that white evangelicals are more individualistic, relational, and antistructural than other Americans *and that their theology has contributed to the manifestation of these characteristics.* Unlike African Americans who experience personal and structural forms of discrimination daily, the vast majority of white evangelicals simply do not have these experiences. Lack of personal experience with discrimination in a racialized society causes white evangelicals to deny racialization even exists. And, most compellingly, their theological commitments rooted in freewill accountable individualism along with their racial isolation from minority groups causes white evangelicals not only to miss the deeper effects of a racialized society but also to reproduce these effects. Emerson and Smith assert:

> Ultimately, such a [individualistic] perspective effectively reproduces racialization. Because its existence is not recognized, action is not taken to overcome it. Attempts at corrective action, perhaps by black Christians, may be countered by white evangelicals because such action simply seems wrong from their vantage point. . . . We stand at a divide. White evangelicals' cultural tools and racial isolation direct them to see the world individualistically and as a series of discrete incidents. They also direct them to desire a color-blind society. Black evangelicals tend to see the racial world very differently. Ironically, evangelicalism's cultural tools lead people in different social and geographical realities to assess the race problem in divergent and nonreconciliatory ways. This large gulf in understanding is perhaps part of the race problem's core, and most certainly contributes to the entrenchment of the racialized society.[13]

Individualistic theology, nurtured in isolation from those who most acutely feel the effects of a racialized society, causes white evangelicals to be blind and insensitive to the realities of their brothers and sisters of color. Thus, this spiritualized individualism persists in keeping American Protestant Christians divided along racial lines. This argument is the crux of *Divided by Faith*. And this provocative and compelling argument has fostered intense discussion and debate within the evangelical community since its publication. Given the ever-shifting nature of America's racial and ethnic landscape, *Divided by Faith* is poised to have continued importance for years to come.

Christians and the Color Line: Race and Religion after Divided by Faith

In October 2010, the John Wesley Honors College at Indiana Wesleyan University hosted a conference commemorating the tenth anniversary of *Divided by Faith*'s publication. At this conference a multidisciplinary collection of scholars offered papers that both complemented and challenged Emerson and Smith's findings. True to the spirit of *Divided by Faith*, this gathering permeated the boundaries of a traditional academic conference by drawing in church practitioners who eagerly discussed how they might implement the presenters' research in diagnosing and overcoming racial divides in their own congregations.

Birthed out of the papers presented at the *Divided by Faith* anniversary conference, the present volume seeks to achieve the same standard of scholarly rigor and broad accessibility that was the hallmark of Emerson and Smith's original study. Written from diverse disciplinary perspectives, each chapter in this collection has a common starting point in *Divided by Faith* but analyzes Emerson and Smith's findings to different ends. Some of the essays bolster Emerson and Smith's arguments while others complicate *Divided by Faith*'s claims. Still other chapters explore new areas of research that have opened up in the years since *Divided by Faith* first appeared. Regardless of the respective ways they interact with Emerson and Smith's original thesis, the rigorous and judicious scholarship put forth in every chapter of *Christians and the Color Line* advances our understanding of the interplay between race and religion in the United States.

The authors in this volume have grappled with the complicated entanglement of race and religion in American history and contemporary society. As readers will see, the essays found in this collection contest claims that a post-racial era has arrived and yet also document changes in America's racialized religious order. Many of the chapters tackle various aspects of the black–white divide within American Christianity, while others address questions surrounding Asian American Christianity. Like any essay collection, *Christians and the Color Line* does not include all possible topics and issues considered germane to racialized religion. Instead, it further opens the door for continued critical engagement with additional dimensions of racialized American Christianity such as class, ethnicity, Latino religion, and immigration.

Following this introduction, the book's chapters are separated into two sections. The chapters in the first section expound on and complicate the history of American evangelicalism and race as portrayed in *Divided by Faith*. In the first chapter, Miles S. Mullin, II, provides an extensive survey of neoevangelical periodicals from the movement's formative period in the postwar era. Mullin uses these newspaper and magazine sources to explain how neoevangelical leaders were forced to embrace an individualistic and gradualist approach to racial equality for the sake of the movement's unity. This moderate approach toward race relations in neoevangelicalism's nascent state, Mullin suggests, planted the seeds for the individualistic and relational response to calls for racial equality that have blossomed in evangelical churches today.

If the diffused, decentralized polity of neoevangelicalism was partially to blame for the entrenchment of broad individualistic trends in the movement, Karen Joy Johnson demonstrates in chapter 2 that even a centralized, top-down approach to race relations could not guarantee racial egalitarianism in ecclesiastical communities. Using an interracial movement that took place within the Catholic Church in Chicago as her case study, Johnson documents the efforts of a group of Catholic women to overcome the color line in Chicago in the middle of the twentieth century. A central finding of Johnson's narrative is that extensive cross-racial exposure allowed white Catholics to begin to see racialized structures of discrimination that existed in American society in ways unavailable to their white peers.

In the third chapter, Brantley W. Gasaway continues the theme of alternate possibilities born from interracial exchange by tracing a different strand of evangelicals than those highlighted by Mullin. Although the vast majority of evangelicals held to individualistic explanations for racial inequality and offered gradualist, if not simplistic, ideas for correcting racial ills, Gasaway demonstrates that a minority group of progressive white evangelicals saw the problem of race being as equally tied to structural issues as it was to personal prejudices. As Gasaway argues in this chapter, these progressive evangelicals possessed a broader, structural conception of racial sin that, similar to Johnson's Catholic women, was due in part to experiences they had with African Americans. These first-hand experiences allowed Gasaway's subjects to offer a structural critique of the problem of race that moved beyond the individualistic notions of their conservative white coreligionists.

Tobin Miller Shearer follows Gasaway's lead in the fourth chapter and provides a narrative analyzing one suburban Chicago congregation's historical struggle with issues of race. Shearer suggests that, contrary to causing racial division as suggested in Emerson and Smith's research, the cross-racial relationalism that marked this particular congregation actually fostered healthy interracial networks and provided a framework for identifying and critiquing systematic and structural sin. In this way, Shearer posits that establishing and nurturing cross-racial relationships at the individual level may ultimately yield a corporate response to the problem of race that transcends individualism.

Ryon J. Cobb's survey of white evangelical explanations of racial inequality through 2010 is the final chapter in the first section. Despite the fact that their attention to racial diversity has grown exponentially in recent years, Cobb argues that white evangelicals remain more individualistic in their understanding of racial inequality than any other group of Americans. Given that hyperindividualism was at the heart of Emerson and Smith's explanation for the racial divide in the evangelical church, Cobb's findings hint that the road to racial unity remains long indeed for American evangelicals.

The second set of chapters pick up where Emerson and Smith left off with *Divided by Faith* in 2000. This section consists of essays that explain both how evangelicals might contribute to overcoming the problem of race by embracing a multiracial church model and how evangelicals' persistent individualism continues to create problems within multiracial churches. Mark T. Mulder begins this section with a chapter that surveys the worship practices of churches. Mulder's year-long study of congregational worship services concludes that the racially isolated nature of American churches (both evangelical and nonevangelical) is unintentionally encouraged by an overriding desire to avoid potential conflicts on Sunday mornings. Mulder finds that the homogeneity of American churches is reinforced not only by the substance of worship services but also by the patterns of those gatherings. Mulder suggests that churches interested in becoming racially diverse must begin to recognize and challenge the unarticulated desire for corporate peace that undergirds most worship services.

In chapter 7, Edward J. Blum examines where, why, and how black and white evangelicals historically occupied the same worship space but were, ironically, divided based on religious arguments. Blum shows that despite the historical white anxiety and fear about black and white miscegenation, the growing number of multiracial families sound a hopeful note for the future of multiracial congregations. Blum concludes that the historical meanings ascribed to black and white physical bodies may be redeemed as evangelicals reconsider what it means to participate in the multicolored corporate body of Christ.

Jerry Z. Park specifically considers Asian Americans' role in the multiracial church movement in the eighth chapter. Surveying Asian American demographics, Park finds that most Asian Americans who participate in multiracial churches are highly skilled, highly educated beneficiaries of particular immigration policies and familial networks. However, Park argues that many white congregants of multiracial churches view their Asian American coreligionists as "model minorities" who advanced in American society solely as a result of hard work and determination, ignoring the structural factors that also contributed to their success. In this way, Park asserts that Asian American Christians can actually unintentionally help maintain racial divides by allowing churches to have "color diversity" without critiquing the deeper structural systems at the heart of American society's racialization. Park argues that it is incumbent upon Asian Americans in multiracial churches to use their position to speak and act on the behalf of other racial minorities who continue to be impeded by America's racialized structures.

In chapter 9, Erica Wong problematizes our understanding of multiracial congregations. Drawn from her study of multiracial churches, Wong argues that it is possible for multiracial congregations to exist without significant cross-racial interaction among church members. Wong suggests that for a multiracial church to reap the full benefits of its diversity, the cross-racial relationships within the congregation must be nurtured and encouraged. Without intentionality in the organizational vision and leadership style of multiracial churches, Wong asserts, these congregations can reproduce racial isolation rather than bridging racial divides.

Concluding the second section, Korie Edwards calls into question the efficacy of multiracial church movements for racial justice. In Edwards's analysis, multiracial churches overemphasize interracial relations at the expense of critiquing structural inequalities. Edwards concludes that until multiracial churches combine their desire for racial diversity on Sunday morning with a desire for racial justice throughout society, these congregations will ultimately produce little, if any, societal change for the people of color who attend them.

Finally, philosopher Darryl Scriven's theological afterword is a powerful coda to this collection and builds on the volume's historical reflection and sociological analysis of evangelicalism's race problem. Scriven draws from recent scholarship on racialized religion to document the historical development of white evangelicals' race problem and to demonstrate how everyday actions—while well-meaning and rooted in white evangelicals' commitment to Jesus and the Bible—subtly reinforce patterns of discrimination through the persistence of white privilege. Saddled with centuries of privilege, Scriven argues that white evangelicals' purported love of neighbor can only be realized by embracing ontological blackness as an act of Christian unity.

As Michael Emerson and Christian Smith suggested in *Divided by Faith*, the most realistic strategy for bringing about constructive change on matters of racial diversity in American evangelicalism starts with "engaging in more serious reflection on race-relations issues, in dialogue with educated others." These dialogues "ought adequately to account for the complex of factors that generate and perpetuate the problems, and then faithfully, humbly, carefully, and cooperatively work against this." Emerson and Smith concede that this vision for change is a tall order, something that "will require attention to multiple factors—from historical forces to subcultural tools to the very organization of American religion" but that "educated, sacrificial, realistic efforts made in faith across racial lines can help us move toward a more just, equitable and peaceful society."[14] Our hope is that this volume contributes to that end.

Notes

1. John Piper, *Bloodlines: Race, Cross, and the Christian* (Wheaton, IL: Crossway, 2011). Piper's confession to be a former racist appeared in the article, "I Was a Racist," *ChristianityToday.com*, September 21, 2011, accessed July 11, 2012, http://www.christianitytoday.com/ct/2011/septemberweb-only/john-piper-racism-bloodlines-excerpt.html. Piper's free version of his book and exultation to Christians to read it can be found on his website: http://www.desiringgod.org/blog/posts/download-bloodlines-for-free.
2. David Van Biema, "Can Megachurches Bridge the Racial Divide?" *Time*, January 11, 2010.
3. For his personal account of fighting against racial injustice in Mississippi, see John Perkins, *Let Justice Roll Down* (Ventura, CA: Regal Books, 1976). For more on Perkins's status in the evangelical world today, see his biography page on Seattle Pacific University's webpage for the John Perkins Center: http://www.spu.edu/depts/perkins/john-perkins/index.asp.
4. Karen L. Willoughby, "Historic: Fred Luter Elected SBC President," *BPnews.net*, June 19, 2012, accessed July 11, 2012, http://www.bpnews.net/bpnews.asp?id=38081.

5. Phillip Luke Sinitiere, "'Will the Evangelical Church Remove the Color Line?': Historical Reflections on *Divided by Faith*," *Christian Scholar's Review* (Fall 2013), 41–62.
6. *Christianity Today*, January 3, 2012.
7. Since the publication of *Divided by Faith*, Christian Smith has publically converted to Roman Catholicism. Interestingly, Smith cited evangelicalism's racial divide as one reason for his conversion. See Christian Smith, *How to Go From Being a Good Evangelical to a Committed Catholic in Ninety-Five Difficult Steps* (Eugene, OR: Cascade Books, 2011), 45–46.
8. Van Biema, "Can Megachurches Bridge the Racial Divide?"
9. Michael O. Emerson and Christian Smith, *Divided by Faith: Evangelical Religion and the Problem of Race in America* (New York: Oxford University Press, 2000), 7.
10. Ibid., 11–17, 21–68.
11. Ibid., 19.
12. Ibid., 74.
13. Ibid., 90–91.
14. Ibid., 171–172.

SECTION ONE

Looking Back – Failures and Successes in Erasing the Color Line

I

Neoevangelicalism and the Problem of Race in Postwar America

Miles S. Mullin, II

IN DIVIDED BY *Faith*, a sociological study of racial divisions in late twentieth-century America, Michael Emerson and Christian Smith demonstrate the manner in which evangelicalism unintentionally reinforces these divisions. According to their research, this division is not malicious but occurs because white evangelicals view the problem of race in America individualistically, failing to perceive the systemic and structural challenges to overcoming the racial divide. Historically, this late twentieth-century reality was far from a foregone conclusion. In fact, it might be expected that such systemic inequalities would have been addressed during the 1940s and 1950s as "the vigor of the new evangelicalism" reawakened evangelical concern for society at the same time that African Americans were bringing attention to racial problems through their own efforts.[1] Instead, during that formative period, the historic evangelical emphasis on personal conversion combined with other factors to shape a moderate, individualistic approach to race relations. This approach focused on church integration but obscured systemic and structural factors involved in racial discrimination. Moderate individualism became the dominant evangelical approach to the problem of race for the remainder of the century.[2]

During the 1940s and 1950s, American evangelicalism was undergoing a transition from an older, culturally isolated fundamentalism to a more socially engaged evangelicalism. At Wheaton College (Illinois), which often stood as a microcosm of the larger realm of the evangelical movement, this change was readily observable at many levels, including attitudes toward the problem of race. Several events related to the civil rights struggle of the 1960s, for instance, were felt across Wheaton's campus. First, in 1960, the son of David Otis Fuller, Sr., a well-known fundamentalist pastor and Wheaton trustee, publicly denounced segregation as a racist practice, a "vestige of slavery" that demanded elimination.[3] Second, by 1965, students had organized a chapter of the NAACP on campus. And third, two Wheaton students had been assaulted while participating in the Selma March for African American voting rights in Alabama. While not insignificant, these occurrences at Wheaton did not represent an organized, coherent, social effort toward the achievement of African American equality either at the college or within the larger evangelical movement. Contrary to the hopes of some, a unified assault on a racism that was manifested in the systematic exclusion of African Americans from the full benefits of citizenship was not forthcoming from evangelicals, despite the fact that their own desire to engage social problems had been reawakened in the 1940s and 1950s.[4]

Neoevangelicalism

In the years immediately following World War II, the United States entered a period that shaped the contours of American society for the rest of the century. Serious changes were afoot in American evangelicalism as well. Transitioning toward greater intellectual, cultural, and social engagement, a new spirit of cooperation and unity simultaneously drew all manner of northern conversion-oriented Protestants together. Embodied in the "Spirit of St. Louis" that resulted in the formation of the National Association of Evangelicals (NAE) in 1943, this cooperative mood attracted Wesleyans, Presbyterians, Baptists, Pentecostals, and other sorts of "born-again" Protestants.[5] Early leaders such as Harold Ockenga, Carl F. H. Henry, and E. J. Carnell envisioned a public and socially active evangelicalism that would shape culture, society, and the world by applying "the genius" of the evangelical position "constructively" to social problems.[6] Increasingly interested on recapturing the historic evangelical emphasis on social concern and action, they were careful to distinguish themselves from the Social Gospel movement of yesteryear, whose great error as they viewed it was to abandon the historic evangelical emphasis on personal conversion. For them, personal conversion was the foundational element of the Christian life, the essential part of evangelical identity. As such, personal conversion remained the focus of evangelicalism's solidarity as a cooperative movement. Hence, any successful social effort would have to connect itself to this central aspect of evangelical identity.[7]

In retrospect, it appears clear that some of the emerging leaders of the new evangelicalism desired to address the subject of racial equality but could not gain traction on the issue for a variety of reasons. First, the very nature of evangelicalism made such an effort challenging. Beyond a fairly cohesive, if not always well-articulated, theology of personal conversion and its corresponding theological commitments, the theological basis of the evangelical movement was thin. In the end what unified these mid-century evangelicals was a commitment to personal conversion as the foundational experience of the Christian life. Personal conversion was a good basis from which to launch a cooperative evangelistic effort—hence Billy Graham's popularity—and even certain types of social efforts (i.e., hunger relief efforts, orphan care, traditional rescue missions) but not one from which to address a systemic issue like racial inequality.[8] Second, the movement itself was fairly amorphous, encompassing all manner of conversion-oriented Protestants, including committed segregationists. Third, some well-established understandings of race, mingled with a peculiar biblical interpretation that supported racial segregation, percolated in the evangelical subculture.

And yet the situation of African American inequality could not be ignored forever, particularly as African Americans were doing so much on their own behalf for full inclusion as citizens. Even so, it would not be until the mid-1950s that external factors—mostly created by the efforts of African Americans themselves—would cause some evangelical leaders to begin taking a consistent stand for African American equality, pressing the issue to their constituency. Of course, their evangelical identity shaped their approach: their vision was not for a beloved community but for a beloved church. Unfortunately, the net effect of all these factors was a social gradualism that focused on interpersonal interactions while accommodating latent racism. These developments are observable in the main evangelical media venue of that day—print periodicals.

Rumblings of Concern

In the 1940s, the inequitable treatment of African Americans in the United States began to garner some attention among a few leaders affiliated with the emerging new evangelicalism. In fact, even in the midst of the war, some began to intimate that this issue needed to be addressed.

Evangelical Northern Baptist churchman Earl Pierce briefly raised the issue of race in his 1943 book, *The Church and World Conditions*, while in *The Uneasy Conscience of Modern Fundamentalism* Carl Henry attacked "racial intolerance" and "racial hatred" in a litany of "social evils" that evangelical leaders and pastors needed to address. Both books were issued by trusted evangelical publishing houses. In the 1940s, at least some evangelical leaders (writers and publishers) were beginning to raise the issue in print.[9]

In the latter half of the decade, *Moody Monthly*, *Christian Life & Times* (*CL&T*), and *HIS* magazine all published short articles on the same topic. All three were stalwart evangelical magazines, and reflected in varied ways the ethos of the new evangelicalism. *Moody Monthly*, the latest permutation in Moody Bible Institute's official periodical, represented the important Bible College constituency. Aimed at college students, *HIS* was published by InterVarsity and represented the growing evangelical emphasis on engaging the intellectual centers of society. *CL&T*, with its news reports, personal interest stories, and large photos, mirrored Henry Luce's *Life* magazine, connecting across the broad spectrum of an evangelical constituency. George Horner, who also wrote a similarly themed article for *Moody Monthly* the prior year, published an article on racial discrimination in *CL&T* in 1947. In his provocatively titled article, "Are Negroes Cursed?" Horner dealt with the racial issue in a straightforward manner. William A. Smalley did the same in his 1949 *HIS* article.[10] The articles attempted to persuade their readers, as Horner put it, that African Americans "should have a right to economic, educational, and social equality."[11]

The evangelical credentials of both Horner and Smalley were unassailable, and both would go on to impeccable evangelical careers—Smalley as a missionary linguist with the Christian and Missionary Alliance denomination and Horner as a professor at Eastern Nazarene College. Further, they embodied the intellectual engagement that was coming to characterize the new evangelicalism: both were trained anthropologists. At the time these articles were written, Horner was a visiting professor of Anthropology and Archaeology at Wheaton College, and Smalley was a Ph.D. candidate in anthropology at Columbia University. Both men, therefore, brought anthropologic insights to bear on the topic at hand. During the early half of the twentieth century, American anthropologists were aggressively challenging some of the mistaken racial theories of the nineteenth-century American School. Thus, both Horner and Smalley argued that race was an artificial category that did not gel with newer anthropological insights. Horner irritably called it "fiction," suggesting that people could be classed into races based on body weight as easily as skin color. In *HIS*, Smalley drew a distinction between biological and cultural factors as Horner had in his earlier article for *Moody Monthly*. There, the linguistic emphasis prevalent in mid-twentieth century American anthropology came through as Horner noted that the characteristics and practices of a "people" have more to do with common language and cultural practices, rather than pigmentation-defined race.[12]

As evangelicals, both Horner and Smalley denied that the Christian faith allowed for any sense of racial superiority. Horner went further, giving theological weight to the issue by categorizing the deleterious effects of American racism as sin, even intimating that evangelicals bore a corporate responsibility for this societal sin due to their explicit and complicit participation in it. Also concerned with effects that racism imposed upon African Americans, Horner lamented that it stifled "a large mass of intellectually capable human beings, the Negroes." The picture that headlines the article emphasizes the last point. Two attractive African Americans in white lab coats work in a laboratory, utilizing a microscope, test tubes, and other scientific equipment. While her male colleague looks on, the woman records observations in a lab book. It appears that both are scientific researchers, not just performing a perfunctory laboratory task. In reality, the picture did not capture much of the general thrust of the article at all, but it further communicated the message that the editors desired to convey: African Americans are working in science, a widely respected profession in the 1940s. In 1947, such an article was bound to elicit reader reaction—and it did.[13]

Initial reader reaction to Horner's article in *CL&T* was not good; at least three readers took time to write and criticize the author. Taking issue both with Horner's interpretation of the meaning of the story of Ham and his understanding of race, an anonymous writer complained that the essay "would be a splendid article for the *Chicago Defender*, *The Pittsburg* [sic] *Courier*, *The Afro-American*, or other papers of their ilk," but did not belong in such a "high class magazine" like *CL&T*. Fellow reader James F. Dew compared Horner to "Father Divine," accusing him of attempting to "destroy the truthfulness and trustworthiness of the Bible," which clearly endorsed a curse upon Ham's descendants. The following month, some readers defended Horner against these detractors, while two others were glad to see this important social issue addressed. Yet three more readers took issue with Horner's conclusions, vehemently opposing him. The editors would only address this issue once more in the decade.[14] When reader reaction was once again mixed, the editors retreated, failing to publish anything more on the race issue until the middle of the next decade. Neither did any other evangelical magazine. On the one hand, the decisions to publish these articles in the late 1940s in *Moody Monthly*, *CL&T*, and *HIS* cannot be understood as haphazard but must be viewed with the intentionality with which all editorial decisions are made. On the other hand, the decision to abandon the issue when some readers objected reflects the editors' unwillingness to press the issue in the face of a divided constituency. A similar pattern developed at Wheaton.

Opinion regarding integration and the full equality of African Americans was uneven on Wheaton's campus. Although many students participated in interracial ministry each Sunday on Chicago's South Side and others praised integration efforts in America, the opposite attitude pervaded campus as well. In 1948, a graduating senior complained of the racist attitudes on campus, specifically manifest in an attitude of racial superiority, racist jokes, and opposition to Horner's article in *CL&T*.[15] In addition, C. Gregg Singer served as chair of the faculty at Wheaton in the 1940s. A strong advocate for unified evangelical social action in that decade, Singer was also an unequivocal segregationist. At the same time that a staunch segregationist served as faculty chair, George Horner taught at Wheaton from 1945 to 1948, and Billy Graham credited his anthropology studies at the college with disabusing him of any latent racial superiority that had adhered from his southern upbringing.[16] United regarding the necessity of the "new birth" and the necessity of evangelical social engagement, on the critical issue of African American equality, evangelicals were divided.

The story was the same within the ranks of the NAE. In 1948, President Harry Truman sought to revive Franklin Roosevelt's Fair Employment Practices Committee (FEPC). Although not exclusively focused on the equitable treatment of African Americans, this issue remained a critical component of the committee's efforts. On the FEPC, the NAE was divided. While the leadership agreed in principle that evangelicalism had something to say about the pressing social issues of the day, they could not agree on what that something ought to be. NAE vice-president Dr. Frederick C. Fowler and James DeForest Murch, editor of the NAE's semi-monthly paper *United Evangelical Action* (*UEA*), opposed the FEPC legislation. Other evangelical leaders such as Baptist General

Conference youth leader and InterVarsity associate Gunnar Hogland, Asbury Seminary professor George Turner, and Gilbert James, Superintendent of the Department of Interracial Evangelism of the Free Methodist Church, supported the FEPC's revival. As a result, the NAE issued a fairly anemic statement on "inter-racial relations" in 1949. Clearly meant to say something rather than nothing, it was vague and equivocal on the specifics that really mattered: African American equality and segregation. In fact, the whole resolution might be read as an exhortation to seek more conversions among "under-privileged races"—something on which every evangelical, including the most ardent segregationist, could agree.[17]

A similar scenario played out in the Social Action Committee of the NAE as it was getting off the ground in 1951. Meeting as the Social Action Forum at the NAE's 1951 annual convention in Chicago, its final panel focused on "race relations," demonstrating that the organizers knew this crucial issue ought to be addressed. Although cordial, the panel demonstrated the divide among evangelicals on this most critical of social issues. Along with Gilbert James, the speakers included missionary director Erwin Wedel, George A. Turner, African American Pastor William Houston, and Roy Nicholson of the General Conference of the Wesleyan Methodist Church of South Carolina. While Turner and James attacked institutionalized racism, Nicholson's position sounded strangely like the position of eighteenth-century plantation missionaries.[18]

Despite the "Spirit of St. Louis," those evangelicals who desired to develop a cohesive, unified, evangelical approach to the problem of racial inequality in America were frustrated. As this reality set in, so did gridlock. This impasse is not to deny the strong sense of solidarity and unity among these "new evangelicals." In fact, Gilbert James, one of the strongest evangelical advocates for racial equality, was sorely disappointed that C. Gregg Singer could not attend the 1951 NAE Social Action Forum. His affection toward and sense of kinship with fellow evangelical Singer was real. Like others in the group, he fully expected that sharing a born-again experience and the theological convictions associated with it would be a sufficient base from which to launch an assault on systemic American racism. That would not prove to be true. Further, many pro-integration evangelicals did not want to endanger the newfound evangelical unity by pressing a divisive issue too strongly.[19]

Thus, approaching the middle of the twentieth century, the issue of African American equality was rarely addressed by evangelicals, much less in a cohesive unified manner. Some pro-integration leaders such as James, Horner, Smalley, and the editorial staffs of *CL&T*, *HIS*, and the organizers of the Social Action Committee tested the issue but retreated rather than pressing their case and endangering the nascent evangelical unity. These new evangelicals could hardly take a strong stance against segregation at the same time that they were trying to court conversion-oriented southern denominational bodies like the Southern Baptist Convention and Southern Presbyterians (Presbyterian Church United States). Along those lines, southern luminaries and staunch defenders of segregation like Bob Jones and Bob Jones, Jr., were deeply involved in the neoevangelical movement during its early years. After 1951, when hopes for a southern connection had been effectively dashed, the NAE adopted a stronger statement on "Christian Race Principles" during its 1951 convention. Even so, it would take events external to the new evangelical movement to change the cultural climate, enabling pro-equality evangelicals to address segregation directly.[20]

In the Wake of Brown

The three years at the middle of the 1950s were momentous for the African American struggle toward equality. After decades of legal efforts by the NAACP, on May 17, 1954, the United States Supreme Court handed down its famous *Brown v. Board* decision. In 1955, the brutal murder of Emmett Till and the acquittal of his killers shocked the nation, changing the overarching moral climate of tolerance toward segregation. In December that same year, Rosa Parks refused to give up her seat on a bus, launching the famous Montgomery bus boycott that ended in a victory for integration the following year. Taken as a whole, these events changed the cultural climate in which discussions regarding African American equality were taking place. For integration-oriented evangelical leaders, this cultural shift tilted the playing field in their direction, allowing more space for discussion. Unsurprisingly, their efforts appeared both in the evangelical print culture of the 1950s and within the NAE, the organizational manifestation of new evangelicalism.[21]

In a pattern often repeated in the years to come, the *Brown* decision did not immediately have an impact on evangelical discourse regarding African American equality, but its effects were gradually felt. For instance, the *Brown v. Board* decision had been handed down two weeks after the end of the NAE's annual convention, held in Cleveland the last week of

April 1954. While even such conservative southern denominations as the Southern Baptist Convention and the Presbyterian Church of the United States addressed the landmark ruling, the NAE did not even adopt a resolution at its next convention in 1955. As became clear in the public space of its print media, its constituency was divided on the ruling. For example, following a rather lukewarm editorial endorsement of *Brown* in the March 1, 1956, issue of *UEA*, two readers were incensed, vehemently opposing integration and intermarriage. Days later, NAE delegates addressed racial discrimination in an official resolution, proclaiming the equality and value of each individual person, clearly condemning discrimination, and urging its "constituency" to action on the issues. Although not radical in its rhetoric, it went much farther than the NAE had heretofore. In the evangelical periodicals of the day, editors pressed further.[22]

In 1954, *Christian Life* (*CL*) reported on the *Brown* decision without much acclaim. Looking back from the vantage point of 1955, however, the editors lauded 1954 as "a big year for the U.S. Negro."[23] That same year, the magazine conducted a survey of racial attitudes, seeking the opinions of over six hundred churches; ninety-two responded. Not a random sampling by any means, it does reflect an effort to move racial issues back on to the table. The editors followed through by running more stories on such topics, referring to segregation as a sin, embracing integration, and even reporting on a Lutheran church on Chicago's South Side that had successfully integrated. Unlike in the late 1940s, the printed responses to these *CL* articles were all positive. Either segregationists were no longer as vocal, or the editors did not feel compelled to publish their letters. Either way, the moral climate within the new evangelicalism had changed.[24]

Along the same lines, beginning with the September 1955 issue, the editors of *CL* began to give more coverage to African American life in general. Positive reports of the efforts of African Americans on their own behalf peppered its pages while the editors criticized the NAE for failing to bring black evangelicals into its ranks and praised the success of the Free Methodist Church's Department of Interracial Evangelism. In addition, greater coverage was given to African American evangelicals such as evangelist Howard Jones and future Olympic Gold Medalist Rafer Johnson. After *Brown*, a similar phenomenon occurred in *HIS* magazine.[25]

Beginning in the mid-1950s, a plethora of articles devoted to some aspect of race relations began to appear in *HIS*, including news briefs on the civil rights movement and full articles directly devoted to the issue of African American racial inequality. Other articles dealt with racial prejudice in other parts of the world, such as South Africa. Although the severest criticism was directed toward South African apartheid, the surrogacy was thinly veiled—at times the comparison with America's Jim Crow was made explicit. Without fail, each article took a stance in favor of desegregation and for African American equality. Several were even authored by African Americans, embodying the equality that the magazine's editors were promoting. A regular section comprised of news briefs taken from other contemporary publications as well as quotes from literary works, regularly incorporated pro-civil rights news blurbs.[26]

In *HIS*, just as in other venues, the tenor of the discussion had changed as prejudice began to be labeled in no uncertain terms: it was a sin, "wrong, degrading, and blasphemous."[27] In 1956, a sharply worded editorial by Joseph Bayly expressed incredulity at the lack of concern within evangelicalism for "social righteousness." He was explicitly referencing segregation, lamenting the fact that the *Christian Century*, which was "theologically liberal," continued to be "outspoken on such matters as economic, educational and political equality for the Negro" while most evangelical people and publications were muted. Of course, like some other evangelical leaders, he was doing his (or *HIS*'s) part to change that. Of the four letters received (and printed) in response to Bayly, only one reacted negatively; the other three were commendatory.[28] For these periodicals, *Brown* had changed things—at least a little bit. *The King's Business* (*TKB*), the in-house organ of the Bible Institute of Los Angeles (BIOLA), would follow suit, but only after events more jarring than *Brown*.

Prior to 1955, *TKB* had presented a moderate approach to questions surrounding racial equality. In the late 1940s and early 1950s, few pages addressed racial equality even though the more egregious forms of segregation and racial prejudice were declaimed at times. Overall, however, writers were ambivalent regarding the drawbacks of voluntary segregation and the benefits of mandatory integration, even seeing racial differences as biblical. This ambivalence was sometimes even reflected in the same writer. Thus, it is not surprising that *Brown* did not receive much attention. The events of the mid-1950s would change things, however.[29]

In 1955, press coverage of both Emmett Till's funeral—complete with pictures of the open-casket insisted upon by his mother—and the trial of his killers in Tallahatchie County, Mississippi, put the brutality of Jim Crow racism on full display across the country. Further, in 1957 the absurdity of segregation was in view as nine African American students in Little Rock, Arkansas, required military escorts to comply with *Brown*. As the moral climate regarding toleration of segregation changed, these two events turned prior vacillation among the editors of *TKB* into a pro-equality position.[30]

In their December 1955 issue, the editors of *TKB* reprinted *Life*'s eulogy of Emmett Till. Condemning the miscarriage of justice in the Till murder case, it also attacked the overall system of Jim Crow that made such an atrocity possible. The editors reached a boiling point less than two years later, when President Eisenhower had to deploy the 101st Airborne Division to protect the Little Rock Nine—the first African American students to attend Little Rock's Central High School. Although Reinhold Niebuhr and Billy Graham equivocated, *TKB* managing editor Lloyd Hamill drew a line in the sand and issued a strong statement opposing segregation, supporting integration, and defending President Eisenhower's actions in enforcing federal law in no uncertain terms. The same issue included a full article attacking segregation, racial prejudice, and declaring equality between African and white Americans.[31]

For these efforts, the editors of the magazine received a deluge of letters from writers who decried their stance, accusing them of falling victim to communist propaganda, abandoning the "King's business" for politics. Several asked for their subscriptions to be canceled. Although the editors conceded that letters ran ten to one against their "stand on segregation" in the early going, they did receive several commendatory letters and additional contributions for compensatory "gift subscriptions." Perhaps it was concerns over these developments that spurred the editors to run a page full of endorsements from prominent evangelical ministers in its April 1958 issue, shoring up their evangelical credentials.[32] In the context of the changing cultural climate, the evangelical elites that served as the editors of *TKB* were willing to take a stronger stance against segregation. At the same time, it seems clear that at least a sizeable portion of its constituency did not follow suit.

A similar pattern emerged in *Eternity*, edited by former BIOLA student and evangelical luminary Donald Grey Barnhouse.[33] What makes the transformation that took place in the pages of *Eternity* so remarkable is that Barnhouse himself had supported segregation in the 1940s, endorsing Booker T. Washington's paradigm of a shared economy but separate social lives in *Revelation*, the evangelical magazine he edited in the 1940s. Gradually moderating his position, by the mid-1950s, his own internal conflict was on full display: he supported school segregation in the North—ostensibly due to the challenges of heterogeneously mixing advantaged and disadvantaged children together—while heaping lavish praise on Thurgood Marshall for his efforts. Further, Barnhouse condemned South Africa for apartheid, even choosing to publish an article that suggested that the American form was even worse. Throughout the rest of 1956 and through 1957, "race relations" became a recurring topic in *Eternity*.[34]

In August 1956, an article in *Eternity* by Fuller Seminary faculty member Harold Lindsell sided with pro-integration evangelicals, declaring integration biblically and legally correct. Unsurprisingly, he advocated gradualism as the only workable solution. Perhaps more significantly, the Lindsell article demonstrated successful integration in action, including a half-page photograph of six African American and three white children praying together. Pressing the issue two months later, *Eternity* published a meandering article by *HIS* editor Joseph Bayly who unreservedly supported full integration. Again, photographs accentuated the content, showing a middle-class African American couple being turned out of a northern all-white neighborhood, while National Guardsmen dispersed a crowd protesting African Americans moving into an all-white neighborhood in Chicago. The comparison with images from Little Rock could not have been missed.[35]

On these issues, readers were split. The next year, the editorial staff of *Eternity* published a rebuttal article to Bayly's. Yet giving equal time to both sides hardly seems the motivation as in that same issue they included a strong counter-rebuttal, "The Church Must Be Color Blind." In general, published letters to the editor favored integration; even those that supported segregation demonstrated a markedly more genteel tone than writers from the 1940s. The climate was shifting.[36]

By 1957, *Eternity* began to embody integration, publishing an article by black pastor B. M. Nottage. A dispensationalist with a weekly show on Moody Bible Institute's radio station (WMBI, Chicago), Nottage's evangelical credentials were never in doubt.[37] Labeling evangelicalism's lack of concern toward the plight of blacks in America as a sin, he also saw reason to be hopeful.[38] The editors would follow this pattern again in 1960, publishing Orthodox Presbyterian Church pastor C. Herbert Oliver's synopsis of his recent book, *No Flesh Shall Glory* (Presbyterian and Reformed Publishing, 1959). In it, Oliver praised those who spoke out against "the sin of racial discrimination," while criticizing American society for denying justice to African Americans and evangelical churches for participating in "the disease" of segregation.[39]

Approaching the end of the 1950s, even though they were still meeting resistance, the tenor of the discussion had changed as pro-racial equality evangelical leaders were regularly addressing segregation, inequality, and racism—things they now openly referred to as sin—in the public space of the print media. In some ways, they were quite progressive, employing anthropology and sociology to make their case, aligning themselves with mainline thinkers on the issue, and even (tentatively) supporting interracial marriage. Even so, resistance still existed among many born-again laypeople, church leaders, and even elites, preventing the development of a consensus on the topic. For mid-century evangelicals, the firm belief in conversion as the foundation of authentic Christian life that unified them simultaneously contributed to a latitudinarianism that meant that segregationists, pro-integrationists, and the unconcerned all moved comfortably in evangelical circles. Thus, although the solidarity of the new evangelicalism was real and its commitment to greater social engagement was sincere, unified action on this all-important issue was elusive. This scenario played out most clearly within the pages of what became the standard bearer—and at times the mirror—of the new evangelicalism: *Christianity Today* (*CT*).[40]

When it first appeared in October 1956, *CT* was poised to become the intellectual pacesetter for the new evangelicalism on social issues. By the time he became founding editor of *CT*, Carl Henry had been advocating for a more socially concerned evangelicalism for over a decade. In his first editorial at the helm of *CT* he did the same. He had even expressed an eagerness to provide evangelical leadership on the "race issue" well before the first issue was published. Yet, in the late 1950s, the magazine printed relatively few articles on this most pressing social question of the day. In addition, when taken as a whole, those few articles demonstrate a marked propensity toward moderation and gradualism.[41]

In general, the positions of *CT* in the 1950s were less settled, perhaps even malleable (or at least muddling) than the hardened positions it would take (or not take) on a variety of social issues in the 1960s. This position was even true regarding African American equality. For instance, editors followed E. Earl Ellis's pro-segregation article in 1957 with a pro-integration article by Timothy L. Smith the following year. Henry's own internal conflict (or inconsistency) on this issue is evident in the pages of the magazine.

While he criticized evangelical "failure to seek social justice for the Negro," referencing the "evils of segregation," he hesitated to endorse a "specific 'program of integration' as the Christian solution." Henry's position and equivocation led to a de facto moderate position, something Henry explicitly embraced a few months later. In this, Henry and *CT* are a microcosm of the overall trajectory of evangelicalism and an example of how a moderate, gradualist position developed by the end of the 1950s.[42]

The reasons for this moderate position, likewise, reflect the trouble with evangelicalism on this all-important issue. First, although erudite, like all mid-century evangelicals, Carl Henry believed that conversion was the foundational Christian experience.[43] Yet, like many evangelicals, he struggled to tie a serious social program to this defining characteristic of evangelical identity. Although he repeatedly insisted that regeneration must be incorporated into any *evangelical* social effort, he was never able to give serious theological content to such statements. Further, when personal conversions failed to transform many individual perspectives regarding race, Henry, like many evangelicals, was at a loss. Second, Henry's equivocation-cum-moderation highlights the challenge of evangelicalism *as a movement*: maintaining evangelical solidarity meant not pressing issues beyond the rather minimalist orientation of evangelical identity, which centered on conversion. Unfortunately, at *CT*, this challenge was even more acute. In the 1950s, evangelicalism never excluded avowed segregationists from its midst. Henry's managing editor, Billy Graham's father-in-law, L. Nelson Bell, believed that the races should be kept separate. These positions were hardly the conditions under which to work out a cohesive evangelical approach toward integration; they were precisely the conditions for evangelical gridlock leading to de facto moderation. In fact, because of behind-the-scenes machinations, the pages of *CT* were even less moderate on these positions than in some other evangelical venues.[44]

Scripture and Conversion

Despite the gridlock caused by internal disagreement in the 1950s, pro-equality evangelicals continued to advocate for a cohesive evangelical position toward African American equality, appealing to both Scripture and conversion. Although neither would provide the basis of a unified evangelical position, both would contribute to what became the dominant evangelical approach to the issue of racial equality through the remainder of the twentieth century.

Because most evangelicals could affirm the Bible as "the inspired, the only infallible, authoritative word of God," it might be expected that the Scriptures could provide the final word regarding African American equality. Some, such as Lloyd Hamill of *TKB*, believed that integration was "the plain teaching of the Bible." But this position seemed plainly wrong to others. And thus, just as Mark Noll has shown in his work on the Civil War, sometimes the Bible simply does not provide a way forward. The disagreement did not hover around the Bible's authority but rather its interpretation.[45]

During the 1940s and 1950s, African American religious intellectuals insisted that the biblical account of creation meant that all human beings are of "one blood," sharing the same ancestral parents. It seems that such a straightforward interpretation of Genesis 1–3 would have gained traction among evangelicals, who should have appreciated the manner in which it took the biblical story seriously as primordial history. Although there is little evidence that white evangelical thinkers engaged with these African American intellectuals, some embraced similar understandings. Unfortunately for those who saw in scripture a mandate for integration, other biblical passages—particularly Genesis 9—were construed in a manner that undercut that interpretation.[46]

In Genesis 9, Noah imbibes too much wine after the floodwaters recede. While he is inebriated, Ham, Canaan's father, acts shamefully toward him while the other two brothers "walked backward and covered the nakedness of their father." After recovering, Noah issues a blessing upon two brothers while cursing Ham's son Canaan, proclaiming, "lowest of slaves shall he be to his brothers." Throughout the centuries, many biblical interpreters have taken this as a racial text. By the nineteenth century, Noah's three sons were often construed to be the progenitors of the three different races of humanity—white, black, and yellow. Additionally, since "Ham" is etymologically related to the Semitic words for black and dark, some contended that this "curse" was both descriptive and prescriptive, indicating that the races were intended to be separate. These interpretations fit nicely with the American School of anthropology, which argued for polygenism of races, thus offering an exegetical legitimacy to the "scientific racism" prevalent in the nineteenth century.[47]

Some recent scholarship has suggested that most southern theologians had abandoned employing Genesis 9 as a racial text, even before the

Civil War, and that "Noah's curse" was not widely employed as a biblical justification for segregation or at least that its use was "frail." However, Stephen Haynes has offered a different perspective, arguing that "Noah's curse" served racism well after the Civil War and into the twentieth century, making a comeback of sorts in the 1950s as part of the backlash against integration. Both Horner and Smalley's articles in the 1940s had addressed this peculiar interpretation, as did Gilbert James, Superintendent of the Department of Interracial Evangelism of the Free Methodist Church, in his advocacy for the FEPC laws in the pages of *UEA*. They were not just tilting at windmills. Rather, this racialized interpretation of Genesis 9 persisted.[48] Because pro-equality evangelicals were as committed to the historical veracity of Genesis as their opponents, they were compelled to address Genesis 9 to dilute it of its power as a text of racial superiority. Pro-equality evangelicals addressed this challenge in a variety of ways, but in each case their positions derived from particular biblical interpretations, around which they hoped to achieve a consensus.[49]

Interpretive consensus on such issues was not forthcoming. Even the same verse could elicit conflicting interpretations. For example, a second biblical passage, Acts 17:26, was cited by both segregationists and integrationists as support for their position. Whereas the segregationists insisted that Paul's words that God had "determined . . . the bounds of their habitation" meant separation of the races, pro-equality evangelicals pointed to the first half of the verse whereby all human beings are said to be of "one blood." In the end, biblical exegesis could not settle that issue. And if the Bible could not settle the issue, neither could conversion overcome the challenge.[50]

A commitment to conversion as the foundational religious experience that fundamentally changed people for the better led equality-oriented evangelicals to genuinely believe that converted individuals would transcend societal and personal racial prejudice through individual transformation. Thus, when Billy Graham opined that a "man who has a genuine conversion experience will find his racial attitudes greatly changed," he was not making a simple equivocation; he was speaking out of the core of his religious identity, and his words resonated with an evangelical constituency that had themselves experienced conversion and believed it had changed them.[51] Three corollaries emerged from this perspective. First, evangelicals had confidence that those who held racist views but had truly been born again would eventually arrive at the right perspective as they "matured in Christ." In their minds, only being converted to Christ and the subsequent transformation by the Holy Spirit could overcome racial prejudice. Second, because their religious identity revolved around individual, personal conversion, evangelicals were prone to think in personal terms. As a result, despite the historical realities of racism in America (especially in the South), they expected that interpersonal contacts would lead to greater acceptance and the overcoming of "ignorance" regarding racism. Yet in reality, conversion did not seem to guarantee that people would disavow segregation and racism. When it did happen, of course, pro-equality evangelicals gleefully recounted how people renounced their racism when they were born again. But such "racial conversions" seemed rare. Both of these perspectives meant that they were slow to realize that whatever interpersonal strategies might be employed in overcoming American apartheid and racism, systemic problems enforced by legal measures had to be addressed by counter systemic alternatives and legal measures. A third corollary, the preeminent evangelical perspective on the church, would help leaders set in motion forces that were helpful in overcoming at least some of the racial prejudices of many evangelicals in the years to come.[52]

The Beloved Church

Historically, the evangelical focus on personal conversion had always maintained a corresponding emphasis on the church as the place in which converted persons lived out their Christian faith with each other. Most postwar evangelicals who argued for African American equality did so in the context of the new community that Christ had established—the church. Thus, their focus and point of argument, although not their sentiment, was slightly different than that of the African American religious leaders. For them, hope did not lay in the vision of a "beloved community," but a "beloved church," an emphasis they perceived in Scripture.[53]

In the 1950s, these pro-equality evangelicals recognized the impasse that confronted them regarding such passages as Genesis 9 and Acts 17. However, unsurprisingly unwilling to leave the Bible behind, they employed a different, but richly biblical tact that emphasized personal conversion as lived out in the life of the church. *HIS* author Ben Marais provided an example of this overarching argument: the flow of the biblical narrative of redemption does not stagnate in Genesis 1–2, Genesis 9, or even Acts 17 but continues through the epistolary literature, particularly regarding the organizational "body of Christ" comprised of converted, born-again believers. In a quick biblical gloss, Marais described how, in the biblical narrative, the promise to bless all nations through Abraham comes immediately after the flood and the scattering of nations at Babel: it is a promise ultimately fulfilled in the incarnation, the day of Pentecost, and the breaking down of the barrier between Jew and Gentile in the church through the work of Christ. By focusing on the unity "in Christ" that all evangelicals—regardless of race—shared, pro-equality evangelicals avoided Acts 17 and the treacherous waters of Genesis 9, tying evangelical arguments for racial equality to evangelical conceptions of their solidarity with other born-again believers. Whatever division might exist in society, those divisions are completely irrelevant for evangelicals because "in Christ all barriers fall away."[54]

Equality-oriented evangelicals, such as C. Herbert Oliver, also emphasized the unity all human beings share with Adam as sinners. Part and parcel of that identity with Adam as sinners is the "sin of racial discrimination." To the contrary, believers are unified because "his blood" truly cleanses them of sin, making them new creatures. Therein lay the hope of real unity.[55]

Along these lines, Robert James St. Clair insisted in a provocative article in *TKB* that in the church all "born-again" believers are equal regardless of their racial classification. The church then, made up of those who have been born again, ought to demonstrate the unity for which Christ prayed because all believers, regardless of "race," are "one in Christ." To this end, several Pauline texts were cited with regularity: Galatians 3:28, Ephesians 2, Colossians 3:10–11 While the Ephesians text emphasizes the manner in which the work of Christ had broken down barriers between Jew and Gentile, those from Galatians and Colossians emphasize the eradication of distinctions of all sorts—racial, ethnic, social, gender—for those who were "in Christ." Besides grounding its appeal in Scripture, the genius of this approach was three-fold. First, it moved beyond the exegesis of a handful of passages, framing the discussion in the context of evangelicalism's larger understanding of the work of Christ and the solidarity of born-again persons. Second, it brought the discussion to bear upon the one institution of indisputable importance to evangelicals, the group of born-again persons known as the church. Because most evangelicals were primitivists of one sort or another, they believed that their local congregations ought to embody the principles for church life found in the New Testament. By this line of argument, integrating them would be doing just that. Finally, it placed local churches, something to which all evangelicals belonged, at the center of the maelstrom regarding racial equality, circumventing other discussions. For example, whether the federal government had overstepped its bounds had little if anything to do with whether a church allowed African Americans into membership. Evangelical leaders who advocated for equality made this particular point, poignantly asking the question: "Is the individual Christian willing to worship with a person of another race?" For a group of people whose whole religious identity revolved around an individual decision to "trust Christ," this piercing question could not be evaded. The answer—either yes or no—revealed everything.[56]

In addition to the biblical case against segregation, these postwar evangelicals were concerned for "the exemplary function of the church."[57] They had an overarching sense that the church ought to be "salt and light" in the world, providing an example to the rest of society in every area, including racial equality. Thus, in the wake of *Brown v. Board*, Billy Graham lamented that the federal government had to compel citizens to do what "the church should voluntarily be doing." Even as late as 1956, the editors of *CL* were hopeful that the churches of the South might cast aside their longstanding practices of racial exclusion to "guide [integration] into peaceful channels." Building from the Pauline corpus, in the pages of *TKB* Robert St. Clair expressed his lament for the church's failure to provide an example and witness to Christ, acting as a "city on a hill" in the midst of a racist society. Rather than being a barrier to others coming to Christ, they were confident that an integrated church would draw many people to Christ. Thus, for the sake of Christ's "beloved church," they urged pastors to stand for racial equality—even against their congregations if necessary.[58]

Conclusion

Overall, a confluence of factors led postwar evangelicalism as a whole to adopt a moderate position on integration and racial equality by the end of the 1950s. First, there was disagreement as to whether integration was even desirable. In the late 1940s and early 1950s, although some evangelical leaders tried to address the issue of African American equality, there was opposition at every level of the movement. At a time when the newfound evangelical unity seemed tenuous, and when postwar evangelical leadership was still trying to attract greater southern participation in the movement, these leaders retreated rather than risk splitting the movement. As a result, even though the NAE adopted a few anemic resolutions on "race relations," no strong positions were taken and no real efforts emerged.

However, toward the middle of the decade, when African American efforts on their own behalf began to change the moral climate regarding their full inclusion as citizens, pro-equality evangelical leaders began to press the issue *despite* continued opposition. By the late 1950s they had articulated a biblically informed vision for a beloved church that resonated with the historic evangelical commitments to conversion and Biblicism while challenging some racialized biblical interpretations. Comfortably denouncing segregation and racial inequality as sins, they focused their attention on the more comfortable arenas of interpersonal relationships and church life rather than the more difficult ones of polis and society. This position left the systemic issues present in American racism largely unchallenged by evangelicalism as a movement.

Not until the late 1960s and early 1970s would a consistent evangelical voice aim to address the systemic nature of racism in America (see chapter 3 of this volume). Even so, they would remain a minority, as the evangelical approach to racial equality stressing individual relationships that developed during the formative immediate postwar period has remained dominant. Perhaps the most public example was observed in the mid-1990s as the popular evangelical men's movement Promise Keepers enshrined "reaching beyond racial barriers" as one of its seven promises and pressed a strong message of "racial reconciliation" on its constituents. For them, this reconciliation did not mean tackling the issue systemically through legal or socio-economic channels but encouraging individual repentance and the development of intentional, long-term relationships with men from different ethnic backgrounds, preferably in one's local church. Thus, the formative postwar years shaped the next half century of evangelical approaches to racial equality in America as even today many good-hearted evangelicals often fail to see the racialized nature of American society, embracing an individualistic, moderate approach to racial issues that centers on the beloved church.[59]

Notes

1. Carl F. H. Henry, "The Vigor of the New Evangelicalism," *CL&T* 1 (January 1948); 1 (March 1948); 1 (April 1948).
2. Michael O. Emerson and Christian Smith, *Divided by Faith: Evangelical Religion and the Problem of Race in America* (New York: Oxford University Press, 2000).

For more on the concept of a "formative period" in religious history, see Sidney E. Mead, *The Lively Experiment: The Shaping of American Christianity* (New York: Harper & Row, 1963), 107–108.

3. David Otis Fuller, Jr., "Conscience of America," *The Wheaton Record (TWR)*, December 1, 1960, 2.

4. Paul M. Bechtel, *Wheaton College: A Heritage Remembered, 1860–1984* (Wheaton, IL: Harold Shaw Publishers, 1984), 285–286. The best accounts of the mid-century evangelical renaissance are Joel A. Carpenter, *Revive Us Again: The Reawakening of American Fundamentalism* (New York: Oxford University Press, 1997); and Garth M. Rosell, *The Surprising Work of God: Harold John Ockenga, Billy Graham, and the Rebirth of Evangelicalism* (Grand Rapids: Baker Academic, 2008). Carpenter's work is more detailed and thesis driven; Rosell's is more accessible.

5. Although there were some significant exceptions, the "new evangelicalism" tended to be a northern movement as evangelicals in the South did not embrace it in the 1940s and 1950s. For a good, albeit brief, discussion of *born again* as a synonym for conversion, see Miles Mullin, "Born Again," in *The Encyclopedia of Christian Civilization*, ed. George Kurian (Malden, MA: Wiley-Blackwell, 2012).

6. Carl F. H. Henry, *The Uneasy Conscience of Modern Fundamentalism* (1947; reprint, Grand Rapids, MI: Eerdmans, 2003), xvii.

7. On evangelical identity, David Bebbington's evangelical quadrilateral—biblicism, crucicentricism (an emphasis on the cross), conversionism, and activism—has gained ascendancy in recent years. See David Bebbington, *Evangelicalism in Modern Britain: A History from the 1730s to the 1980s* (London: Routledge, 1989; reprint, Grand Rapids MI: Baker Book House, 1992); and *The Dominance of Evangelicalism: The Age of Spurgeon and Moody* (Downers Grove, IL: InterVarsity Press, 2005). My own contention is that evangelicalism qua evangelicalism is possessed of a core identity that is more minimalist, revolving around the experience and theology of conversion. Such a minimalist definition explains, among other things, both the real sense of solidarity and kinship that evangelicals have for one another as well as their failure to agree on many other issues (e.g., politics, sacraments, ordination, etc.). This position is developed more fully in my dissertation, "Postwar Evangelical Social Concern: Evangelical Identity and the Modes and Limits of Social Engagement, 1945–1960," (Ph.D. Dissertation, Vanderbilt University, 2009).

8. For a good discussion of how a conversion parlayed nicely into *certain forms* of social action, see Mullin, "Postwar Evangelical Social Concern."

9. Earl V. Pierce, *The Church and World Conditions* (New York: Fleming H. Revell, 1943), 103–106; Carl F. H. Henry, *The Uneasy Conscience*, 17, 77–78.

10. George R. Horner, "A Christian View of Race," *Moody Monthly* 9, no. 12 (August 1946); Horner, "Are Negroes Cursed?" *CL&T* 2, no. 10 (October 1947); William A. Smalley, "What About Race Prejudice?" *HIS* 10, no. 2 (November 1949).

11. Horner, "Are Negroes Cursed?" 32.
12. Ibid., 31–32; Smalley, "What About Race Prejudice?" 7–8; Horner, "A Christian View of Race," 735, 778. For a good summary of the history of the American School, see Adam Dewberry, "The American School and Scientific Racism in Early American Anthropology," in *Histories of Anthropology Annual*, Vol. 3, ed. Regna Darnell and Frederic W. Gleach (Lincoln, NE: University of Nebraska Press, 2007). For broader treatments of how these ideas fit into the history of anthropology more generally, see C. Scott Littleton, "Anthropology," *New Dictionary of the History of Ideas*, Vol. 1, ed. Maryanne Cline Horowitz (Detroit: Charles Scribner's Sons, 2005); Ann M. Kakaliouras "Ethnicity and Race: Anthropology" in ibid., Vol. 2; and Julia E. Liss, "Anthropology and Ethnology," in *Dictionary of American History*, Vol. 1, 3rd ed., ed. Stanley I. Kutler (Detroit: Charles Scribner's Sons, 2003).
13. Horner "Are Negroes Cursed?" 30, 32; Smalley, 7; Photo, *CL&T*, 2, no. 10 (October 1947), 30. In the 1950s, confidence in science and respect for scientists was at an all-time high, trending toward a near religious faith in science that some have labeled "scientism." See, for example, James Hudnut-Beumler, *Looking for God in the Suburbs: The Religion of the American Dream and Its Critics, 1945–1965* (Brunswick, NJ: Rutgers University Press, 1994), 8–15.
14. E. Finkenbiner, "Anonymous," and James F. Dew, Letters to the Editor, *CL&T* 2, no. 12 (December 1947), 6–9; E. B. Charles and Waldo Richardson, and Alice E. Norris and John Barbee, Letters the Editor, *CL&T* 3, no. 1 (January 1948), 12–13; "Jane Doe," J. H. Armfield, and David Peterson, Letters to the Editor, *CL&T* 3, no. 1 (January 1948), 10–11. *CL*, the successor to *CL&T* after its merger with *Sunday* magazine in July 1948 published "A Matter of Understanding" by Bernard Palmer in its October 1949 issue (11, no. 6).
15. Bechtel, *Wheaton College*, 203–204; Sherwood Ebey, "Wheatonites Carry Story of Christ to Children of Rickety Tenements," *TWR*, October 2, 1952, 2. Schmid, "Columnist Schmid Urges Students to Study Racial Equality Problem," *TWR*, January 13, 1949, 2; Schmid, "Blowing the Lid with Schmid," *TWR*, January 20, 1949, 2; Harry Cook, "Illinois Joins United Nations in Honoring Human Rights," *TWR*, December 11, 1952, 2; R. G., Class of 1948, Letter to the Editor, *TWR*, March 18, 1948, 2.
16. When forced to leave Wheaton in 1949 (Bechtel, *Wheaton College*, 190–192), Singer landed in North Carolina where he participated in the "Dixiecrat" movement: C. Gregg Singer to Carl F. H. Henry, April 4, 1951; Singer to Henry, March 22, 1951. Both are found in the Unprocessed Henry Papers, Rolfing Library, Trinity Evangelical Divinity School (Deerfield, Illinois), Folder: NAE Commission on Social Action (1951–52). Steven Miller describes how Billy Graham's major in anthropology "had given him some awareness of the cultural relativity of race": see Miller, *Billy Graham and the Rise of the Republican South* (Philadelphia: University of Pennsylvania Press, 2009), 18. Similarly, William Martin

records that Billy Graham's "anthropology studies taught him that race is a quite imprecise term and concept often used by laypeople to explain such obviously nongenetic traits as language, religion and social values." Martin also recounts Graham's own references to anthropology in this regard: *A Prophet With Honor: The Billy Graham Story* (New York: William Morrow and Company, 1991), 169, 171–172.

17. "New Bills Peril U.S. Freedom," *CL* 11, no. 2 (June 1949), 23; James DeForest Murch, "UEA Editorial: FEPC Legislation," *UEA*, June 1, 1949, 7; Gunnar Hogland, Letter to the Editor, *UEA*, August 1, 1949, 2; "Capital Chat," *UEA* August 15, 1949, 6; George A. Turner, Letter to the Editor, *UEA*, September 15, 1949; Gilbert James, "What's Right With FEPC," *UEA*, September 15, 1949; George A. Turner, "Evangelicals and the Social Gospel," *UEA*, December 1, 1949, 9. In this resolution, the NAE urged "its constituent denominations and other membership to address themselves earnestly to the sincere application of the Christian message to under-privileged races and minority groups, and to promote legislation in keeping wherewith." See "Evangelicals at Chicago United for Action," *UEA*, May 1, 1949, 6.

18. "The NAE Faces Issues in National Crisis: A Report of the Ninth Annual Convention in Chicago," *UEA* May 1, 1951, 15–16. Nicholson reminded listeners that, even in the face of segregation, evangelism could still take place.

19. Both Henry and James had urged Singer to come, but due to a heavy teaching load at Salem, he could not. C. Gregg Singer to Gilbert James, March 22, 1951; C. Gregg Singer to Carl F. H. Henry, April 4, 1951; C. Gregg Singer to Carl F. H. Henry, March 22, 1951. All these letters are in the Unprocessed Henry Papers, Folder: NAE Commission on Social Action (1951–52).

20. In these early years threats to unity were keenly felt. In its institutional form (i.e., the NAE), the new evangelicalism had already lost potential constituents to Carl McIntire's American Council of Christian Churches. On the American Council of Christian Churches vis-à-vis NAE vis-à-vis National (née Federal) Council of Churches, see Carpenter, *Revive Us Again*, 147–154; Rosell, *The Surprising Work of God*, 91–96; D. G. Hart, *That Old Time Religion in Modern America: Evangelical Protestantism in the Twentieth Century* (Chicago: Ivan R. Dee, 2002), 55–56; and Jon R. Stone, *On the Boundaries of American Evangelicalism* (New York: St. Martin's Press, 1999), 73–116; "NAE Convention Resolutions," *UEA*, May 1, 1954, 6.

21. *Brown* reversed the earlier ruling of *Plessey v. Ferguson* (1896) by unanimously declaring, in the opinion of the court expressed by Chief Justice Earl Warren, "Separate educational facilities are inherently unequal." *Brown v. Board of Education of Topeka*, 347 U.S. 483, p. 486. For a good account of the Emmett Till Story and the historiography associated with it, see Stephen J. Whitfield, *A Death in the Delta: The Story of Emmett Till* (Baltimore, MD: Johns Hopkins University Press, 1998), 33–69.

22. James DeForest Murch, "Editorial: Racial Integration," *UEA*, March 1, 1956, 7; Don B. Card and Coulson Shepherd, Letters to the Editor, *UEA*, April 1, 1956, 2; "Human Rights," NAE Convention Resolutions, *UEA*, May 15, 1956, 7.
23. "Supreme Court Aftermath," World Wide News, *CL* 16, no. 4 (August 1954), 58–60; No Title, *CL* 17, no. 5 (September 1955), 15. In light of the *Brown* decision, desegregation of public facilities in Washington, DC, the vocal support of many national religious bodies, and the fact that the armed services were nearly completely desegregated it *was* a "big year."
24. "The Christian and the Color Line," *CL* 17, no. 5 (September 1955), 15–17; "Integration Can Work, Says Bethel Lutherans," *CL* 17, no. 5 (September 1955), 16–17; Letters to the Editor, *CL* 17, nos. 6–7 (October–November 1955).
25. "Watch the Negro," Prospects, *CL* 17, no. 12 (April 1956), 9; "Nation Eyes Dixie Christians," *CL* 18, no. 2 (June 1956), 13, 43–44; "Answering an African S.o.S.," *CL* 17, no. 11 (March 1956), 62–63; "Africans Hear American Negro," *CL* 19, no. 1 (May 1957), 24; "Olympic Challenger," *CL* 18, no. 6 (October 1956), 80–81.
26. Al Fairbanks, "The American Negro Student," *HIS* 15, no. 6 (March 1955), 6–8; "The Cost of Prejudice," *HIS* 15, no. 6 (March 1955), 8; Joseph T. Bayly, "Editorial: He Died to Make Us Good," *HIS* 16, no. 6 (March 1956), 34 (inside back cover); William Pannell, "The Evangelical and Minority Groups," *HIS* 20, no. 1 (October 1959), 11–13; Arthur F. Glasser, "Hastening Day" *HIS* 15, no. 8 (May 1955), 8–13, 29–31; Robert O. Stephens, "Race Relations in Congo," *HIS* 18, no. 7 (April 1958), 15–16; Dudley Reeves, "Costly Prejudice," *HIS* 19, no. 3 (December 1958), 11–12; Mohandas K. Gandhi, "My Year in South Africa," *HIS* 19, no. 3 (December 1958), 6–10; "The Deep South and South Africa" Trend of Thought, *HIS* 16, no. 3 (December 1956), 20. See also Peter Letchford, "Dialog on Racial Prejudice," *HIS* 20, no. 1 (October 1959); "The Southern Case for Segregation" *HIS* 16, no. 7 (April 1956), 19; "What Does the Negro Want?" *HIS* 16, no. 8 (May 1956), 20; "Desegregation for Missionary Candidates," 17, no. 1 (October 1956), 21; "Students and Segregation" *HIS* 17, no. 3 (December 1956), 19; "Public Opinion Quarterly" *HIS* 17, no. 6 (March 1957), 20; "On A Christian Attitude Toward the Negro," *HIS* 19, no. 2 (November 1958), 17; "New Republic," *HIS* 20, no. 8 (May 1960), 17–18.
27. Letchford, "Dialog on Racial Prejudice," 7.
28. Bayly, "Editorial: He Died," 34; Letters to the Editor, *HIS* 15, no. 8 (May 1956), 35–34. By contrast, only one commendatory letter had been forthcoming after the publication of Smalley's 1949 article: Donzel E. Betts, Letter to the Editor, *HIS* 10, no. 8 (May 1950), 35.
29. James H. Jauncey, "Christian Citizenship Overcomes Prejudice (Race Relations Day): Acts 10:19–28," *TKB* 43, no. 1 (January 1952), 23–25.
30. The Little Rock event made national and international news, occurring at the time when television news programs were beginning to blossom. A good narrative account, illustrated by photographs, is "Hall Monitors from the 101st: The

Little Rock Story" in Juan Williams, *Eyes on the Prize* (New York: Viking Penguin, 1987).

31. The eulogy assessed the Till incident as "another blot . . . added to [the South's] already ugly record in the field of human justice"; Robert James St. Clair, "Segregation: Spiritual Frontier," *TKB* 48, no. 11 (November 1957); Lloyd Hamill, "Editorial: The Problem of Segregation and the Christian," *TKB* 48, no. 11 (November 1957), 6. *TKB* 46, no. 12 (December 1955), 11. On Billy Graham and Reinhold Niebuhr's reaction to Little Rock, see Miller, *Billy Graham and the Rise of the Republican South*, 68.

32. Reader Reaction, *TKB* 49, no. 1 (January 1958), 8; *TKB* 49, no. 2 (February 1958), 8–9; *TKB* 49, no. 3 (March 1958), 6; *TKB* 49, no. 4 (April 1958), 6; Editorial Response to a Letter from the Editor and Mrs. O. L. Hambrick, Letter to the Editor, both in *TKB* 49, no. 2 (February 1958), 9; "What Do Ministers Say About *The King's Business?*" *TKB* 49, no. 4 (April 1958), 2 (inside front cover). The ministers who endorsed it were without a doubt evangelical: R. S. Beal, Percy Crawford, M. R. DeHaan, Charles Fuller, Richard Halverson, Albert J. Lindsay, Wilbur E. Nelson, Bob Pierce, and Jack Wyrtzen. Ironically, Lindsay, a Tacoma, Washington, pastor was vehemently opposed to interracial marriage (see Albert J. Lindsey, "Shall We Have World Centralization?" *UEA*, March 15, 1955, 4).

33. *Eternity* was not quite as obscure as has been suggested by Curtis J. Evans: "White Evangelical Protestant Responses to the Civil Rights Movement," *Harvard Theological Review* 102, no. 2 (Spring 2009), 270. Barnhouse, who edited it until his death in 1960, was well connected to neoevangelicalism, particularly as the 1950s wore on, developing a close friendship with World Vision founder, Bob Pierce, even traveling with World Vision alongside other evangelical luminaries such as Carl Henry, Bernard Ramm, and Richard Halverson. Further, Barnhouse brought respected evangelical journalist Russell Hitt to *Eternity* as co-editor in the 1950s and published articles by well-known evangelical luminaries. As a result, *Eternity* was also consumed by a great number of leaders of the "new evangelicalism." For more on this topic see C. Allyn Russell, "Donald Grey Barnhouse: Fundamentalist Who Changed," *Journal of Presbyterian History* 59 (Spring 1981), 33–57.

34. Donald Grey Barnhouse, "Racial Difficulties," *Revelation* 15, no. 5 (May 1945), 224–227. Barnhouse and Russell T. Hitt, "Negro Population Shift," *Eternity* 6, no. 1 (January 1955), 12; Barnhouse, "Editorial: Race," *Eternity* 6, no. 4 (April 1955), 8–9; Editorial Response to a Letter from the Editor, *Eternity* 7, no. 1 (January 1956), 2; Barnhouse, "A Survey of 1955," *Eternity* 7, no. 1 (January 1956), 9, 42; Ben Marais, "The Church and Racial Tension in South Africa," *Eternity* 7, no. 6 (June 1956), 6–7, 47–48.

35. Harold Lindsell, "The Bible and Race Relations," *Eternity* 7, no. 8 (August 1956), 12–13, 43; Joseph T. Bayly, "A Northern Christian Looks at the Race Question," *Eternity* 7, no. 10 (October 1956).

36. Letters to the Editors, *Eternity* 7, no. 12 (December 1956); Letters to the Editors, *Eternity* 8, no. 1 (February 1957); Guy T. Gillespie, "A Southerner Looks at the Race Question," *Eternity* 8, no. 7 (July 1957). Gillespie was a southern Presbyterian (Presbyterian Church U.S.) minster and Belhaven College (Jackson, Mississippi) president. Martin H. Scharlemann, "The Church Must Be Color Blind," *Eternity* 8, no. 7 (July 1957); Letters to the Editors, *Eternity* 8, no. 9 (September 1957); for example, Charles McDowell, Letter to the Editors, *Eternity* 8, no. 11 (November 1957), 4.

37. Born in the Bahamas, Nottage experienced an evangelical conversion in 1904 before coming to America in 1910. He would later become a mentor of sorts to more famous African American evangelicals such as Howard Jones and William Pannell: Albert G. Miller, "The Rise of African-American Evangelicalism in American Culture," in *Perspectives on American Religion and Culture*, ed. Peter W. Williams (Malden, MA: Blackwell, 1999), 262–265.

38. B. M. Nottage, "You've Neglected My People," *Eternity* 8, no. 12 (December 1957), 12–13.

39. C. Herbert Oliver, "The Christian Negro: What Should He Do?" *Eternity* 11, no. 11 (November 1960), 15–16, 57–88. Eventually, Oliver became a veteran of the civil rights movement. For more on this topic, see Andrew M. Manis, *A Fire You Can't Put Out: The Civil Rights Life of Birmingham's Fred Shuttlesworth* (Tuscaloosa: University of Alabama Press, 1999), 234, 263, 290, 295, 368, 379–380; and Clarence Taylor, *Knocking at Our Own Door: Milton A. Galamison and the Struggle to Integrate New York City Schools* (New York: Columbia University Press, 1997), 195–202.

40. The employment of anthropology is addressed in the previous discussion. As an example of aligning with mainline thinkers, Robert St. Clair recommends mainline elite Liston Pope's perspective on race vis-à-vis evangelical segregationists. He also endorses a pamphlet series entitled, *Sense and Nonsense About Race* published by Friendship Press, the press of the National Council of Churches. Although supportive of interracial marriage, like other Americans most evangelicals cautioned regarding its difficulties. For example, James H. Jauncey, "Christian Citizenship Overcomes Prejudice (Race Relations Day): Acts 10:19– 28," *TKB* 43, no. 1 (January 1952), 23–25; Lindsell, "The Bible," 12–13, 43. In an article in *HIS*, the author deals with an American's marriage to an (Asian) Indian but intentionally leaves the terms of discussion broad: Name Withheld, "Inter-racial Marriage," *HIS* 18, no. 4 (January 1958), 38–41, 48.

41. Carl F. H. Henry, "Editorial: Why Christianity Today," *CT*, October 15, 1956, 20; Carl F. H. Henry to Billy Graham, May 26, 1956, Unprocessed Henry Papers, Folder: Graham, William Franklin [Billy]—Correspondence, 1955–1968; Henry, *Confessions of a Theologian* (Waco, TX: Word Books, 1986), 158–159; John W. Oliver, Jr., "Evangelical Campus and Press Meet Black America's Quest for Civil Rights, 1956–1959: Malone College and *Christianity Today*," *Fides et Historia* 8

(1975), 54–70; Mark J. Toulouse, "*Christianity Today* and American Public Life: A Case Study," *Journal of Church and State* 35, no. 2 (1993), 241–284; Evans, "White Evangelical Protestant Responses to the Civil Rights Movement," 246–273. Although dated, Oliver's conclusions are still generally correct, and he rightly cordons off the 1950s as a separate era. Toulouse's lengthy article is full of helpful information. Evans's article is the best of the three and incorporates the others into his work. Although it is difficult to quibble with Evans's thorough work and thoughtful analysis on this topic, I perceive two main differences in our approach: first, I tend to look at evangelicalism from the religious side, that is, the nature of evangelical identity and its character as a religious movement vis-à-vis political, social, and economic influences. Second, I see a marked difference between what was developing within evangelicalism in the 1950s and the later period.

42. E. Earle Ellis, "Segregation and the Kingdom of God," *CT*, March 18, 1957; Timothy L. Smith, "Christians and the Crisis of Race," *CT*, September 29, 1958; Henry, "Editorial: Desegregation and Regeneration," *CT*, September 29, 1958, 20; Ibid., "Editorial: Race Tensions and Social Change," *CT*, January 19, 1959.

43. Henry recounts his own conversion experience in *Confessions of a Theologian*, 42–48.

44. A "moderate" segregationist, Bell strongly advocated for *voluntary* segregation. Several letters from the L. Nelson Bell Papers (Collection 318) at the Billy Graham Center Archives (BGCA) demonstrate this position. From Box 1, Folder 18: L. Nelson Bell to Mrs. Russell H. Carter, November 22, 1957; Carter to Bell, June 12, 1957; Bell to Carter, June 26, 1957. From Box 15, Folder 15: Bell to W. E. Kibler, November 1, 1958. See also Julia Kirk Blackwelder, "White Southern Fundamentalists and the Civil Rights Movement," *Phylon* 40, no. 4 (4th Quarter, December 1979), 334–336. Steven Miller's assessment ("The Rise of African-American Evangelicalism," 18–19, 61–62) is also helpful. In addition, whatever he thought of integration, chief *CT* financier J. Howard Pew feared the growth of federal power. Evidently, the publication of the Smith's article and Henry's editorial "Desegregation and Regeneration" in the September 29, 1958 issue concerned Pew because it "put us on the side of the Supreme Court," which had overstepped its authority (Pew to Bell, October 1, 1958): J. Howard Pew to L. Nelson Bell, October 1, 1958; Bell to Pew, October 3, 1958, Carl F. H. Henry to Pew, October 7, 1958; Pew to Henry, November 3, 1958. All of these are found in the unprocessed Henry Papers at TEDS, Folder: Pew, J. Howard, 1959.

45. NAE *Statement of Faith*, Article 1. The NAE's *Statement of Faith* was unanimously adopted in 1943 by the Constitutional Convention of the NAE meeting in Chicago, IL; Hamill, "Editorial: The Problem of Segregation," 6; Mark A. Noll, "The Bible and Slavery," in *America's God: From Jonathan Edwards to Abraham*

Lincoln (New York: Oxford University Press, 2002), 386–401; "The Crisis over the Bible," in *The Civil War as a Theological Crisis* (Chapel Hill, NC: University of North Carolina Press, 2006), 31–50.

46. On African American intellectuals' use of the "one blood" motif, see Mark Chapman, "'Of One Blood': Mays and the Theology of Race Relations," in *Walking Integrity: Benjamin Elijah Mays, Mentor to Martin Luther King, Jr.*, ed. Lawrence Edward Carter (Atlanta: Mercer Press, 1998).

47. Genesis 9:23, 9:25. The entire story recounted here is found in Genesis 9:18–29 Stephen R. Haynes, *Noah's Curse: The Biblical Justification of American Slavery* (New York: Oxford University Press, 2002), 27–40.

48. Eugene D. Genovese, *A Consuming Fire: The Fall of the Confederacy in the Mind of the White Christian South*, Mercer University Lamar Memorial Lectures, No. 41 (Athens: University of Georgia Press, 1998), 73–98; Haynes, 116–121, 135–160; James, "What's Right With FEPC?" 3–4. Even such a revered evangelical figure as BIOLA president Louis Talbot perceived that Genesis 9 had to do with the origin of the races. "Dr. Talbot's Question Box," *TKB* 44:12 (December 1953), 24; "Dr. Talbot's Question Box," *TKB* 45, no. 2 (February 1954), 24. Mark Noll has suggested that this interpretation of Genesis 9 had "considerable currency" among lay people who supported segregation (Mark A. Noll, *God and Race in American Politics* [Princeton, NJ: Princeton University Press, 2008], 133). From my study, it was not uncommon among evangelical laity *and* ecclesiastical leaders. In addition to the "Dr. Talbot's Question Box" previously cited, see, for example, Chester J. Padgett, "Color is Skin Deep," *TKB* 44, no. 1 (January 1953), 24.

49. P. B. Fitzwater, review of *The Negro Community Within American Protestantism*, by Leonard L. Haynes, in *Moody Monthly* 54, no. 7 (March 1954), 68; Ben Marais, "Scripture and the Race Problem," *Eternity* 10, no. 8 (August 1959), 15; Mrs. Jane P. Lewis, Letter to the Editor, *CL* 17, no. November 7, 1955), 4–5; Peter Letchford, "Dialog on Racial Prejudice," 9; Bayly, "A Northern Christian," 42; "The Christian and the Color Line," 16; Miller, "The Rise of African-American Evangelicalism," 41–42.

50. In Acts 17:26, Paul addresses a group of men in Athens. Proclaiming the relevancy of the Christian message to the whole of humanity, Paul asserts that God "hath made of one blood all nations of men for to dwell on all the face of the earth, and hath determined the times before appointed, and the bounds of their habitation (KJV)." For examples of those who interpreted this verse as teaching segregation see the following: Chester J. Padgett, "Color is Skin Deep," *TKB* 44:1 (January 1953), 24; Padgett was a Bible professor at BIOLA. Another good example can be observed in *Sunday School Times* (*SST*) Associate Editor John W. Lane, Jr.'s regular column based on the Christian Endeavor Bible Study Plan, "The Young People's Prayer Meeting:" "My Neighbor the Negro (Rom. 15:1–7; Ruth 4:1–12)" *SST*, January 29, 1944; "The Myth of Racial Superiority (Acts

10:34, 35)," *SST*, January 27, 1945; "Being Christian in Race Relations (Acts 17:22–29)," *SST*, May 3, 1947; "Has Our Nation a Caste System (Gal. 3.26–29; Acts 10:9–18, 34, 35)," *SST*, January 29, 1949; "Progress in Race Relationships (Gal. 3:28)," *SST*, January 24, 1959. For examples of those who understood this verse to teach integration of the races, see the following: Bayly, "A Northern Christian," 42; Donald Grey Barnhouse and Russell T. Hitt, "Southern Pastors Hit at Klan's Misuse of Scripture," *Eternity* 8, no. 3 (March 1957), 14. "Christians and the Color Line," 16; H. H. Barnett, "What Can Southern Baptists Do?" *CT*, June 24, 1957, p. 15.

51. Billy Graham, "Billy Graham Makes a Plea for an End to Intolerance," *Life*, October 1, 1956, 146, quoted in Miller, *Billy Graham*, 43. Mid-century evangelicals—even staunch integrationists—sincerely believed in conversion as a transformative event. Thus, a premillennial dispensationalist who somewhat simplistically insisted that the real need was salvation because "real world equality can only exist among Christians" found theological affinity with the more erudite and prolix arguments of Carl Henry, who pointed to regeneration as the basis (although not necessarily solution) of a lasting solution to any protracted social problem. Carl Henry, "Editorial: Desegregation and Regeneration," *CT*, September 29, 1958; Walter L. Wilson, "World Peace Possible Through Missions: Matthew 23:8," *TKB* 38, no. 10 (October 1947), 15.

52. Clyde M. Narramore, "Talking It Over," *TKB* 47, no. 9 (September 1956), 39; Robert O. Stephens, "Race Relations in Congo," *HIS* 18, no. 7 (April 1958), 15–16; Horner, "Are Negroes Cursed?" 32; Billy Graham, "No Color Line in Heaven," *Ebony*, September 1957, 100; Nottage, "You've Neglected My People," 13; Bayly, "A Northern Christian," 47–48.

53. Lindsell, 12. The NAE's 1951 resolution is another good example: "NAE Convention Resolutions," *UEA*, May 1, 1954, 6.

54. Marais, "Scripture and the Race Problem," 14–15. Here, Marais references or alludes to the following passages: Genesis 12:1–3, John 1:1–18, Acts 2:1–47, and Ephesians 2:11–22.

55. Oliver, "The Christian Negro," 15–16, 58.

56. St. Clair, "Segregation," 13; V. Raymond Edman, "Personal Problem Clinic," *CL* 20, no. 7 (November 1958), 80; Horner, "Are Negroes Cursed?" 32; James, "What's Right With FEPC?" 3; Jesse Albergotti in "Pro–Con: What do YOU Say . . . " *TWR*, November 3, 1955, 2; Barnhouse and Hitt, "Southern Pastors," 14; St. Clair, "Segregation," 14; Edman, "Personal Problem Clinic," *CL* 20, no. 7 (November 1958), 80; Marais, "Scripture and the Race Problem,"14; Pannell, "The Evangelical and Minority Groups,"13; "The Christian and the Color Line," 15.

57. Bayly, "A Northern Christian," 40–41.

58. Ibid., 9, 41. In his comments on this topic, Billy Graham sounded strangely like Martin Luther King, Jr., lamenting that when "the church should have been the

pacesetter" on this critical issue, it was not; see Martin, *A Prophet with Honor*, 172. "Nation Eyes Dixie Christians," *CL* 18, no. 2 (June 1956), 13; St. Clair, "Segregation," 14–15; Martin, *A Prophet with Honor*, 72; Bayly, "A Northern Christian," 9, 41; Nottage, "You've Neglected My People," 13.

59. For more on the racialized nature of contemporary American society, see Emerson and Smith, *Divided by Faith*, 9–18.

2

Healing the Mystical Body: Catholic Attempts to Overcome the Racial Divide in Chicago, 1930–1948

Karen Joy Johnson

WHEN, IN 1938, Ann Harrigan, a twenty-six-year-old Irish Catholic school teacher from New York City, decided to skip a movie with friends to attend a talk at a local parish hall, she could not have known that the decision would change her life and, indeed, change history. The speaker that night, the Russian Baroness Catherine de Hueck, presented a Christian faith that emphasized the sinfulness of racial discrimination present in American society and argued that true Christians would work to overcome it. De Hueck thundered that to help God save the world, the Catholic laity (not just the priests) must work for social justice for all Americans because "before the war-torn, hungry, naked, miserable world can listen to [Catholic] voices, they must alleviate its material misery."[1] Sending more money to support missionary priests who were working among African Americans was not the solution de Hueck offered, even though this practice was the extent of white Catholic religious involvement with African Americans if they participated at all. White Catholics, de Hueck argued, must actually cross racial boundaries.

In doing so, white Catholics would keep their "date" with "Christ in the Negro." De Hueck was using the reemerging doctrine of the Mystical Body of Christ to argue that Jesus Christ actually—not symbolically—lived and breathed among America's black population. Few American Catholics pondered the humanity of African Americans, much less their union with Jesus. But if they wanted to know Jesus, de Hueck claimed, they had to get to know African Americans. To that end, she invited her listeners to join her at the Friendship House she was opening in Harlem. Harrigan accepted de Hueck's offer and became a great proponent of "Christ in the Negro."

In Harlem, Harrigan met Ellen Tarry, a black woman who had a different perspective about how white and black Catholics should work together for civil rights.[2] Tarry was drawn to Friendship House less as a way to meet Jesus and more because of de Hueck's charisma, focus on civil rights, and emphasis on what de Hueck argued was true Catholicism. When she first visited de Hueck's Harlem flat, Tarry found a group of mostly white young people gathered around de Hueck. "I could catch phrases like 'the Fatherhood of God, and the Brotherhood of man' or 'the Negro and the Mystical Body' which indicated much more depth than I had attributed to these youngsters," Tarry recalled. She "entered the room as a Doubting Thomas and left as an ardent disciple."[3]

But Tarry did not adopt de Hueck's, and later Harrigan's, language of "Christ in the Negro." Instead, Tarry changed it to "God *and* the Negro," reflecting a different perspective than her white counterparts.[4] And Tarry also knew that the white people who were trying to serve God and the Negro had a lot to learn. Of her first encounter with Friendship House in 1938, Tarry wrote

> I was convinced that Friendship House needed me and many other Negroes if it was to be the Catholic Center the Baroness said was needed to combat the forces of Godless Communism in Harlem. But I would have to get more Negroes to help me and we would have to explain to these well-intentioned white boys and girls that, instead of working *for* the Negro, they would have to work *with* us.[5]

Tarry knew that this perspectival shift would disrupt traditional power hierarchies and elevate African Americans, which was necessary for their own well-being and to make interracial justice meaningful.

Tarry, Harrigan, and de Hueck were lay leaders in the Catholic interracial movement. This movement was a response to the discrimination built into Catholic institutions and American society, and its participants—men and women, black and white, clergy and lay—worked together to create a more integrated and just Church and society. Catholic interracialism was most dominant in northern cities. Its growth surged by the 1920s but declined in the late 1960s. In 1942, as the Catholic interracial movement gained momentum, these three women founded a Friendship House in Chicago. Their struggle to work together and work with Chicago's black community reveals the complicated nature of Catholic interracialism.

Their story complements *Divided by Faith*'s focus on evangelicals by shifting attention to the intersection of race and religion among Catholics. Like Emerson and Smith's work, this study shows how religion shaped racial perceptions and how race shaped religion. Not surprisingly, Catholic interracialists' experience of Catholicism—just as black and white evangelicals' experience of evangelicalism—was racialized. In addition, like the evangelicals of the late twentieth century, Catholic interracialists used their religious tools, shaped by their culture, to forge a theology and practice of Catholic interracialism.

This essay also illuminates the value of historical context. That de Hueck, Harrigan, and Tarry were members of the Catholic Church and worked out their notion of Catholic interracialism in the context of the Depression and World War II matters tremendously. First, they lived in a time in which society, even northern society, was explicitly and implicitly racialized. Their battles, therefore, were different from those of late-twentieth-century evangelicals. Second, in contrast to Emerson and Smith's white evangelicals, De Hueck, Harrigan, and Tarry were able to forge a notion of Catholic interracialism that did, in many ways, help to overcome racial hierarchies in America. Their success was due, in large part, to the origin of their theology of Catholic interracialism, which grew out of the corporatist ethos of the Depression era and Catholic social thought. Catholic interracialists, quite simply, had more tools in their theological tool kits to deal with questions of race. In addition, particularly because the white women lived with African Americans, they made race a central, not a peripheral, category to their understanding of their faith.

Next, their theology addressed individual relationships and society. They worked on an individual level by emphasizing relationships and on the corporate level by emphasizing social justice. Despite these Catholic interracialists' focus on structures, however, one of their primary solutions was to build relationships, which is what Friendship House would be known for in the 1960s. The individualism of the American ethos was always in tension with the corporatism of Catholicism, to some extent foreshadowing the individualism and anti-structuralism of the white evangelicals Emerson and Smith studied.

Finally, this essay also takes Emerson and Smith's work a step further by exploring the internal relational dynamics of Catholics committed to racial justice and ultimately reveals the challenges of interracial relationships and organizations. In the end, de Hueck, Harrigan, and Tarry failed to bring about the full measure of justice in both their own relationships and in society that they were honestly seeking. But their story nonetheless offers insights to all Americans about some potential ways that faith can help break down the barriers of race.

How Catholicism Shaped Race in the Early Twentieth Century

In the late nineteenth and early twentieth centuries, Chicago's parishes followed a national model, which seemed justified given the city's incredible growth in the second half of the nineteenth century, much of it due to immigrants from the Old World coming to Chicago. John McGreevy, the preeminent historian of race and Catholicism in the urban North noted, "African-American Catholics, like Poles, Italians, and other Euro-American groups, were expected to worship in their own parishes, receive the ministrations of religious-order priests specially trained for work in their community, and learn from nuns who were devoted to working in their parochial schools."[6] Because the city had so many immigrants, its bishops had supported churches that catered to specific ethnic groups, particularly by holding services in a group's native language. The leaders of the Church believed that the best way to minister to Catholics was by grouping them according to ethnicity.

The national parish model matched the racial dynamics of the United States in the late nineteenth and early twentieth centuries. At the turn of the century, Americans conflated ethnicity and race, treating groups like the Irish and Polish as racial categories.[7] *White* did not have the same meaning that it developed after the 1924 Immigration Act. Each parish, therefore, was a racial/ethnic enclave, and as late as 1910, Italian immigrants were more segregated than black Chicagoans.[8] Although Chicago was a city divided among ethnic lines at the turn of the century, African Americans were treated by nonblacks as a group apart, and that pattern would only increase.

Racial discrimination in Chicago grew because of the tensions that arose as more black people moved north as part of the Great Migration. Between 1910 and 1940, 1.75 million southern African Americans moved to northern cities. Between 1910 and 1920, Chicago's black population increased by 148%, going from a population of 44,103 to 109,458. Ten years later, the black population had again more than doubled, reaching 233,903 by 1930.[9] As a result, during the first few decades of the twentieth century, Chicago's parish model began to shift slowly away from an ethnic parish model as the racial order of the city gradually became a black/white binary. This process was by no means uniform, unidirectional, or universal. In ebbs and flows, black Chicagoans began to experience more discrimination that was tied to their skin color. By 1915, most of Chicago's black population lived in a narrow strip of land on the south side of the city, which became known as the Black Belt. The belt extended from the railroad yards on the west to Cottage Grove Avenue on the east and from the central business district into the Woodlawn and Englewood neighborhoods.[10] As the rate of black migration from the South increased beginning in 1900, two interrelated things happened. First, middle- and upper-class black families began to look for homes on blocks where they had previously not lived. Second, the white ethnic residents of those blocks became upset. The movement of African Americans combined with the developing anti-black racism, therefore, shaped Chicago's racial dynamics in a sharper, new way.

White Catholic practice and theology upheld the growing exclusion of African Americans. The movement of black families to white neighborhoods was particularly troubling to white Catholics because they merged their neighborhood and religious lives. The Catholic Church maintained a parish model, meaning that all members of a particular geographic area were cared for by the local church. Local priests encouraged parishioners to commit themselves to their parish by buying a house, pouring their lives' savings into brick and mortar. Parishioners gave their tithe to the church to support new buildings, schools, and programs for their children and in the process created a nearly separate Catholic world. The reaction to a black family moving into a white ethnic neighborhood, then, was a mix of racism and economic self-interest as white families feared dropping property values. The new black residents, furthermore, were unlikely to be Catholic, and so the priests could not expect them to support church programs. White responses to these changes tightened a noose around black Chicago through improvement associations, community newspapers, boycotts, restrictive covenants, and racial violence in an attempt to contain all black Chicagoans within strict geographic boundaries.[11]

In 1916, Chicago's Catholics celebrated the installation of George Mundelein as their new archbishop. As an iron-fisted leader, Mundelein tried to make the Church more Catholic, or universal, by pushing forward an Americanization campaign among his parishioners. He pushed his agenda in three ways. First, he attempted to shift the city's parishes from the national parish model to a territorial parish model, which was based on geography rather than race or ethnicity. Second, he standardized the school curricula so that all children were receiving similar educations. Third, he created a seminary for Chicago's priests so they could be trained uniformly in one location. Overall, the thrust of Mundelein's work was toward universalizing Catholicism in Chicago, a move that many of his ethnic parishioners fought tooth and nail. But they agreed with Mundelein on the one important exception that he made to his universalizing program.[12]

Mundelein helped his all-white priesthood and white laity discriminate against black Catholics.[13] During World War II, Mundelein began to talk with J. A. Burgmer, SVD, the provincial of the Society of the Divine Word with North American headquarters north of Chicago in Techny, about taking over the administration of St. Monica's parish, which had a predominantly black population but also included several white families. By placing the responsibility for the care of African Americans in the hands of missionaries trained to serve in foreign lands, Mundelein separated African Americans from the rest of the ethnic groups as a missionary population. Naming the city's African Americans a missionary population ignored and demoted families who had been members of the Church for generations and removed them from the concern of the Archdiocese's diocesan priests. In a letter dated October 26, 1917, Mundelein announced his intention that the Society of the Divine Word take over the care of St. Monica's parish and also declared St. Monica's to be "reserved entirely for the Colored Catholics of Chicago and particularly of the South Side; all other Catholics of whatever race or color are to be requested not to intrude."[14]

To many people Mundelein's intentions seemed benign, and, indeed, he believed his course of action would bring more black converts into the Catholic fold. He stated, "It is, of course, understood that I have no intention of excluding colored Catholics from any of the other churches in the diocese, and particularly if they live in another part of the city, but simply excluding from St. Monica's all but the colored Catholics." To support his decision, Mundelein argued first that the white Catholics who had been attending St. Monica's would not be too inconvenienced because they could go to other white parishes nearby. Second, Mundelein suggested that the intrusion of people who were not black into a parish that had originally been founded as a black parish had caused crowding, disturbance, and embarrassment for the black parishioners at St. Monica's. Finally, Mundelein wanted to give the parishioners at St. Monica's an opportunity to prove to others that they could support their own school and church. Mundelein summed up his reasoning:

> Because of the circumstances that exist in this city I am convinced that our colored Catholics will feel themselves much more comfortable, far less inconvenienced and never at all embarrassed if, in a church that is credited to them, they have their own sodalities and societies, their own school and choir, in which they alone will constitute the membership, and for even stronger reasons the first places in the church should be theirs just as much as the seats in the rear benches are.[15]

Mundelein's arguments about how Catholic theology spoke to race are important. He did not suggest that the Catholic faith had anything to say about what African Americans were seeing as an increasingly oppressive racial order. Mundelein acknowledged that "a distinction of color" often shaped "the daily happenings of our city," but he refused to comment on that fact:

> I am not going to argue as to the reasons for or against this line of distinction which causes so much bitterness, nor will I say anything as to the justice or injustice of it. It is sufficient to say that it does exist and that I am convinced that *I am quite powerless to change it*, for I believe the underlying reasons to be more economic than social. What I am concerned about is that my colored children shall not feel uncomfortable in the Catholic Church.[16]

Mundelein admitted that Chicago's white Catholics treated their black brethren poorly and was concerned that their racist practices would hinder the expansion of the Church among African Americans. But rather than addressing white Catholics' habits and beliefs, Mundelein created a separate church where black parishioners would not have to interact with white parishioners. He saw it as a refuge for black Catholics. Chicago's African Americans, Mundelein concluded, "are as dear to me as their white-skinned brethren, and that for them and for their children too, I must one day render an accounting before the Eternal Judge Who looks not at the color of our faces, but searches for the purity of our hearts and judges us by the fruits we have to show."[17] Catholic religion, Mundelein said, was color blind; God loved all people. But the manifestation of that love did not extend to material, or "economic," realities. In Mundelein's mind, Catholic faith had nothing to say to a racial social order. Many black Catholics challenged this understanding of Catholicism almost immediately, but it took the city's white Catholics years to reach the same conclusion.

African Americans' responses to Mundelein's letter show the diversity of opinions on how the city's shifting racism should be handled. Some, like the Pullman Porter's review editor, praised Mundelein. Although he and his staff, the editor wrote, were Protestants, "never in my life time have we heard or read of such a beautiful tribute as you pay the colored race."[18] On the other hand, a group of eighty-one black Catholics from St. Monica's immediately asked Mundelein to reverse his action. They suggested that Mundelein had distinguished black Catholics from other Catholics and put them in an "anomalous position" by his "policy of segregation in relation to the affairs of St. Monica's." These parishioners did not want whites barred from St. Monica's because they knew it would be unlike other national churches.

Mundelein's response was swift and unmoving. First, through his chancellor, Mundelein asserted his authority, telling the protesters that he had consulted ecclesiastics "who were engaged in zealous work among the colored people long before many of your signatories were born as well as of more than one active and even prominent colored Catholics here and elsewhere."[19] Then, he reminded the protesters that they could go to any church they wanted because he had "given to the colored Catholics of this city the entire liberty of attending and affiliating themselves with any other parishes," and insisted that "nothing was further from [his] mind than to insist on or even suggest anything as segregation."[20]

But most of Mundelein's white priests, nuns, and laity thought otherwise. They used Mundelein's dictum to justify second-class citizenship in black parishes and African Americans could only participate fully in the black parish. Although Mundelein had made it clear that black Catholics could attend any church they wanted, during his tenure he allowed white diocesan priests to deny the sacraments to black parishioners and force them to go to St. Monica's. In addition, priests and nuns frequently denied black children admission to the local parish school. Culturally and theologically the school issue was a major problem for black Catholics. At the Third Plenary Council of Baltimore in 1884, the American bishops emphasized the importance of Catholic education, decreeing that "near every church a parish school, where one does not yet exist, is to be built and maintained *in perpetuum* within two years of the promulgation of this council. . . . All parents," the legislation continued, "are bound to send their children to the parish school."[21] This decree became Church policy in the United States. But if a black Catholic child applied for admission to his or her local parish and that parish was not a black parish, the nuns denied admission.

Policies like Mundelein's, which Church leaders across the North enacted, not only used the Church to support black/white racial division but also racialized the experiences of parishioners, priests, and nuns. For instance, Ann Harrigan grew up in the insular bosom of the immigrant Catholic Church in New York City, largely unaware of the discrimination that African Americans faced. Even though she was deeply concerned about social justice in 1938, the year she met Catherine de Hueck, Harrigan could legitimately claim that she knew, and cared, little about black people's struggles. She recalled, "All kinds of mixed feelings clamored inside me—gnawing regret, the turmoil of wondering how I ever could make amends for these terrible injustices, alternating with an immense relief at knowing that perhaps I could do something, and the sensation of sweet joy of having come upon a precious treasure—the truth."[22] Even in the liberal Catholic circles Harrigan traveled, race clearly demarcated her realm of existence.

When Mundelein died in 1939, he left a quite a racial legacy. He constructed a Catholic church that provided for the unification of white ethnic Catholics, while fostering the exclusion of black Catholics from white divisions. A generation of Catholics had grown up under this developing binary racial hierarchy, the vast majority of white Catholics favored the racial order, and most of the city's African Americans who were not Catholic thought the Church was racist. This was the situation into which de Hueck, Harrigan, and Tarry would step three years later. But there was also a countervailing force to the racialized Catholicism from which they could draw.

Catholic Interracial Organizations

Catholic interracialism drew on the corporatist ethos of Catholic social thought and was initially rooted in the black community. Unlike evangelicalism in the late twentieth century, Catholic doctrine in the United States did not support laissez-faire capitalism. It also opposed the increasing inequality and dehumanization of the new industrial order that was in full bloom at the end of the nineteenth century. Instead, it argued for a more corporatist view of society. Pope Leo XIII's 1891 encyclical *Rerum Novarum* was a key document for defining, as he put it, "the relative rights and mutual duties of the rich and of the poor, of capital and of labor."[23] Leo emphasized the dignity of each person; the commitment that individuals must have to the common good, the charity, or concern for others; and the rightness of labor unions and other interest groups if they promoted love and worked for the good of society. This encyclical laid the groundwork for Catholic social thought.[24]

Catholic social thought flourished during the financial crises of the Depression, when Americans began to question laissez-faire capitalism and business authority.[25] Before becoming an interracialist, Harrigan had blossomed as a volunteer in the most radical Catholic response to the Depression: the Catholic Worker movement, founded by Dorothy Day, who was also a friend of de Hueck and Peter Maurin in 1933. Through her friendship with Day, Harrigan began to live an alternate life to the "bourgeoisie" manner of her upwardly mobile family. Harrigan remembered "the thrill of that wet Saturday afternoon in 1933 when, arms full of packages, I pushed my way out of Macy's on 34th Street and stood waiting for the rain to stop." She recalled hearing "a voice near me yelling, '*Catholic Worker!* Buy the *Catholic Worker!*'" Her ears perked up. "Could I have heard right? *Daily Worker*, yes—This was their favorite spot to hawk—but the *Catholic Worker*? Incredible, I said to myself, and bought the paper."[26] The *Daily Worker* to which Harrigan referred was the newspaper of the Communist Party; Day had countered it with her *Catholic Worker*. Through the *Catholic Worker*, Harrigan developed a strong structural critique of society that primed her for understanding how race worked. She volunteered at the *Catholic Worker* for five years, working by day as a public school teacher.

African American Catholics complicated the corporatist notions of Catholic social thought by applying it to race. For example, although the *Catholic Worker* newspaper reported on the labor issues faced by both black and white Americans, it was Arthur Falls, a black Catholic doctor from Chicago, who suggested to Day that she change the masthead of the paper to include a black and white worker, instead of just two white workers.[27] Black migrants to northern cities like Ellen Tarry, who moved to Harlem from Alabama, helped sensitize their priests (who were nearly all white) to the injustices African Americans faced in their new homes. At the same time, using the language of Catholic social thought, black lay leaders developed organizations committed to promoting black rights in the Catholic Church.

These organizations were not without internal racial conflict, often along racial and hierarchical lines. In 1917, black layman Joseph Turner founded The Committee Against the Extension of Race Prejudice, which became the Federated Colored Catholics in 1925, a race-conscious organization that worked for African American equality in the Catholic Church.[28] White Jesuit Fathers William Markoe and John LaFarge (who later invited de Hueck to Harlem) both worked in northern cities and supported Turner. But by the end of the 1920s, Markoe and LaFarge shifted the organization's priorities away from black rights toward interracialism. This shift revealed differing priorities between some of the black laymen and the white clerics involved. Turner and many of the other African American laymen in the Federated Colored Catholics wanted to maintain a degree of black autonomy and focus on black rights, while clergymen Markoe and LaFarge wanted to break down boundaries of race and work for interracialism.[29] Catholics on both sides of the debate opposed the inequalities of segregation, but they disagreed on how to achieve parity.

LaFarge became the most prominent interracialist priest, and he contributed greatly to the development of an intellectual and theological framework for Catholic interracialism. Tarry, who knew and greatly admired LaFarge, later recalled, "Father LaFarge reminded white America that there is a problem as far as black Catholics are concerned, and blacks in general."[30] Unlike LaFarge, however, the women of Friendship House did not have easy access to the halls of power and were limited by their status as both women and lay people.

Friendship House Opens in Chicago

In the spring of 1942, Bishop Bernard Sheil invited de Hueck to open a Friendship House in Chicago. Mundelein had promoted Sheil, but Sheil was more racially progressive than his patron.[31] Sheil learned about

Friendship House through a reporter originally from Chicago named Eddie Doherty. On an assignment from *Liberty* magazine to report on the slums of Harlem in 1940, Doherty met de Hueck and became a supporter of Friendship House. Doherty eventually fell in love with his "angel of Harlem" and frequently asked de Hueck to marry him. Spurned by de Hueck, Doherty had moved to Chicago to work for the white daily, the *Chicago Sun*. When de Hueck visited him in Chicago, Doherty introduced her to Sheil, hoping the priest would convince de Hueck to marry him. Instead, to Doherty's chagrin, Sheil agreed that de Hueck should pursue her work in the lay apostolate of Friendship House and a few months later the bishop invited Friendship House to Chicago.[32] De Hueck planned to remain at the Harlem house and so asked Harrigan and Tarry to be the co-directors of the new house.

Harrigan jubilantly agreed, but Tarry hesitated because of her ambivalence and her desire to write as a career. Both women would have to sacrifice something. Harrigan requested a leave of absence from her job teaching in New York City's public schools, giving as the official reason that she would be taking classes in sociology at the University of Chicago. She also left without the support of her family who, at best, did not fully support her interracialist leanings, and at worst, called de Hueck a Communist (which for Catholics of the time was anathema). This opportunity was, however, Harrigan's dream. It was not Tarry's. Moving would require Tarry to leave her job at the *Amsterdam News*, which she felt was her true calling. Nonetheless, Tarry agreed to move to Chicago for a year to serve her race, even though leaving New York was "the last thing [she] wanted to do."[33] De Hueck planned for Tarry to direct the black members and volunteers and for Harrigan to direct the white ones. They moved to Chicago in late summer 1942.

By mid-September, Friendship House was ready for its grand opening. Harrigan and Tarry recruited volunteers from the nearby St. Elizabeth's parish (which had merged with St. Monica's in 1924 and had become the flagship black parish in Chicago) and Chicago more broadly. Two storefronts at 305 and 309 East 43rd Street housed a children's center, a Catholic library, and Friendship House's office. According to Harrigan, "It was the right location. Stores, milling crowds, trolley cars, trucks, the El, all close by. Cheap theatres, taverns, hundreds of kids running around the streets, broken-down houses, with here and there a street of home-owners who kept up their property carefully."[34] Their presence in Chicago and Harrigan's presence on the South Side and as a parishioner at St. Elizabeth's was a protest to the racial hierarchy that had developed. Friendship House in Chicago would have many challenges to overcome, but they also drew from a heritage of strength both within Catholic social thought and from the black community.

The Mystical Body of Christ and the Black Jesus

The key to understanding the strength of Friendship House lies in looking at the theology that implicitly and explicitly shaped the group. More than any other Catholic interracialist group, they emphasized the doctrine of the people of the Mystical Body of Christ. The doctrine reemerged among Catholics at a time in which it was becoming more common to speak of the brotherhood of man under the fatherhood of God as a rhetorical device supporting things from the New Deal to black civil rights. It stated that all men and women were mystically united together by the Holy Spirit as members of the Body of Christ, of which Jesus was the actual head. People were not autonomous with their own rights nor were they just part of an organization. According to this view, just as a human body has millions of cells each living its own life, so the Church had millions of people, each living their own lives who were incorporated into the Body through baptism.

Furthermore, and perhaps most provocatively, the doctrine suggested that Catholics must view all people as potentially part of the Mystical Body because "some there are who are without grace, yet will afterwards obtain it, and some have it already."[35] There would be no exclusion or isolation according to race or even religion. According to Harrigan, "whether a man be a capitalist, a communist, a Negro, a Jew, a Protestant, etc., he is our brother because ALL MEN ARE OUR BROTHERS."[36] This theology, then, allowed Catholic interracialists to argue for the inclusion of black people—not just black Catholics—in the Body. Finally, because all people were members of Christ's body, whatever one person did to another person, he or she actually did to Jesus because each member, in a mystical way not understood through rational means, was actually Christ.

The doctrine became a source of authority to these lay interracialists who in this time would have had otherwise little authority in the Church. The interracialists used this authority to challenge racial hierarchies within the Catholic Church and in American society generally. Priests in this time had all the power. Before Vatican II, the focus of Catholic popular religion had been on pietistic practices like praying the rosary coupled with popular expressions of faith such as street marches, and the Catholic laity's primary job was to receive the sacraments that the priests dispensed. In this atmosphere, Catholic interracialists lived out a corporate expression of Catholic faith that moved beyond traditional parochial boundaries, questioned authority, and did not look like the faith of a generation reared on individual piety and Mass attendance. Indeed, the women involved in Friendship House spoke like prophetic priests not only to the male and female laity but also to the hierarchy, thus contesting the social order within Catholicism.[37] Interracialism had profound consequences.

A Catholic's very soul was in danger of hell unless one worked to liberate Christ in the Negro, said De Hueck. Chapter 25 of the book of Matthew became a key scripture for the women of Friendship House. According to de Hueck, to be accepted by God at the Last Judgment one must "feed the hungry, give drink to the thirsty, clothe the naked, look after the sick, and visit those in prison." In Catholic terminology, these were spiritual and corporeal acts of mercy. To not do these meant eternal punishment. The Gospels, De Hueck observed, are "perfectly clear and quite simple" about what God expects of his people. According to De Hueck, practicing "corporeal and spiritual acts of mercy toward our brethren, especially the least of them . . . was, and is, and always shall be a part of our faith, without which we cannot save our souls."[38]

But by not caring for black Americans, Catholics were not caring for Christ. Christ in the Negro languished, segregated in large cities and towns across America, as De Hueck wrote, by "walls of . . . prejudice and discrimination that most of us have in our hearts." His suffering would condemn American Catholics. De Hueck argued,

> It is quite conceivable that [Christ would say to an American Catholic] I was hungry for the justice of my father and you did not give me to eat. And I was thirsty for friendship and understanding and you did not give me to drink. And I was naked of any privileges and rights belonging to me as a human being such as the right to work, the right to the pursuit of happiness, and you did not clothe me with them. And I was in prison, the bars of which were made not of iron or steel but prejudice and discrimination, and you neither broke these bars nor visited me. And I was sick with despair and loneliness and you did not minister unto me.

And when the poor sinner asked when he could have helped Christ in this way, Christ would respond, "I was in the American Negro, and you—you were a white American Catholic."[39]

How was De Hueck, a white woman, able to portray Christ as a black man deserving justice? Hers was a radical move that made many of her contemporaries uncomfortable. Most Catholic art portrayed Jesus as a white man, and racist and racialized fears of social equality and miscegenation limited white Americans' responses to black civil rights efforts. First, she claimed that she was listening to God and following the tradition of the Church and Scripture. Offsetting her serious message, De Hueck portrayed herself and those who agreed with her as simple, almost child-like people simply seeking to hear from God. This rhetorical move shifted the authority of her message from herself to God and suggested that everyone should be able to understand and obey.

De Hueck, and eventually Harrigan, was also able to argue that Christ was black and become a spokeswoman for black Catholics because they lived with African Americans. When Harrigan began to visit Harlem in 1938, she discovered a black world she never knew existed. Like de Hueck, Harrigan immersed herself in black culture, giving her conversion to interracialism true life. She learned about black history and read Harlem Renaissance-era luminaries such as James Weldon Johnson (*The Autobiography of an Ex-Colored Man*) and Richard Wright (*Native Son*) and poets like Countee Cullen and Claude McKay. She prayed to black saints and holy men, developed friendships with African Americans like Ellen Tarry, and developed black love interests.[40] Harrigan helped lead the only black Catholic Youth Organization in the country, and, as her interracialist consciousness grew, began to lecture on Catholic interracialism, becoming a public mouthpiece for Friendship House's message. Harrigan recalled, "[I] ate, drank and slept Friendship House . . . spending all my waking time there except for teaching and travelling to [and] from Brooklyn."[41] After spending a summer running Friendship House while de Hueck was abroad, Harrigan described her work there as, in part, "an extended hangover—heat, noise, endless itching b./c of the bed bugs, and little sleep."[42] Above all, Harrigan began to understand her faith in such a way that it became impossible to separate it from serving Christ in the Negro.

The interracial justice for which Friendship House worked and prayed matched the concerns that African Americans had in the long civil rights movement: fair employment, equitable payment, increased educational opportunities, and an end to segregation in businesses, public places, and housing. Friendship House, because of its grounding in the Catholic Church, also worked to end to segregation in churches. White members followed de Hueck's model and moved to black neighborhoods to live and work. The longer the white members were involved with black people, the more their religious views changed and the more they adopted black perspectives on American society. Black members and volunteers taught the white members about black culture and helped pave the way for Friendship House in their communities.

Because of their grounding in black culture and thinking, Friendship House's members did not claim that black people should—or even could—simply pull themselves up by their own bootstraps. Instead they blamed white Americans for structurally excluding black Americans from opportunities open to other Americans. They called the Catholic Church, and society at large, to turn from segregation and immediately create an integrated society, modeled on what they were seeking to practice at Friendship House. The social interactions that Friendship House promoted led to a number of interracial marriages striking at the heart of many northerners' fears about miscegenation. They flipped their contemporaries' parlance of a "Negro problem" on its head, saying that the nation's racial problems were actually a white problem. Thus, unlike Emerson and Smith's white evangelicals, this interracial group was able to connect personally with structural sin.

But despite their structural critique, the Friendship House group shared the hope that they could change the world by building cross-racial friendships and reforming themselves. From there, they hoped to help rebuild all of society from the inside out. Of these early days, Harrigan wrote,

> The ambience was unforgettable: walls lined with books, a place of not many lights, muted by smoke. (The "B" [de Hueck] as we called her smoked like a chimney then.) White faces, black faces, talking, laughing, friendly, sipping coffee. How simple the solution all seemed then: the sooner we of different races learned to work together, to pray together, to eat, to study, to laugh together, the sooner we'd be on the way to interracial justice.[43]

But as Harrigan would learn, interracial justice—indeed sometimes even living peacefully with people from a different race and culture—would be much harder to attain.

Black Responses to "Christ in the Negro"

Despite closely identifying with African Americans and entering into their suffering, white members of Friendship House found their efforts limited by the powerful effects of race in American history and society. Many black people would not accept them, and they often failed to see eye to eye with black friends. Even for Ellen Tarry, who was committed to Friendship House, working with de Hueck and Harrigan was a struggle because of how hard it was for them to understand one another. Some of their conflict was related to personality; other parts were related to race. Tarry wrote to de Hueck in 1942, "Lordy, Lord! We need to ask the Holy Ghost to tell us what *not* to say, more than what *to* say, because my folks are so sensitive. There are times when I want to choke you so you can't say another word, and at the same time, I know there will be a day when others feel the same way about me."[44] Although de Hueck offended some African Americans, Tarry was willing to stick by de Hueck because of their friendship.

But even Tarry vacillated in her views toward loving white people. Her letters from the summer of 1940, when she returned to the South to see family and conduct research, reveal her ambivalence about interracialism despite her deep commitment. As war raged in Europe, she observed that southern African Americans seemed indifferent to the death toll in Europe, thinking, "Heck! The white man has been killing us all along, so maybe he'll give us a rest and kill his blood brothers for a while." But, Tarry wrote to de Hueck, "I can't condemn my folk for their bitterness . . . but I try to see or understand my white brother's point of view."

Tarry believed, however, that her faith could unite black and white people across racial lines. Tarry concluded in a letter from the South, "So many of my brothers in Christ are white. And my blood brothers are black. Why we can't see the folly of hatred between us is perplexing at times." The kinship she experienced with white people at Friendship House, to whom she was linked by the Mystical Body of Christ, made her unable to condemn white people. Tarry came to believe that friendship was essential for interracial justice. Then, referring to her friendship with de Hueck, Tarry wrote, "I know we share a similar slogan, 'God and the Negro' and that is a powerfully strong connecting link."[45] Notably, Tarry's rallying cry differed from de Hueck's and Harrigan's "Christ in the Negro." Perhaps because the phrase sounded odd or patronizing to black ears, Tarry did not talk about Christ in the Negro. Her struggle was to see Christ in white people.

More whites than African Americans associated with Friendship House, especially as staff workers. To be a staff worker—which meant that one lived and worked at Friendship House and was devoted full-time to interracial justice—one had to commit to live in voluntary poverty. They made this commitment as a way to stand outside and witness against the unfettered capitalism and racism of American society and to identify with the poorest African Americans. Harrigan explained that voluntary poverty meant "limiting your DESIRES to fewer things so that you have more time to spend in the service of others. Possessions tend to possess you. The more you have, the less there is for others."[46] In practice for members of Friendship House voluntary poverty meant earning no wage, wearing second-hand clothing, holding no health insurance, and eating whatever they could buy with the donations they received. But few African Americans found voluntary poverty appealing; they wanted to participate in the fruits of American capitalism. Also, because of job discrimination, they often needed the money to contribute to their family incomes. Tarry reflected, "Voluntary poverty is neither attractive nor practical for the average trained Negro" and so "the first staff members of Friendship House were all white."[47] Only white, middle class individuals like Harrigan and De Hueck had the luxury of adopting voluntary poverty. On the rare occasion that a black person was a member, he or she was paid—as Tarry was in her time as a staff worker. Thus, voluntary poverty, which de Hueck intended to help Friendship House staff workers identify with poor African Americans, actually limited full black participation in the group because it made little sense to African Americans struggling to get by.

Finally, many African Americans never fully accepted Friendship House's vision. As Tarry remembered, de Hueck

> knew that a white woman of Russian birth, noble or otherwise, living in Harlem would cause talk, it was difficult for [de Hueck] to understand how the Negroes she had come to serve could question her motives.... Once, when she was very weary, [de Hueck] told me that working with the Negro was like walking on eggshells. As the years rolled by she came to understand the background which had bred so much suspicion.[48]

Friendship House had a few hundred years of history to overcome, and the social, religious, and interpersonal work was hard.

Struggles in Chicago

From the time that Harrigan and Tarry arrived in Chicago, they faced adversity and within a few months of Friendship House's opening, Tarry left Chicago and returned to New York City. The problems began with the seemingly simple question of where they would live. In the midst of Chicago's housing shortage on the South Side, caused largely by restrictive housing covenants and white-on-black violence, the only place Tarry and Harrigan could to stay was an upstairs room at Sunshine Edwards's funeral parlor on south Michigan Avenue. Tarry could never tell Harrigan "how many times I had found living quarters for us and was told 'Oh, that's different,' when I explained my roommate was white."[49] Then, when Harrigan was out at night without Tarry, Tarry stayed up until Harrigan returned home, fearing for Harrigan's safety.[50] Tarry could not describe her feelings to Harrigan and "felt disloyal to my own kind and equally disloyal to these two friends who had joined hands with me to launch this interracial venture."[51]

Next, Tarry disagreed with de Hueck about how Friendship House should approach charity. De Hueck, for instance, insisted that Friendship House host a clothing room to provide free clothing to local residents. Tarry, however, argued that "the least fortunate of my people needed an opportunity to help themselves instead of an angel of mercy to dole out food and clothing."[52] She wanted African Americans to be served with dignity and to avoid dependence. Bishop Sheil solved the immediate conflict by saying that another Catholic organization in Chicago handled clothing distribution and he did not want Friendship House to focus on that, but the division between de Hueck and Tarry over how to serve black Chicago was deep. Tarry felt that she was being forced to choose between a deep friendship with de Hueck and losing "the respect of [her] people."[53]

Harrigan, too, felt isolated from her new neighbors. Her diary reveals that she fought off depression stemming from her surroundings, which she despised as a "den of iniquity" with the "liquor, drugs, prostitution, juvenile delinquency—toughs, embittered Negroes, hard shell Protestants," likening the Church on the South Side to a "nice stony portion of the Lord's vineyard."[54] Her skin, the very thing that would allow her to leave the South Side if she so desired, acted as a barrier between her and the people with whom she wanted so desperately to fellowship, work, and know. De Hueck later wrote of this sort of experience, saying "we find it hard to see that our identification with the Negro is not complete ... sorry to have the pass-key, with which we can pass through the thick folds of the Veil. WE ARE WHITE.... We can stay and we can go.... THE NEGRO CAN'T."[55] Even within Friendship House, Harrigan felt excluded. Sheil had hired black Chicagoan Mildred Wiley to help get Friendship House up and running. Harrigan envied the close relationship Tarry and Wiley developed.

Harrigan gave meaning to her situation by receiving it as a corporeal and spiritual discipline from God. She told herself she needed "to be weaned away from people" and instead depend on God.[56] Sometimes Harrigan berated herself for her sense of aloneness: "why should the fact that N[egroes] take care of N[egroes]—and leave you out in the cold—that's not so terrible—and yet it cuts me to the heart.... Why should I get attentions—why do I expect them?"[57] At other times, overwhelmed by the number of tasks and a "bitter sense of futility" that her efforts would accomplish anything, Harrigan wrote that she was "a hostage to the negro in earnest of all the white folks who've done wrong to the colored."[58] She struggled with anger toward African Americans and desperately consoled herself with the idea that God needed to break her of self-love and her need for other people's affirmation.

When Tarry left, Edwards, the funeral director, asked Harrigan to find another place to stay. In the weeks it took Harrigan to find a new place to live, she described her suffering as she typically did, believing her physical suffering and aching loneliness made her able to identify with Christ. She consoled herself by reminding herself that "Christ was lonely too."[59]

Harrigan, in essence, tapped into a theology of suffering to sustain her efforts to cross racial boundaries. She gave theological meaning to the challenges that she was facing and was thus able to persevere on Chicago's South Side for another six years, until she moved to Canada to marry. Harrigan believed that her suffering helped to sanctify the entire Mystical Body. If one member of the Mystical Body suffered, that suffering would, in a mystical way, help to heal the Mystical Body. She also knew that American society needed pioneers in interracialism so that one day black and white Americans could live together in true—and just—friendship.

Conclusion

Despite her suffering, Harrigan managed to lead Friendship House to become one of the pillars of the Catholic interracial movement in Chicago.[60] By mid-1943, Chicago's Friendship House boasted a kitchen; a library; an office; a publicity department; family visiting crews; a liturgy study group; adult activities, which included Monday night lectures, a labor school, Spanish lessons, and black history; and children's activities, which included crafts; classes in religion, black history, and reading; and library time. Busily involved in overseeing these activities, Harrigan also lectured to white and black audiences to help fund Friendship House, which thrust her into the ferment of lay Catholic activism in Chicago.[61] In 1943, de Hueck moved to Chicago but, claiming she could not find a place to stay in Bronzeville, lived in a white neighborhood on the North Side. Her apartment acted as another interracial bridge because she hosted the "Outer Circle," a group of white and black Catholics who met to discuss a range of topics. In the ensuing years, Friendship House opened branches in Marathon, Wisconsin, Washington D.C., Portland, and Shreveport.[62] In 1945, de Hueck, with her husband Eddie Doherty, moved to Canada to open a branch of Friendship House there and oversee the national Friendship House movement.

Friendship House helped shape American Catholic views on race through its newspapers, lecturing, and the actual house, where scores of Catholics stopped by to visit. Friendship House also helped black Americans in its immediate environment see a less racist iteration of the Catholic Church. As Tarry wrote in her autobiography, although she was one of Friendship House's "most severe critics," she believed that Friendship house "held the line in Harlem for the Church."[63]

The successes and the limitations of Catholic interracialism at Friendship House highlight the nature of racialized religion and the possible responses of people of faith. De Hueck and Harrigan became Catholic interracialists only when they began to live and work with African Americans and listen to the wisdom of friends like Tarry. Like the evangelicals Emerson and Smith address that have strong networks with African Americans, living with African Americans changed the white women's perspective on race. They began to view society from the perspective of African Americans, seeing the racism inherent in northern institutions. Their integration of black neighborhoods—even if it was on a small scale—shows the significance of where people live for their racial and social perspectives.

For these white women, working for black civil rights and building interracial friendships became a marker of their faith, even if it was at times a costly endeavor. For Harrigan, only the religious belief that her suffering for interracialism was right in God's eyes enabled her to persevere in a difficult setting. But these women's application of the doctrine of the Mystical Body of Christ to racism and racialization in American society expanded the cultural tool kit of American Catholics, and they influenced a generation of Catholic liberals who would work for racial justice. A new generation of leaders eventually replaced de Hueck, Harrigan, and Tarry. De Hueck experienced a deep split with Friendship House in 1946 and moved to Canada to start a rural lay apostolate, and in 1948 Harrigan left the movement to marry.

Part of the Friendship House creed, as created in 1943, read:

> AS LONG AS A NEGRO IN AMERICA HAS TO SUBMIT TO THE UNCHRISTIAN UNDEMOCRATIC LAWS OF JIM CROWISM AND SEGREGATION . . . *Friendship House has work to do.* AS LONG AS A NEGRO IN AMERICA CANNOT VOTE . . . *Friendship House has work to do.* AS LONG AS A NEGRO IN AMERICA HAS TO LIVE IN GHETTO-SLUMS . . . *Friendship House has work to do.* AS LONG AS A NEGRO IN AMERICA IS REFUSED A BED IN A HOSPITAL BECAUSE OF COLOR . . . *Friendship House has work to do.* AS LONG AS A NEGRO IS REFUSED ADMITTANCE TO A GRADE, PAROCHIAL HIGH SCHOOL OR COLLEGE BECAUSE OF COLOR . . . *Friendship House has work to do.* AS LONG AS A NEGRO IS REFUSED A JOB IN AMERICA BECAUSE OF COLOR . . . *Friendship House has work to do.* AS LONG AS A NEGRO IN AMERICA IS NOT TREATED AS OUR BROTHER IN CHRIST AND A CHILD OF OUR FATHER WHO ART IN HEAVEN, NOR GIVEN HIS DUE DIGNITY AS A MAN, AS WELL AS HIS JUST AND DEMOCRATIC RIGHTS . . . *Friendship House has work to do.*[64]

Many of the causes for concern Friendship House laid out in the creed have been legally put to rest; discrimination in voting, housing, hospitals, education, and employment are no longer legal. In Chicago, Catholics participated in transforming the racialized church Mundelein had helped create. Yet society remains racialized. If history is any indicator, it may take interracial living, working, and worshipping for white Christians to appreciate fully the meaning and significance of racial justice. And the path—for people of all races—may be rough. But the prophetic call of these Catholic interracialists still demands a response to the question "How now shall we live?"

Notes

1. I draw this material from Harrigan's description of that first night and from the stock speech de Hueck gave. Catherine de Hueck Doherty, *Friendship House* (New York: Sheed and Ward, 1947), 12.
2. Tarry, like Harrigan and De Hueck, sought to promote understanding between white and black people. She also worked hard as a writer to foster pride among African Americans. By the 1940s, she was famous for her children's stories with strong black characters and tales of interracial cooperation and admiration. In 1940, she published her first children's book *Janie Bell* in which "a little colored baby" abandoned in a rubbish can is rescued by a white woman and white postman, saved by white doctors, and eventually adopted by a white nurse. Nurse Moore, the adoptive mother, names the little girl Janie Belle. In the end, the infant "was no longer the little colored baby no one seemed to want, but Nurse Moore's Janie Belle" (Ellen Tarry, *Janie Belle*, New York City: Garden City Publishing Co., Inc., 1940). White people could love a black child. Tarry based her second children's book, *Hezekiah Horton*, on Eddie Doherty, a white reporter who became an intimate part of Friendship House. Published in 1942, the book was "a happy bit of Harlem living" and describes the adventures of Hezekiah Horton and Mister Ed in Mister Ed's "shiny red convertible" (Ellen Tarry, *The Third Door: The Autobiography of an American Negro Woman*, London: Staples Press Limited, 1956, 174.) Like *Janie Bell*, *Hezekiah Horton* reflects a significant aspect of Friendship House in which white adults took an interest in and were changed by black children.
3. Tarry, *The Third Door: The Autobiography of an American Negro Woman*, 144.
4. Emphasis added. Ellen Tarry, letter to Catherine de Hueck, July 9, 1941, folder Ellen Tarry 1940–1942 1992 042-250, Madonna House Archive (Combermere, Ontario, Canada).
5. Tarry, *The Third Door: The Autobiography of an American Negro Woman*, 144.
6. John T. McGreevy, *Parish Boundaries: The Catholic Encounter with Race in the Twentieth Century Urban North*, Historical Studies of Urban America (Chicago: University of Chicago Press, 1996), 29.
7. Matthew Frye Jacobson, *Whiteness of a Different Color* (Harvard University Press, 1998).
8. Allan H. Spear, *Black Chicago: The Making of a Negro Ghetto, 1890–1920* (Chicago: University of Chicago Press, 1967), 15.
9. Harry C. Koenig, *A History of the Parishes of the Archdiocese of Chicago* (Chicago: Archdiocese of Chicago, 1980), 357. See also Roger Biles, *Richard J. Daley: Politics, Race, and the Governing of Chicago* (DeKalb: Northern Illinois University Press, 1995), 85.
10. Spear, *Black Chicago: The Making of a Negro Ghetto, 1890–1920*, 5–27.
11. Arnold R. Hirsch, *Making the Second Ghetto: Race and Housing in Chicago, 1940–1960*, Historical Studies of Urban America (Chicago: University of Chicago

Press, 1998); Spear, *Black Chicago: The Making of a Negro Ghetto, 1890–1920*. This pattern made black ghettoes very lucrative for many white entrepreneurs. See Beryl Satter, *Family Properties: Race, Real Estate, and the Exploitation of Black Urban America* (Metropolitan Books, 2009).

12. For more on the significance of Mundelein's tenure in Chicago, see Edward R. Kantowicz, *Corporation Sole: Cardinal Mundelein and Chicago Catholicism*, Notre Dame Studies in American Catholicism (Notre Dame, IN: University of Notre Dame Press, 1983). Lizabeth Cohen emphasizes that although Mundelein tried to Americanize his parishioners, many of them resisted. She highlights Italian and Polish resistance. See Lizabeth Cohen, *Making a New Deal: Industrial Workers in Chicago, 1919–1939* (Cambridge, UK: Cambridge University Press, 1990), 83–94.

13. Although Chicago was home to a black priest in the nineteenth century, under Mundelein, no black priests were appointed to positions in the city. Only in 1940, eleven years after Mundelein's death, was a black priest named Vincent Smith assigned to a parish. In keeping with Chicago's overwhelming pattern of segregation, Smith was assigned to St. Elizabeth's. At the time, he was only one of two black priests in the entire nation.

14. Archbishop George Mundelein, "Letter in Favor of the Negro Parish of St. Monica, Chicago (October 26, 1917)," in *Two Crowded Years* (Chicago: Chicago Extension Press, 1918).

15. Ibid.

16. Ibid., 294. Emphasis added.

17. Ibid., 300.

18. "Pullman Porters Review Editor to Mundelein," November 13, 1917, 1917M166, Madaj Collection, Archdiocese of Chicago (Chicago).

19. Chancellor, letter to James S. Madden, December 11, 1917, 1917M77(18), Madaj Collection, Archdiocese of Chicago (Chicago).

20. Ibid. According to the finding aid of the Madaj Collection, there should be a list of the eighty-one signees of the petition to Mundelein included with the letter, but unfortunately that list is missing.

21. Quoted in James W. Sanders, *The Education of an Urban Minority: Catholics in Chicago, 1833–1965* (New York: Oxford University Press, 1977), 14–15.

22. Harrigan may have accentuated the new perspective that de Hueck exposed her to in her memoirs to emphasize the significance of her own transformation. But it is more likely that she was telling the truth; her life experiences had not cued her into the destructive power of race for black and white Americans because her life had been shaped by the boundaries of race. Harrigan's diaries before Friendship House reveal none of the anguish over African Americans' situation that they demonstrate later, suggesting that the subject was not on her radar. Ann Harrigan Makletzoff, memoir draft, Ann Harrigan Makletzoff Papers, box 3, folder 5b, University of Notre Dame Archive (Notre Dame, IN). Hereafter, University of Notre Dame Archive is referred to as UNDA and the Ann Harrigan Makletzoff Papers as CMAK).

23. Leo XIII, "Rerum Novarum," 1891, accessed April 30, 2013, http://www.vatican.va/holy_father/leo_xiii/encyclicals/documents/hf_l-xiii_enc_15051891_rerum-novarum_en.html.
24. One of the most significant groups in the radicalization of Catholic social thought was Dorothy Day's and Peter Maurin's Catholic Worker, founded in New York City in 1933. Harrigan was involved with the Catholic Worker for five years before she joined Friendship House. See Mel Piehl, *Breaking Bread: The Catholic Worker and the Origin of Catholic Radicalism in America* (Philadelphia: Temple University Press, 1982).
25. See Wendy Wall, "'Are We a Nation?'" In *Inventing the "American Way": The Politics of Consensus from the New Deal to the Civil Rights Movement* (Oxford: Oxford University Press, 2008), 5–33.
26. Ann Harrigan Makletzoff, "Canadian Recalls Impact of Dorothy Day," *Catholic New Times,* December 28, 1980.
27. Arthur Falls, letter to Dorothy Day, November 3, 1933, box 1, folder Falls, Arthur G. 1933–36, Dorothy Day Catholic Worker Series W-2.2, Dorothy Day Catholic Worker New York Catholic Worker Records, General Correspondence, Incoming by Correspondence, 1933–, Marquette University Archives (Milwaukee, WI).
28. Thomas Joseph Harte, "Catholic Organizations Promoting Negro-White Race Relations in the United States" (Thesis, Catholic University of America, 1947). Marilyn Wenzke Nickels, *Black Catholic Protest and the Federated Colored Catholics, 1917–1933: Three Perspectives on Racial Justice* (New York: Garland Publishing, 1988).
29. Harte, "Catholic Organizations," 7. See also David W. Southern, *John La Farge and the Limits of Catholic Interracialism, 1911–1963* (Baton Rouge: Louisiana State University, 1996). But some members of the Federated Colored Catholics, like Arthur Falls and other black Catholics in Chicago, did want to change the name. They believed that because of the hierarchical nature of the Catholic Church, they needed the support of white priests to change the Church.
30. Ellen Tarry, oral history interview conducted by Lorene Hanley Duquinn, 1991, folder People—Tarry, Ellen (Harlem) 1998.052-072, Madonna House Archives (Combermere, Ontario, Canada).
31. In 1930 he founded the Catholic Youth Organization that facilitated some institutional crossing of racial boundaries by hosting sporting events that were open to parish teams of all races. See Timothy B. Neary, "Crossing Parochial Boundaries: African Americans and Interracial Catholic Social Action in Chicago, 1914–1954" (PhD diss., Loyola University Chicago, 2004).
32. De Hueck and Doherty did eventually marry on June 25, 1943 at a private ceremony that Sheil performed.
33. Tarry, *The Third Door: The Autobiography of an American Negro Woman,* 185.
34. Quoted in Doherty, *Friendship House,* 86.
35. Fulton Sheen, *The Mystical Body of Christ* (New York: Sheed and Ward, 1935), 80.

36. Ann Harrigan, "Rendezvous with God," *Harlem Friendship House News*, May, 1942. The Chicago History Museum holds an extensive run of the *Harlem Friendship House News*.
37. Unlike later civil rights advocates, the early Catholic interracialists continued to submit to church leadership, at least in their rhetoric. See James Terence Fisher, *The Catholic Counterculture in America, 1933–1962* (Chapel Hill: University of North Carolina Press, 1989).
38. "The Yardstick of Heaven," *Harlem Friendship House News*, August 1941.
39. Ibid.
40. Makletzoff, memoir draft, box 3, folder 5b, CMAK, UNDA (Notre Dame, IN). Claude McKay became a Catholic and was very involved in Friendship House both in New York and Chicago. See Tarry, *The Third Door: The Autobiography of an American Negro Woman*, 178, 253–255.
41. Makletzoff, memoir draft, box 3, folder 5b, CMAK, UNDA (Notre Dame, IN).
42. Ibid.
43. Ibid.
44. Ellen Tarry, letter to de Hueck, July 4, 1942, folder Ellen Tarry 1940–1942 1992 042-250, Madonna House Archive (Combermere, Ontario, Canada).
45. Ellen Tarry, letter to de Hueck, July 9, 1940, folder Ellen Tarry 1940–1942 1992 042-250, Madonna House Archive (Combermere, Ontario, Canada).
46. Ann Harrigan, "Chicago House," *Harlem Friendship House News*, September, 1941.
47. Tarry, *The Third Door: The Autobiography of an American Negro Woman*, 148.
48. Ibid., 147.
49. Ibid., 202.
50. Ibid., 209.
51. Ibid., 202.
52. Ibid., 203.
53. Ibid., 212.
54. Ann Harrigan Makletzoff, diary, September 22, 1942, box 1, folder 4 diaries, 1942–1943, CMAK, UNDA (Notre Dame, IN). The dates that Harrigan wrote on in her diary frequently do not match the actual dates.
55. Doherty, *Friendship House*, 60. In addition, this section of Catherine's book is included in Paula M. Kane, James Kenneally, Karen Kennelly *Gender Identities in American Catholicism* (Maryknoll, NY: Orbis Books, 2001), 103–104.
56. Ann Harrigan Makletzoff, diary, September 29, 1942, box 1, folder 4 diaries, 1942–1943, CMAK, UNDA (Notre Dame, IN). UNDA.
57. Ann Harrigan Makletzoff, diary, October 21, 1942, box 1, folder 4 diaries, 1942–1943, CMAK, UNDA (Notre Dame, IN).
58. Ann Harrigan Makletzoff, diary, October 23, 1942, box 1, folder 4 diaries, 1942– 1943, CMAK, UNDA (Notre Dame, IN).
59. Ann Harrigan Makletzoff, diary, January 10, 1943, box 1, folder 4 diaries, 1942–1943, CMAK, UNDA (Notre Dame, IN).

60. By World War II, Catholic interracialism was flourishing in northern cities, and by the 1950s, Chicago was at the center.
61. Steven M. Avella, *This Confident Church: Catholic Leadership and Life in Chicago, 1940–1965* (Notre Dame, IN: University of Notre Dame Press, 1992).
62. De Hueck moved to Canada in 1947 to open a rural apostolate called Madonna House, which still functions today. Harrigan stayed in Chicago for six years, leaving to marry and move to Canada in 1948.
63. Tarry, *The Third Door: The Autobiography of an American Negro Woman*, 146.
64. "Manifesto," *Harlem Friendship House News* (December, 1943).

3

"Glimmers of Hope": Progressive Evangelicals and Racism, 1965–2000

Brantley W. Gasaway

ON THE FIFTIETH anniversary of the Supreme Court's 1954 ruling in *Brown v. Board of Education*, *Sojourners* magazine—the flagship journal of evangelical progressivism—published an editorial entitled "Still Separate, Still Unequal." The promise of racial equality remained unfulfilled, *Sojourners* declared. Indeed, the "structural violence" of American society kept many African Americans just as segregated and even more endangered than fifty years before. Discriminatory zoning laws, lack of affordable housing, and underfunded schools institutionalized patterns of segregation and poverty. "Most of us who don't suffer from the violence of our structures don't see it," the editorialist claimed. "We live the myth of equal opportunity and don't see our opportunities for the privileges they are." If privileged Americans continued to fail to recognize how social structures sustain racial inequalities, the author wrote, they will never embrace substantive solutions such as increased anti-poverty programs, access to affordable housing, and more equitable funding of schools.[1]

This *Sojourners* editorial epitomized how politically progressive evangelical leaders analyzed racial inequalities in ways that distinguished them from the majority of evangelicals. As Michael Emerson and Christian Smith demonstrated in *Divided by Faith: Evangelical Religion and the Problem of Race in America*, most evangelicals in the late twentieth century interpreted racial problems almost exclusively in terms of discriminatory attitudes and actions of individuals. To be sure, Emerson and Smith noted, beginning in the mid-1960s black evangelicals such as John Perkins and

Tom Skinner developed robust theological models for racial reconciliation that addressed not only personal prejudices but also social structures of racial inequality. As the message of reconciliation became popularized in subsequent decades for white audiences, however, Perkins and Skinner's more radical goals—"to challenge social systems of injustice and inequality" and "to confess social sin"—largely disappeared. In surveys and interviews, Emerson and Smith discovered that most white evangelicals proposed simplistic, individualistic, and spiritualized solutions to overcome racial divisions and inequalities. Ultimately, the authors concluded, white evangelicals seemed to perpetuate rather than to reduce America's racialized society. Yet Emerson and Smith noted that there had been "glimmers of hope" in the 1970s: a minority of white evangelicals such as Jim Wallis of *Sojourners* and Ronald Sider of Evangelicals for Social Action (ESA) began proclaiming that racial reconciliation must address structural racism and racialized inequality. This chapter offers an account and assessment of how progressive evangelical leaders like Wallis and Sider represented exceptions to Emerson and Smith's otherwise bleak analysis of evangelicals' responses to the problem of race in America.[2]

Despite its minority status within American evangelical circles, contemporary progressive evangelicalism has represented a dynamic religious and political movement dedicated to social justice. Although the political conservatism of the Religious Right became the popular face of evangelicals' public engagement beginning in the late 1970s, progressive evangelicals have promoted alternative agendas that prioritize reforms of injustice and inequalities. In 1994, Wallis, editor of *Sojourners* and the most visible leader, described progressive evangelicalism as a "prophetic" movement that, "at its best, transcends the categories of liberal and conservative that have captivated both religion and politics." "This spiritual movement existed before the Religious Right burst upon the national scene with Ronald Reagan's 1980 presidential victory, and the more prophetic commitment it represents has grown ever since," he wrote. "It relates biblical faith to social transformation; personal conversion to the cry of the poor; theological reflection to care of the environment, core religious values to new economic priorities; the call of community to racial and gender justice; morality to foreign policy; [and] spirituality to politics." To both participants and critics, progressive evangelicalism has represented the evangelical alternative to the Religious Right.[3]

This study focuses upon three of the most prominent representatives of evangelical progressivism from the mid-1960s through the twenty-first century: *Sojourners* under the leadership of Wallis; a journal entitled *The Other Side*, which served as the second major periodical for progressive evangelicals; and ESA and its president Ron Sider. These two journals and ESA date to the formative period of the contemporary progressive evangelical movement. *The Other Side*, started in 1965 as *Freedom Now*, and *Sojourners*, launched in 1971 as the *Post-American*, contributed to the rise of evangelical progressivism by creating a forum and network for a cadre of like-minded evangelicals to champion social justice. ESA formed following the 1973 "Thanksgiving Workshop on Evangelicals and Social Concern," a meeting that marked the self-conscious emergence of the progressive evangelical movement. Over the past four decades, these three representatives produced the most regular and most read progressive evangelical publications. While *The Other Side* ceased publication in 2004, *Sojourners* remains the foremost journal of evangelical progressivism. ESA began publishing newsletters in 1980 and its own magazine, *Prism*, in 1993. Collectively, *The Other Side*, *Sojourners*, and ESA's publications offer a lens through which to analyze progressive evangelicals' responses to the problem of race in America.[4]

Throughout the final third of the twentieth century, these progressive evangelical representatives identified persistent racial inequality as one of the most egregious forms of injustice. In the mid-1960s, growing recognition of inequities faced by blacks inspired many leaders' early activism and became a central concern of the emerging progressive evangelical movement. Throughout the following decades, *Sojourners*, *The Other Side*, and ESA repeatedly highlighted and condemned the unremitting nature of these structural inequalities, especially gross economic disparities between whites and blacks. Leaders debunked "the myth of black progress," opposed fiscal policies that exacerbated African Americans' disproportionate poverty, campaigned against the racial segregation of South Africa's apartheid system, and used prominent public events such as the 1992 Los Angeles riots and holidays such as Martin Luther King, Jr.'s birthday to refocus attention on racial problems in America. Two factors led progressive evangelical leaders to view racial inequalities as rooted not only in personal prejudice but also in unjust social systems. First, they believed that both personal immorality and social injustice represented offenses against God. This comprehensive interpretation of sin fueled progressive evangelicals' social activism and shaped their perception of oppressive social structures such as institutional racism. Second, personal exposure to the experiences of African Americans sensitized key leaders to the persistent effects of racism. To address the racial isolation of most white evangelicals that limited their understanding of racial injustice, *The Other Side*, *Sojourners*, and ESA's publications carried didactic articles and analyses to increase their audience's awareness of racial problems. Thus progressive evangelical leaders represented an important exception to most evangelicals' deficient grasp of racial inequality in America.

Activists for Racial Equality

A sense of Christian responsibility to oppose racism and reverse its unjust social effects played an integral role in the rise of contemporary evangelical progressivism. While the civil rights movement inspired the social activism of many mainline Protestants and significant numbers of Catholics and Jews, most evangelicals distanced themselves from public and political efforts to advance racial equality. Some evangelicals, especially in the South, defended segregation, while almost all others viewed social activism as a distraction. Even those committed to racial equality typically preferred a gradualist approach toward civil rights and focused on opposing personal prejudices and discrimination—a position exemplified by Billy Graham. In response to evangelicals' meager support for the civil rights movement, in 1965 Fred Alexander and his son John began publishing *Freedom Now*, the earliest progressive evangelical journal, to challenge racism, segregation, and the apparent naiveté regarding social problems within their white evangelical subculture. Fred, a Baptist minister in Cleveland, and John, a recent graduate of Trinity Evangelical Divinity School, became committed to working for blacks' equality and integration after they began teaching at a black Bible college. The Alexanders intended the journal's title to underscore that blacks needed more than religious salvation to overcome social and economic problems. In the initial issue, John Alexander insisted that "the simple message of salvation" did not accelerate integration, end discrimination, improve educational facilities, or fight poverty. The editors urged readers to empathize with the struggles of blacks and to understand white Americans' complicity in creating them. "The reason Negroes have so many problems is precisely because whites have treated them so wretchedly," John Alexander wrote in 1966. "First we broke their legs, and now we criticize them for limping." By 1969, their initial focus on racial inequalities had sensitized the editors and contributors to other forms of injustice, and the Alexanders changed the name of the journal to *The Other Side* to reflect their broadened focus. In contrast to prosperous and healthy white Americans, they explained, "the other side of America is hungry, defeated and miserable." Representatives resided in "migrant working camps, Indian reservations, inner-city ghettos," and international sites devastated by hunger, war, and tyranny. As they called upon evangelicals to confront all forms of social injustice, contributors to *The Other Side* continued to promote racial equality as a priority for the early progressive evangelical network.[5]

The founders of the magazine that became *Sojourners* likewise identified racism as one of the most pressing forms of injustice. Led by Jim Wallis, a group of seminarians at Trinity Evangelical Divinity School began publishing the *Post-American* in 1971 to challenge evangelicals' social and political conservatism. They described themselves as "a grassroots coalition calling for people committed to the revolutionary Christian message" that both "changes men's lives and generates an active commitment to social justice." As evangelicals recovered this biblical balance, the group believed, they would work for social and political reform. In the initial issue of the *Post-American*, Wallis condemned what he regarded as a "society cancerous with racism." Another author identified "Black liberation" along with the Vietnam War as one of the two paramount issues Christians must face. As part of their insistence that "Christians must be active in rejecting the corrupt values of our culture," the editors called upon readers to become "prophetic in our resistance and activism against the injustice of a racist society." Although the magazine devoted more attention to condemning the Vietnam War and American civil religion, the *Post-American*—renamed *Sojourners* in 1975—joined *The Other Side* in ensuring that the emerging progressive evangelical movement would make racial equality a prominent objective within its political engagement.[6]

The 1973 "Chicago Declaration of Evangelical Social Concern" made this intention clear. This pioneering manifesto of evangelical progressivism marked the public coalescence of the movement and the genesis for ESA. The declaration itself first contained a clear, strong repudiation of evangelicals' responsibility for racial inequalities and estrangement. "We deplore the historic involvement of the church in America with racism and the conspicuous responsibility of the evangelical community for perpetuating the personal attitudes and institutional structures that have divided the body of Christ along color line," the signers stated. The document then emphasized the financial consequences of such attitudes and actions. "Further, we have failed to condemn the exploitation of racism at home and abroad by our economic system." For progressive evangelical leaders, equitable access to economic resources would become a litmus test for determining the state of racial equality. Over the next three decades, they continued to identify social and economic inequalities faced by racial minorities as evidence of structural barriers to their substantive equality.[7]

The first issue of *The Other Side* in 1974 featured several paradigmatic articles. Despite the passage of civil rights legislation, Fred and John Alexander argued that attempts at integration had failed to achieve the supreme goal: "justice and human development." In response, the Alexanders urged financial redistribution from wealthy white Christians to black Christians to enable more equal opportunities for development than forced integration efforts. Two prominent black contributors to *The Other Side* reached similar conclusions. "Integration isn't the answer," argued John Perkins, a leading advocate for racial reconciliation. Instead African Americans needed "an equal economic base" that allowed for "self-determination" and "human development." Activist Ron Potter insisted that "equal footing" was in fact a prerequisite to equitable integration and racial reconciliation. "Before reconciliation takes place there must be an equal distribution of power across the board," he wrote. As progressive evangelical leaders pointed out, power proved inextricably tied to money.[8]

As the 1970s progressed, the sagging American economy continued to lead evangelical progressives to frame discussions of racial inequality within attacks upon economic injustice. Not since the Great Depression four decades earlier had Americans experienced such a severe economic recession. Budget deficits grew as the government financed both the social programs of President Lyndon Johnson's "Great Society" and America's military involvement in Vietnam. The 1973 oil embargo by the Organization of Petroleum Exporting Countries (OPEC) precipitated soaring energy and gas costs. Sluggish business, dramatic increases in unemployment, and historically high inflation produced the economic quagmire of "stagflation": rising prices and low growth. This economic uncertainty reinforced progressive evangelicals' sensitivity to issues of poverty and unequal distribution of wealth. In many ways, these economic crises seemed more urgent than racial prejudice. An end to legalized segregation, a reduction in overt racism, and affirmative action policies had created greater economic and educational opportunities for some African Americans. Yet while the black middle class expanded, many inner-city blacks without the same social opportunities remained trapped in poverty. William Julius Wilson, an influential black sociologist at the University of Chicago, suggested in *The Declining Significance of Race* that class had become a more important factor than race in determining African Americans' welfare. Economic justice and opportunity appeared a decisive factor in the extent to which racial minorities achieved substantive equality.[9]

While not discounting racism, therefore, progressive evangelical leaders stressed the significance of socioeconomic factors that perpetuated inequalities. In his 1976 *Agenda for Biblical People*, for example, Jim Wallis addressed "the division of the world" not in terms of race but along the lines of "powerful and powerless, rich and poor, strong and weak, those who benefit and those who are victimized." Yet within these dichotomies, he consistently acknowledged that racial minorities were overwhelmingly confined to the latter category. "Race and sex are still the basis for denying people their basic human rights," Wallis wrote, "and class and color continue to be the primary factors in determining a person's share of justice, education, health, respect, income, and society's goods and services." Authors in both *Sojourners* and *The Other Side* consistently subsumed discussions of racial inequalities under broader evaluations of social and economic injustice.[10]

Two articles from the late 1970s demonstrate how arguments regarding economics served as vehicles for expectations of racial equality. In 1978 John Perkins described in *Sojourners* the hostility shown toward black evangelical leaders by white conservative Christians, not when they denounced racism, but when the former challenged economic inequalities. "As soon as I question the economic order that has made America unfairly rich and is creating massive poverty," he wrote, "I find myself in very, very hot water." He accused the leadership of white evangelicalism of defending a system that prevented substantive equality for African Americans by unfairly distributing wealth and perpetuating poverty. When black leaders such as evangelists Tom Skinner and Bill Pannell and National Black Evangelical Association president William Bentley highlighted the association between economic and racial inequalities, they had been called communists and barred from white evangelical institutions. Perkins identified this treatment as the "institutional assassination of prophetic black leaders," and he pleaded for white evangelicals to "stop stoning our black prophets." In 1979 Mark Olson, an editor of *The Other Side*, cited statistics showing the ongoing economic, social, and educational inequalities faced by African Americans. Despite "the myth of black progress," he claimed, "racism is not over." Olson described Jimmy Carter as a "huge disappointment" for African Americans and accused the president of "establishing an economic philosophy that ignores the plight of ghetto-dwelling blacks." The slow advance toward racial minorities' substantive equality under the Carter administration caused Olson to anticipate that "the 1980s may see a resurgence of black activism." Yet even Olson could not have predicted the extent to which Ronald Reagan's tenure in the White House would make his speculation appear prescient.[11]

"Ronald Reagan Is Not Their Friend"

The Republican Party's platform in 1980 signaled how the Reagan administration would interpret racial equality. Although affirming that "no individual should be victimized by unfair discrimination because of race" or other personal characteristics, Republicans insisted that "equal opportunity should not be jeopardized by bureaucratic regulation and decisions which rely on quotas, ratios, and numerical requirements to exclude some individuals in favor of others, thereby rendering such regulations and decisions inherently discriminatory." In other words, they repudiated affirmative action. Enforced by the Equal Employment Opportunity Commission and the Office of Federal Contract Compliance, affirmative action programs grew out of the civil rights legislation of the 1960s to prevent discrimination and to increase opportunities for minorities. To meet affirmative action goals, many businesses and institutions gave special preferences to nonwhites to overcome the effects of historical inequalities. By the late 1970s, however, white conservatives became increasingly frustrated by compensatory treatment for past racial oppression and discrimination. Many Americans believed, in fact, that affirmative action programs represented "reverse racism" and subverted the ideal of equal opportunity by giving advantages to certain groups. In a Gallup poll of March 1977, 83% of those questioned opposed preferential treatment of minorities and women in employment and higher education, programs historically associated with the Democratic party. The Republicans now benefited from this backlash against affirmative action.[12]

Reagan's intentions to end affirmative action reflected his opposition both to federal intervention and legal efforts to promote racial equality. He had earlier objected to the 1964 Civil Rights Act and described the subsequent Voting Rights Act of 1965 as "humiliating" for southerners, apparently disregarding the benefits to the region's millions of disenfranchised

African Americans. Not only did Reagan and his conservative supporters hope to end these programs, but they also intended to cut federally financed social programs designed to aid the poor. Reagan's promises to end the intrusion of "big government" tied together his opposition to affirmative action, civil rights regulations, and social welfare. While these themes solidified his appeal to conservative evangelicals as represented by Jerry Falwell's Moral Majority, progressive evangelicals found them deplorable and damaging to racial minorities.[13]

Almost immediately following Reagan's election, progressive evangelical leaders began addressing racial equality with renewed urgency. Many activists had recently neglected explicit issues of race, Jim Wallis admitted early in 1981, but the policies of the new administration were already undermining the precarious hopes of African Americans for equality. Wallis therefore wanted to renew attention to "the vulnerability of black children and of all black people" who "are forced to live on the margins of a society that still refuses to grant them the most basic requirements of human dignity and justice." Wallis accused the Reagan administration of justifying the "official neglect of the poor" in "the name of sound fiscal policy," charging that the disproportionate poverty of racial minorities represented the persistence of white racism. In the same issue of *Sojourners*, contributor Lucius Outlaw stated that the return of conservatives to political power gave him "concern and even fear" for "the future of black people in the United States." Progressive evangelicals' anxiety over prospects for racial equality quickly turned to disillusionment and then disgust with the policies of the Reagan administration.[14]

While the president justified his desire to slash programs that benefited the poor and minorities by appealing to his philosophical commitment to limited government, evangelical progressives interpreted his political agenda as thinly disguised assaults on black equality. "Instead of protecting civil rights and eliminating the demonic effects of racism," wrote Bill Kallio, the executive director of ESA, "our government only talks about reverse discrimination and getting rid of affirmative action." *Sojourners* editor Danny Collum believed that the president had revealed himself "personally and officially" against the needs of blacks. "The signal [his] policies are sending to black people is that Ronald Reagan is not their friend," Collum declared. "The small gains toward racial equality made in the last twenty years are being eaten away by an administration whose officials have made it clear that racial discrimination is a tolerable evil." The combination of Reagan's opposition to affirmative action and domestic spending cuts seemed to reinforce rather than relieve racial inequalities.[15]

For the remainder of Reagan's presidency, progressive evangelical leaders repeatedly denounced the apparent active and passive enforcement of racial inequalities over which the president presided. In its twentieth anniversary issue in 1985, for example, *The Other Side* carried articles by black authors such as John Perkins, Bill Pannell, Coretta Scott King, and civil rights veterans Vincent and Rosemarie Harding that addressed the ongoing challenges faced by African Americans. Pannell especially lashed out at the Reagan administration and the Republican Party, calling the president's professed commitment to civil rights "baloney." "The message out of the Republican convention in Dallas last year was loud and clear: this country is better off in the hands of a few white folks with plenty of money whose businesses can provide gobs of trickle-down fun for the upper-middle class," Pannell stated. *Sojourners* devoted its January 1986 issue to honoring the first celebration of Martin Luther King, Jr.'s birthday as a national holiday. While lauding the inauguration of an annual tribute to "a great prophet of God," Jim Wallis also insisted that King's vision of justice should inspire ongoing efforts to achieve racial equality. Likewise, black theologian James Cone declared that King's dream of racial equality in America must not obscure Malcolm X's message of the nightmare of racial oppression. He asserted that Reagan willingly ignored the existence of poverty and racial discrimination in his proclamations that the American dream had already been realized. Therefore Cone declared that Malcolm X offered a timely corrective to focusing solely on hopes for the "beloved community of integration" envisioned by King. "No promise of equality, no beautiful word about freedom and justice, can serve as a substitute for the bestowal of basic human rights for all people," Cone wrote.[16]

At the end of 1987, *Sojourners* published its most sustained rebuke of racial inequality. On the cover, a white figure stood triumphantly on the back of a kneeling black silhouette next to a title blaring "White Racism: America's Original Sin." Once more, Wallis tried to direct his readers' attention to a matter that no longer seemed a "hot topic." He suggested that improvements in personal attitudes and increased opportunities for some black Americans had caused white America as a whole and even activists like himself to prioritize other concerns. Indeed, combating racism had received less attention from the progressive evangelical movement over the previous decade than protests against nuclear arms,

America's militarism in Central America, and persistent poverty. Yet Wallis argued that racism endured, and he again used financial statistics as the prime evidence of intensifying inequalities faced by African Americas. "The heart of racism was and is economic, though its roots and results are also deeply cultural, psychological, sexual, even religious, and, of course, political," he wrote. "The existence of a vast black underclass, inhabiting the inner cities of our nation, is a testimony to the versatility of white racism twenty years after legal segregation was officially outlawed." Subsequent articles recounted the history of racism in America, gave examples of recent racial violence, and urged white Christians to work for equal educational, economic, and social opportunities.[17] The detrimental effects of the Reagan administration's political agenda upon African Americans had provoked renewed concern among progressive evangelicals for racial equality in the United States. Meanwhile, Reagan's policies toward South Africa had intensified their protests against racism abroad as well.

The Battle Against Apartheid

In the late 1970s progressive evangelical leaders joined the growing international opposition to apartheid in South Africa. Beginning in 1948, the system of apartheid (Afrikaans: *separateness*) extended and institutionalized racial segregation that allowed the minority of white South Africans to dominate the majority nonwhite population. Countries throughout the world opposed this oppression, and in 1962 the United Nations General Assembly urged member nations to end diplomatic and economic relationships with the South African government. Within the country itself, groups such as the predominantly black African National Congress led protests that often ended in arrests and violent suppression. Following the 1977 death of Steve Biko, a black opposition leader imprisoned as a security threat, progressive evangelical publications began exhorting readers to join efforts to fight apartheid. "As Americans we have a personal responsibility to end our corporate and governmental alliances with the racist South African regime," wrote Perry Perkins in *Sojourners*. "We must muster all the energy of nonviolent struggle and end our country's participation in a deeply oppressive system." *Sojourners* began profiling Christians within both South Africa and the United States working to end apartheid. *The Other Side* published articles from authors such as Muhammad Isaiah Kenyatta, who claimed that "our unity with suffering South

African humanity" required American Christians to "disrupt the political, economic, and moral alliance that exists between the United States of America and the fascist Union of South Africa." As with domestic issues of racial equality, the Reagan administration's policies heightened these protests.[18]

In light of President Reagan's unwillingness to distance the United States from South Africa, progressive evangelicals' waged a consistent campaign against apartheid through the 1980s. Reagan understood the primary problem in South Africa not as racism but as the threat of communism gaining a foothold in the region. The Cold War with the Soviet Union dominated his thinking, and he declared that concern for human rights in South Africa "clouds our ability to see this international danger [i.e., Soviet interests] to the Western world." Jeane Kirkpatrick, Reagan's appointed ambassador to the United Nations, even claimed that "racist dictatorship is not as a bad as Marxist dictatorship." In response, progressive evangelical leaders began publicizing the extent to which the American government and industries not only sanctioned but also empowered the repressive system of apartheid. For example, in a *Sojourners* article entitled "Greasing the Wheels of Apartheid: How the Reagan Administration and the U.S. Corporations Bolster the South African Regime," Elizabeth Schmidt detailed the extent to which American diplomatic and economic support for the country had increased since Reagan took office. "In the face of the most racist and totalitarian government on earth today," Jim Wallis concluded in 1986, "Ronald Reagan is trying to do as little as possible." For the rest of the decade, the progressive evangelical movement continued to highlight efforts to end apartheid and to urge participants to contribute to the movement. *Sojourners* in particular publicized and promoted Christian opposition to apartheid by carrying over forty relevant articles between 1986 and the end of apartheid in 1991.[19]

For progressive evangelical leaders, working to end apartheid represented a logical extension of their commitment to racial equality and justice. "To treat any bearer of God's image as sub-human is to contradict the gospel," wrote Vernon Grounds, President of ESA. "And to permit millions of blacks to be treated as sub-human is heresy in act. It is not just heresy. It is sin." Based upon this conclusion, Grounds reflected on the responsibilities of both himself and his audience. "Am I courageously taking my stand against any policy of my government which at bottom is ethnically discriminatory and harmful to a minority group?" he asked. "Am I praying fervently and persistently for the bloodless, non-violent triumph of equality and justice in South Africa?" To spur its members to action, ESA carried regular updates in its publications and encouraged readers to petition the president and congressional representatives for sanctions against South Africa.[20]

Yet even as antiapartheid efforts played a conspicuous role in the progressive evangelical movement in the 1980s, participants knew domestic work remained. "As we are appalled by the institutionalized racism imposed in South Africa," Sharon Temple wrote in 1988 for ESA, "let us not forget our own shamefully recent history of a similar apartheid that denied full rights of citizenship and humanity to our black neighbors—and which continues in many ways today."[21] As prominent public events in the coming decade sparked national conversations regarding issues of race, progressive evangelical leaders reiterated their calls for substantive equality and justice for all people.

The Persistent Problem

The impending five hundredth anniversary of Christopher Columbus's arrival in the Americas encouraged progressive evangelical leaders to reemphasize that African Americans were not the only targets of white racism. In the late 1970s both *The Other Side* and *Sojourners* first gave brief attention to injustices faced by Native Americans. The American Indian Movement (AIM) organized a walk across the United States in 1977 to protest legislation that would abrogate treaties between the American government and Native American tribes. AIM's activities successfully raised progressive evangelicals' consciousness. The sympathetic articles in *The Other Side* and *Sojourners* described threats to "Indian self-preservation" and efforts to "survive the onslaught of anti-Indian legislation being proposed in the U.S. Congress." In the mid-1980s, *The Other Side* ran several more articles that accused the Federal Bureau of Investigations (FBI) of conducting a "secret war" against AIM and framing American Indian activist Leonard Peltier for the murder of FBI agents during a siege of Pine Ridge Indian Reservation in 1975. To progressive evangelicals, these events served as reminders of persecution suffered by Native Americans that called not only for repentance but also for "restitution of stolen land" and "reparation for three hundred years of injustice." As 1992 approached, the opportunity to thrust Native Americans into the public eye alongside Columbus offered a promising strategy to increase awareness of their oppression.[22]

Plans to commemorate Columbus's "discovery" represented a fitting symbol to progressive evangelicals of how celebrations of American history often masked racial oppression. White Americans should realize, wrote Bob Hulteen in *Sojourners*, that "1992 actually marks the 500th anniversary of an invasion and the heinous consequences that resulted for America's indigenous people." Additional articles in *Sojourners*, *The Other Side*, and ESA's newsletter all suggested that anti-Indian prejudice persisted and contributed to the contemporary social and economic inequality of Native Americans. "White America has at least one thing left to discover," Hulteen concluded: "justice for American Indians." Even as they focused primarily on African Americans, progressive evangelicals defended other minorities who suffered discrimination and injustice.[23]

Additional prominent events in the 1990s reconfirmed for progressive evangelicals their perception that racial equality, particularly for African Americans, remained far from realized. At the beginning of the decade, *Sojourners* devoted an issue to re-examining race relations since the civil rights movement. Authors agreed that efforts to achieve an integrated society had failed to produce any semblance of substantive equality. "In the critical areas of income and employment, education, housing, and health," wrote Jim Wallis, "life for most black Americans is still separate and very unequal." He claimed that an ostensible commitment to integration had allowed whites to assimilate blacks selectively into social structures that they still controlled. "White society has preferred integration to equality," Wallis charged, and continued "to cover up the fundamental questions of justice and compassion." Contributors to *Sojourners* called for the goal of social transformation to replace that of integration to create "a multicultural partnership of equals."[24] These calls to revive discussions and efforts to generate racial equality became even more urgent in the wake of the 1992 Los Angeles riots.

In 1991 the violent arrest of a black motorist, Rodney King, by Los Angeles police officers was caught on tape and received extensive media coverage. A year later a jury acquitted the officers of using excessive force, and several days of protests, violence, and vandalism ensued. Progressive evangelicals interpreted the decision as yet another sign of racial injustice. "There was no question that Rodney King was brutalized; the issue was whether it mattered," Wallis wrote. "The verdict, in effect, told every black American that it did not." While condemning the riots, Wallis also insisted that African Americans had just grievances against ongoing discrimination and inequalities that "demonstrate the absolute and persistent reality of racism on every level of American life." Several authors in *Sojourners* again declared that responsibility for racial equality began with white Americans. "The white community needs to move beyond denial to the facing of racism, the naming of racism, and the commitment to do everything in its power to change racist behavior and systems of injustice," argued Yvonne Delk, a *Sojourners* contributing editor. For Wallis, the riots once more manifested the economic and racial divisions that plagued the United States. "This violence is not only rooted in crushing poverty," he claimed, "but also in our painful separation from one another" that reflected Americans' "deep-seated individualism and failure to make community." Thus progressive evangelicals used the Los Angeles riots to underscore again the exclusion of many blacks from authentic participation and equal opportunities in American society.[25]

Three years later, another controversial trial captured the nation's attention and provoked discussions of racial equality. In 1994, football star and actor O. J. Simpson had been charged with murder in the deaths of his former wife Nicole Brown Simpson and her friend Ronald Goldman. Simpson's lengthy televised trial in 1995 fascinated the public. In polls, most Africans Americans expressed sympathy for charges of police misconduct and Simpson's innocence, while the majority of white Americans believed the prosecution's case left little doubt of his guilt. When the predominantly black jury found Simpson not guilty, many African Americans celebrated. Wallis responded to disbelief among whites by explaining how the experience of racism contributed to African Americans' response. "Black jubilation over the acquittal reflected a belief that this case hadn't been proven beyond a reasonable doubt," he wrote, "that it had been tainted by police sloppiness and racial corruption, and that a black man finally had the resources to beat the system, as whites have done for years." In his column for *Prism*, ESA's new magazine, Rodney Clapp interpreted the case's appeal as a reflection of historical racial inequalities in America. "The extraordinary attention devoted to the O. J. Simpson trial can only be accounted for in terms of the passions and fears race engenders in a country with a history of such tortured racial relations," he wrote. Wallis used the Simpson case to illustrate the racial polarization in American culture that demanded "a new conversation on race" led by religious communities. He criticized the Religious Right, whose attempts to repeal affirmative action he considered "a desire to turn back in the struggle for racial justice rather than go forward." "It is absolutely clear," Wallis continued, "that continuing efforts are still vitally needed to open up opportunities for people of color." To progressive evangelical leaders, racism and its legacy made equality elusive.[26]

At the close of the twentieth century, progressive evangelicals remained ambivalent concerning prospects for racial justice. Many signs indicated progress. During Bill Clinton's presidency, African Americans benefited from benign public policies and a robust economy. The growth of the median income for black households exceeded that of whites, while poverty among blacks decreased dramatically. Among their more conservative religious peers, progressive evangelicals noted several encouraging signs. At a 1996 gathering of the National Association of Evangelicals, president Don Argue publicly confessed the sin of racism and committed his group to addressing patterns of racial inequality. The conservative evangelical men's organization of Promise Keepers likewise embraced the goal of racial reconciliation as a prominent part of its agenda. Both Jim Wallis and contributors to ESA's *Prism* expressed cautious optimism. "A deep conviction and growing passion about racial reconciliation is taking root in the very unexpected soil of the white, conservative Christian world," Wallis reported. *Prism* noted that the conspicuous participation of minorities at "Stand in the Gap," Promise Keeper's 1997 assembly in Washington, D.C., "may signal the forging of a powerful multiethnic coalition." Yet other considerations tempered this optimism.[27]

Progressive evangelicals expected not merely advances but the achievement of racial equality. While some socioeconomic gaps had lessened, other glaring disparities endured. The poverty rate among African Americans still stood at two and a half times that of whites. The unemployment rate for blacks remained twice as high. African Americans had significantly less access to health insurance and a lower life expectancy than whites by six years. Although heartened by the rhetoric of racial reconciliation, progressive evangelicals insisted that its actualization required racial justice. "Outside the church meeting rooms and stadium rallies where white and black Christians are hugging each other is a nation where racial polarization is on the rise," Wallis wrote, "where the legacy of slavery and discrimination is still brutally present, and where the majority white population is signaling its tiredness with the 'issue' of race by voting down long-standing affirmative action policies." The same issue of *Sojourners* carried a stinging indictment of white racism by contributing editor Eugene Rivers, an African American pastor and community leader in Boston. The ideological concept of "white identity" was created, he argued, to justify enslavement and oppression. The bifurcation of people into white and nonwhite identities empowered "the demonic ideology of white supremacy" that remained "the dominant principle governing American culture." He challenged white Christians no longer to think of themselves as white, for accepting distinctions based upon constructed racial identity undermined the reality of the equality of all people. Justice for minorities required both social and ideological transformation.[28]

In 1998 both *Sojourners* and ESA's *Prism* marked the thirtieth anniversary of the assassination of Martin Luther King, Jr. by once again reviewing African Americans' disproportionate poverty and the persistence of discrimination and racial estrangement. "The hopes and dreams that followed the 1960s civil rights and voting rights legislation have yet to be fulfilled," Wallis reiterated. "America is still a racially divided society, where diversity is widely perceived as a greater cause for concern than for celebration." Yvonne Delk outlined a strategy to dismantle racism that included acknowledging racism's existence and challenging organizational structures and cultural patterns that reinforce racial inequalities. In *Prism*, editorial board member Harold Dean Trulear pointed to King's vision for social transformation, not superficial integration, as vital to achieving equality for minorities. Americans must change "the quality of inter-racial interaction," he proposed, "so that the gifts of all persons in society come to form what he called 'the beloved community.'" From its inception, the progressive evangelical movement had proclaimed a consistent message that they carried into the beginning of the twenty-first century. White racism endured, and only radical social transformation would begin to dismantle the obstacles that hindered minorities' substantive equality in American society.[29]

A Social and Structural Sin

In *Divided by Faith*, Michael Emerson and Christian Smith demonstrated how the individualistic ethos of most evangelicals limited their understanding of racial inequality. As with most social problems, racism appeared to mainstream evangelicals as the aggregate of magnified personal faults. In other words, social problems such as racial inequality or poverty resulted almost exclusively from the bad decisions and sinfulness of individuals. In the case of racism, Emerson and Smith discovered, most evangelicals believed that the only problems that existed were the prejudice and discrimination of individuals that produced hurtful interpersonal relationships. Yet, the authors noted, "This perspective misses the racialized patterns that transcend and encompass individuals, and are therefore often institutional and systemic." White evangelicals overwhelmingly disregarded relevant social structures that influenced individuals: for example, "unequal access to quality education, segregated neighborhoods that concentrate the already higher black poverty rate and lead to further social problems, and other forms of discrimination." Thus most evangelicals proposed solutions to racial problems based upon personal rather than structural transformation.[30]

In contrast, the most striking aspect of progressive evangelical leaders' opposition to racism was their firm assertion of its institutionalized and structural nature. As early as 1970, *The Other Side* began discussing "institutional racism" and advocating changes in social and economic patterns. Signers of the 1973 "Chicago Declaration" acknowledged not only the "personal attitudes" but also the "institutional structures" that segregated Christians and fed racial injustice. As President Reagan aligned his policies with individualized interpretations of racial problems, evangelical progressives condemned views that discounted structural support for racial inequalities. "Reagan's approach in matters of racial justice, as in economics, is to reduce everything to isolated transactions between individuals," wrote Danny Collum in *Sojourners*. "This is essentially an attempt to escape from history, to abdicate human responsibility for the powerful economic, political, cultural, and spiritual forces that form and feed the racist impulse in people and societies." Jim Wallis argued that the appearance of improved personal attitudes belied the pervasive institutional nature of racism. American economic, education, and judicial systems remained biased toward the benefits of whites and thus perpetuated African Americans' inequality. "Merely to keep personally free of the taint of racial attitudes is both illusory and inadequate," he argued. "Just to go along with a racist social structure, to accept the economic order as it is, just to do one's job within impersonal institutions is to participate in racism." Unlike most evangelicals, therefore, progressive evangelical leaders believed that the primary obstacles to racial equality lay not in individual prejudice but in social patterns and structural injustices.[31]

These convictions regarding institutional racism stemmed from progressive evangelicals' broad understanding of sin. From the early stages of their movement, leaders criticized the ways in which more conservative evangelicals tended to restrict their interpretations of sin to only "consciously willed individual acts." Yet progressive evangelicals insisted that "humanity's proud rebellion against God expresses itself in both personal *and* social sin." These social sins become manifest in unjust laws, inequitable social structures, and oppressive political and economic systems. Ron Sider identified "neglect of the biblical teaching on structural injustice, what we might call institutionalized evil," as "one of the most deadly omissions in evangelicalism today." As a result, when "Christians frequently restrict the scope of ethics to a narrow class of 'personal' sins," he argued, "they fail to preach about the sins of institutionalized racism, unjust economic structures and militaristic institutions which destroy people just as much as do alcohol and drugs." This foundational interpretation of sin animated progressive evangelicals' public activism, for they insisted that Christians must combat all forms of sin. "If sin manifests itself institutionally, politically, and economically as well as personally (and it does)," wrote Jim Wallis, "then our evangelism must bring the gospel into confrontation with both the personal and corporate dimensions of sin." This theology of sin primed progressive evangelicals to recognize and to combat racism as both individual discrimination and social injustice.[32]

Because they accepted the reality of institutional racism, progressive evangelical leaders rejected strategies for improvement based merely upon the transformation of individuals, including spiritual regeneration. Instead, they consistently supported a response repugnant to conservative evangelicals: affirmative action. In response to the Supreme Court's ruling in the landmark 1978 case of *Regents of the University of California v. Bakke*, both *The Other Side* and *Sojourners* defended affirmative action programs for disadvantaged racial minorities. John Alexander even provocatively advocated "reverse racism." To be sure, he admitted, "choosing people on the basis of merit without regard to color sounds fair." Yet in practice, blind meritocracy preserves white privilege and power, Alexander argued, for "it ignores history" and "the long legacy of discrimination in America." He concluded, "Something must be done to correct past crimes." Jim Wallis concurred. "To legally enforce equality in a society of inequities is to perpetuate those inequities," he wrote. "The Blind Lady of Justice has peeked through her blindfold just enough to see race and class and adjust her decisions accordingly."[33]

Throughout the 1980s and 1990s, progressive evangelical leaders employed similar arguments to oppose periodic attempts to dismantle affirmative action programs. In a 1991 newsletter, ESA associate director Van Temple insisted that certain preferential policies do not deprive white men of opportunity but only chip away at unfair advantages those in power have possessed. Wallis likewise emphasized the reality of these advantages. "Affirmative action has always existed in America—for white men from affluent classes, in particular," he wrote. "It is not whether anyone should get affirmative action, but rather whether anyone other than white men should get it." Contributing author Barbara Reynolds encouraged *Sojourners* readers to think of affirmative action not as "preferences" but as a "remedy." "Affirmative action done correctly lifts up, rather than tears down," she declared. "It makes up for past wrongs, while not unjustly creating new wrongs." For progressive evangelical leaders, the legitimacy of affirmative action stemmed from their interpretations of sins such as racism as not only personal but also social and structural. "Can we acknowledge that God exercises impartial justice, but at the same time shows special consideration for victims of structural sin?" asked one author in ESA's *Prism* magazine. "Affirmative action is an important mechanism for compensatory racial justice—perhaps the only mechanism," he insisted. "It deserves the support of evangelicals." As Emerson and Smith showed in their study of evangelicals and race, however, most white evangelicals failed to recognize institutional and systemic forms of racism. Thus wider support for affirmative action remained wishful thinking for progressive evangelical leaders.[34]

Neither Isolated nor Ignorant

In addition to their theology of sin as both personal and social, formative interracial relationships shaped how many progressive evangelical leaders interpreted racial inequality. Such quality exposure to racial diversity was rare among white evangelicals. "We were struck," Emerson and Smith noted, "by how racially homogenous the social worlds of most evangelicals are, particularly those of white evangelicals." Emerson and Smith's study revealed how this racial isolation allowed respondents to downplay the existence and ramifications of racial problems. In contrast, the minority of evangelicals who had meaningful interracial contact expressed a more robust understanding of racism as a persistent, powerful reality. Indeed, the most prominent leaders of *The Other Side*, *Sojourners*, and ESA testified to the catalytic role that interracial relationships had in shaping their understanding of both racism and other forms of injustice.[35]

Fred Alexander, the founder of *Freedom Now* (the predecessor to *The Other Side*), had considered social concern a distraction from his primary evangelistic calling until teaching at a black Bible college and moving into an integrated neighborhood in Cleveland, Ohio. His experience and relationships altered his views of racial problems, theology of social justice, and attitude toward politics, economics, and American history. He confessed that he had always regarded capitalism and states' rights as biblical. Yet Alexander became convinced by the mid-1960s that "it was capitalism which enslaved blacks and that states' rights, supposedly so crucial to freedom, held blacks in slavery for an extra seventy-five years and still causes them to be grossly mistreated." Likewise, preparation for a Thanksgiving sermon disabused him of previous patriotic sentimentality. "So what could I say to a people to whom this 'sweet land of liberty' has been the sour land of slavery and continued oppression?" he realized. "How could a white man preach thanksgiving to a people who were social outcasts and had strong in their memories incidents of lynching, castration, and rape?" The Alexanders' expectations for racial equality came not simply from reading their Bibles but rather from relationships and experiences in these communities. "Our concerns were biblically based and motivated, but to be truthful, that wasn't their origin," remembered John Alexander. "Their origin was in what was happening in society."[36]

Jim Wallis and Ron Sider had similar experiences. Born in 1948 outside of Detroit, Wallis described himself as "a son of the American dream" in the economic boom of the postwar era. As a teenager, however, he became disillusioned with both the suburban lifestyle and conservative evangelicalism of his all-white community. The plight of black Americans particularly troubled Wallis, and the apparent apathy and patronizing attitude of his Plymouth Brethren church led him to inner city Detroit to interact with black communities. There he built relationships with many African Americans. Their stories of suffering and oppression indelibly shaped his views of racism and injustice. "They showed me the other America, the America that is wrong and mean and hateful; the America that we white people accept," Wallis later wrote. In repeated conversations, the refusal of white Christians to acknowledge the contributions of racism to black suffering in general and to the violence of Detroit's 1967 race riot transformed Wallis's faith and catapulted him into progressive politics. During the same period, Ron Sider and his wife lived in a predominantly black neighborhood while he studied for his doctorate at Yale University. Witnessing events through the eyes of the African American couple from whom they rented proved particularly influential. "We actually sat with them the night that Martin Luther King was killed, [and] we felt their pain," Sider remembered. "We got to know their son, who was an angry young man open enough to talk to a white person." As with the Alexanders and Wallis, Sider's relationships with African Americans and exposure to racial inequality played a pivotal role in his interpretation of the Christian responsibility for progressive social action. "Most of what I know about oppression I've learned from black Americans," he declared. These experiences of the Alexanders, Wallis, and Sider indicate how dynamic contact with African Americans enhanced progressive evangelical leaders' interpretations of racial inequality.[37]

Given the racial isolation of many white evangelicals, these leaders made strategic decisions to confront their predominantly white audiences with didactic articles about racial problems. *Sojourners*, *The Other Side*, and ESA's publications regularly published stories that offered the perspectives of racial minorities on injustices and inequalities. In the early stages of the movement, the prominence given by *The Other Side* to black authors stood out within the traditionally white circles of evangelicalism. "It was in the pages of this vital organ that many of us [black evangelicals] were given the opportunity which no other magazine would even consider," recalled William Bentley, president of the National Black Evangelical Association. "There can be no mistake that it was first *Freedom Now*, and then *The Other Side*, which gave our viewpoints a chance at unedited expression." *Sojourners* and ESA also began to carry regular articles by African Americans and added minority representatives to their editorial and advisory boards. In October 1984, for example, *Sojourners* published lead articles by James Cone, the foremost black liberation theologian, and Vincent Harding, a civil rights activist and historian. Because the articles originated as addresses to black Christians, associate editor Danny Collum admitted that "our staff discussed whether this magazine, with a majority-white readership, was an appropriate forum" for them. However, the editors concluded, "God's desire for people of faith is often seen most clearly from the perspective of the oppressed," and therefore white Christians must "listen closely to prophetic voices from the black church." Likewise, ESA invited African American minister Michael McKinley in 2000 to offer "some frank views from within the black church" for "the white evangelical church to be aware of and to act on." Over the years, progressive evangelical publications also featured profiles of nonwhite activists, theologians, and academics addressing racial injustices and inequalities. Through promoting these minority perspectives, evangelical progressives attempted to ensure that white audiences remained neither isolated from nor ignorant of racial problems.[38]

Conclusion

Unlike many evangelicals in the final decades of the twentieth century, the progressive evangelical leaders highlighted in this chapter insisted that blacks had failed to achieve any semblance of equality. "What has not changed is the systematic and pervasive character of racism in the United States and the condition of life for the majority of black people," lamented Jim Wallis in 1994. "Whites in America must admit the reality and begin to operate on the assumption that ours is a racist society. Positive individual attitudes are simply not enough," he declared, for "racism is more than just personal."[39] Wallis and other progressive evangelicals again and again argued that discrimination and injustice persisted, and only a willingness to overhaul social, economic, and political structures would afford minorities truly equal opportunities. By highlighting the social and structural foundations of racial inequality, progressive evangelical leaders distinguished their stance from the individualistic interpretations of most evangelicals.

At the end of their study of evangelicals and race, Michael Emerson and Christian Smith claimed that "with a few exceptions, evangelicals lack serious thinking" regarding "the complexity of American race relations." Progressive evangelical leaders stood among these exceptions. In many respects, they have fulfilled Emerson and Smith's proposal that evangelicals should bring together knowledge based upon sophisticated analyses with "Christian understanding of freedom, love, universalism, justice, unity, and community."[40] While they have remained in the minority, progressive evangelical leaders nevertheless should offer "glimmers of hope" that evangelicals possess the analytical and theological tools to confront the problem of race in America.

Notes

1. David Hilfiker, "Still Separate, Still Unequal," *Sojourners*, May 2004, 7.
2. Michael Emerson and Christian Smith, *Divided By Faith: Evangelical Religion and the Problem of Race in America* (New York: Oxford University Press, 2000), 67, 59.
3. Jim Wallis, *The Soul of Politics: A Practical and Prophetic Vision for Change* (New York: New Press, 1994), 39.
4. For broader analyses of the progressive evangelical movement in the late-twentieth century, see Brantley W. Gasaway, "An Alternative Soul of Politics: The Rise of Contemporary Progressive Evangelicalism," (Ph.D. diss., University of

North Carolina at Chapel Hill, 2008), and David R. Swartz, *Moral Minority: The Evangelical Left in an Age of Conservatism* (Philadelphia: University of Pennsylvania Press, 2012). In 2011, Sojourners boasted that its ecumenical audience included "hundreds of thousands of well-educated and culturally engaged readers through our website, Sojo.net, online e-newsletters, and *Sojourners* magazine, an influential national voice exploring the crossroads of faith, politics, and culture" (Sojourners, "2011 Media Kit," accessed December 27, 2011, http://archive.sojo.net/magazine/MediaKit.2011.pdf).

5. James F. Findlay, *Church People in the Struggle: The National Council of Churches and the Black Freedom Movement* (New York: Oxford University Press, 1993); Emerson and Smith, *Divided by Faith*, 45–48; John Alexander, "Our Name," *Freedom Now*, August 1965, 4; ibid., "The Problems of Integration in the Community," *Freedom Now*, April 1966, 4; Fred and John Alexander, "The Other Side," *The Other Side*, September–October 1969, 31.

6. "What Is the People's Christian Coalition?" *Post-American*, Winter 1972, 7; Jim Wallis, "Post-American Christianity," *Post-American*, Fall 1971, 2; Glen Melnik, "Awake Thou That Sleepest or Who Are You Sleeping With?" *Post-American*, Fall 1971, 7.

7. "The Chicago Declaration of Evangelical Social Concern," in *The Chicago Declaration*, ed. Ronald J. Sider (Carol Stream, IL: Creation House, 1974), 1.

8. Fred and John Alexander, "A Manifesto for White Christians," *The Other Side*, January–February 1974, 51; John Perkins, "Integration or Development," *The Other Side*, January–February 1974, 12, 48; Ron Potter, "Black Christian Separatism," *The Other Side*, January–February 1974, 42.

9. James T. Patterson, *Restless Giant: The United States from Watergate to Bush v. Gore* (New York: Oxford University Press, 2005), 15–19, 62–66; Stephanie A. Slocum-Schaffer, *America in the Seventies* (Syracuse, NY: Syracuse University Press, 2003), 67–70; Sean Dennis Cashman, *African-Americans and the Quest for Civil Rights, 1900–1990* (New York: New York University Press, 1991), 236–241; William Julius Wilson, *The Declining Significance of Race: Blacks and Changing American Institutions* (Chicago: University of Chicago Press, 1978).

10. Jim Wallis, *Agenda for Biblical People* (New York: Harper and Row, 1976), 85. For a paradigmatic example of how Wallis argued that poverty had the most debilitating effects upon racial minorities, see "Mammon's Iron Thumb," *Sojourners*, February 1978, 3–5. James Davison Hunter conducted a statistical analysis of the content of articles within *The Other Side* from 1972 to 1978 and *The Post-American/Sojourners* from 1973 to 1979. During this period, *The Other Side* devoted about 9% (18 out of 205) of its articles primarily to analyzing inequalities faced by African Americans, while *The Post-American/Sojourners* primarily addressed blacks' inequality in just over 1% (5 out of 416) of its articles (James Davison Hunter, "The New Class and the Young Evangelicals," *Review of Religious Research* 22, December 1980, 163). The significantly higher percentage in

The Other Side reflects both its genesis in the civil rights movement and a greater percentage of African American authors. Numerous articles in the *Post-American* and *Sojourners* did discuss racism in the context of other social injustices. But without being the primary focus of the article, such references to inequalities among racial minorities did not appear in Davison's statistical analysis.

11. John Perkins, "Stoning the Prophets," *Sojourners*, February 1978, 8–9; Mark Olson, "White Follies, Black Shackles," *The Other Side*, June 1979, 14, 28.

12. Quoted in Philip A. Klinkner and Rogers M. Smith, *The Unsteady March: The Rise and Decline of Racial Equality in America* (Chicago: University of Chicago Press, 1999), 300; Philip F. Rubio, *A History of Affirmative Action, 1619–2000* (Jackson: University Press of Mississippi, 2001), 144–166.

13. A sympathetic analyst even noted, "A major focus of the Reagan presidency was to curtail federal enforcement of the landmark federal civil rights laws passed during 1960s and 1970s" (Nicholas Laham, *The Reagan Presidency and the Politics of Race: In Pursuit of Colorblind Justice and Limited Government*, Westport, CT: Praeger, 1981, 1). See also Michael Schaller, *Right Turn: American Life in the Reagan–Bush Era, 1980–1992* (New York: Oxford University Press, 2007), 131–133; and Jeremy D. Mayer, *Running on Race: Racial Politics in Presidential Campaigns, 1960–2000* (New York: Random House, 2002), 150–172.

14. Jim Wallis, "The Children Are Getting Hurt," *Sojourners*, May 1981, 3; Lucius Outlaw, "Down to the Crossroads: The Future of Black People in the United States," *Sojourners*, May 1981, 12. See also William Pannell, "Somewhat Short of the Second Coming: Reflections on Black People and the Reagan Administration," *Sojourners*, September 1981, 20–21.

15. Bill Kallio, "Editorial: From the Executive Director," *ESA Advocate*, February 1982, 2; Danny Collum, "Clear Signals," *Sojourners*, March 1982, 4, 6; ibid., "Prophet of Hope for the Sick and Tired," *Sojourners*, December 1982, 4.

16. William Pannell, "Catsup and Baloney," *The Other Side*, October 1985, 33; Jim Wallis, "A Great Prophet of God," *Sojourners*, January 1986, 4; James H. Cone, "A Dream or a Nightmare? Martin Luther King, Jr. and Malcolm X: Speaking the Truth about America," *Sojourners*, January 1986, 28–29.

17. Jim Wallis, "America's Original Sin: The Legacy of White Racism," *Sojourners*, November 1987, 15–16. Other articles in this issue included Calvin S. Morris, "We, the White People: A History of Oppression"; C. T. Vivian, "Target: Democracy—Racial Violence in the '80s"; Catherine Meeks, "At the Door of the Church: The Challenge to White and Black People of Faith"; and Ron Spann, "The Promised Community: The Way Out of the Ghetto and Oblivion."

18. Perry Perkins, "The Loss of Steve Biko," *Sojourners*, November 1977, 7; Nicholas Wolterstorff, "Naude: Prophet to South Africa," *Sojourners*, March 1980, 30–33; Motlalepula Chabaku, "'We Carry the Cross Close to Us:' A South African Woman Talks About Her Land and Faith," *Sojourners*, July 1980, 16–18; Robert Robertson, "The Naidus Started It: How One Family's Resistance to Apartheid

Snowballed," *Sojourners*, September 1981, 12–13; Muhammad Isaiah Kenyatta, "Time to Take Offense," *The Other Side*, November 1981, 20.

19. Donald R. Culverson, *Contesting Apartheid: U.S. Activism, 1960–1987* (Boulder, CO: Westview Press, 1999), 87–88; Elizabeth Schmidt, "Greasing the Wheels of Apartheid: How the Reagan Administration and the U. S. Corporations Bolster the South African Regime," *Sojourners*, October 1983, 10–12; Jim Wallis, "A Lesson for the Long Haul," *Sojourners*, October 1986, 5. See also Danny Collum, "No Apologetics for Apartheid," *Sojourners*, October 1982, 5–6; Vicki Kemper, "Anti-Apartheid Movement Broadens Struggle," *Sojourners*, March 1986, 9–10; and Jim Wallis, "Stand for Truth: From Pentecost to Soweto," *Sojourners*, March 1989, 5–6. In addition, see the February 1985 issue of *Sojourners*, the December 1985 issue of *The Other Side*, and the August–September 1988 issue of *Sojourners* for full issues devoted to racism in South Africa.
20. Vernon Grounds, "Sharing South Africa's Agony: Indifferent Spectators or Empathetic Intercessors?" *ESA Update*, May 1986, 3. See also "Issues in Christian Perspective: South Africa" [insert] *ESA Update*, May 1986; and Ronald J. Sider, "Will Sanctions End Apartheid?" *ESA Advocate*, June 1989, 1–2.
21. Sharon Temple, "Apartheid in America," *ESA Update*, July–August 1988, 4.
22. Phil Shenk, "The Longest Walk: Marching for Indian Self-Preservation," *Sojourners*, July 1978, 10–12; Charlie Garriot, "Captives in Their Homeland" *Sojourners*, July 1978, 12–13; ibid., "Land, Sin, and Repentance," *The Other Side*, June 1985, 23. See also Ward Churchill, "Behind Our Backs: The Seldom-Told Story of America's Secret War Against Leonard Peltier and the Contemporary Indian Movement," *The Other Side*, August 1984, 12–16; "Issues in Christian Perspective: Native Americans" [insert], *ESA Update*, September 1986; and Ward Churchill and Jim Vander Wall, "The FBI Takes AIM: The FBI's Secret War Against the American Indian Movement," *The Other Side*, June 1987, 14–29. In 1987, many progressive evangelical leaders—including Jim Wallis, John Alexander, Ron Sider, and Vernon Grounds—endorsed a petition urging a "stand for justice" by demanding that Congress investigate the 1975 siege of the Pine Ridge Reservation. See "A Call to Action," *The Other Side*, June 1987, 36–37.
23. Bob Hulteen, "Unsettled Scores of History," *Sojourners*, January 1991, 4, 6. See also Carol Hampton, "A Heritage Denied: American Indians Struggle for Racial Justice," *Sojourners*, January 1991, 11–13; Kathleen Hayes, "Columbus and the Great Commission: Did He Help Fulfill It?" *ESA Advocate*, January–February 1992, 1–2; and Little Rock Reed, "Broken Treaties, Broken Promises," *The Other Side*, May–June 1992, 48–54.
24. Jim Wallis, "From Integration to Transformation," *Sojourners*, August–September 1990, 4–5. Additional articles in this issue that examined "What's Wong With Integration" included Anthony A. Parker, "Whose America Is It?"; Manning Marable, "The Rhetoric of Racial Harmony: Finding Substance in Culture and

Ethnicity"; Eugene Rivers, "Separate and Free: The Role of the Black Church in Integration"; and Danny Duncan Collum, "An Interest in Equality: White People's Place in the Rainbow."
25. Jim Wallis, "Time to Listen and Act," *Sojourners*, July 1992, 12; Yvonne V. Delk, "To Move Beyond Denial," *Sojourners*, July 1992, 16.
26. Patterson, *Restless Giant*, 310–313; Jim Wallis, "A New Conversation on Race," *Sojourners*, November–December 1995, 10; Rodney Clapp, "One Afternoon in the Sun," *Prism*, November–December 2000, 4; Jim Wallis, *Who Speaks for God: An Alternative to the Religious Right* (New York: Delacorte Press, 1996), 118, 112, 113.
27. Patterson, *Restless Giant*, 305–307; Jim Wallis, "Evangelicals and Race," *Sojourners* March–April 1997, 11; Andres Tapia and Rodolpho Carrasco, "The High Stakes in Promise Keepers Bid to Reconcile Races," *Prism*, January–February 1998, 15.
28. Patterson, *Restless Giant*, 308; Jim Wallis, "Evangelicals and Race," 11; Eugene F. Rivers, III, "Blocking the Prayers of the Church: The Idol of White Supremacy," *Sojourners*, March–April 1997, 26–31.
29. Jim Wallis, "Why?" *Sojourners*, March–April 1998, 9; Yvonne Delk, "A Time for Action: Building a Strategy to Dismantle Racism," *Sojourners*, March–April 1998, 25; Harold Dean Trulear, "I've Been to the Edge: Martin Luther King's Vision, 30 Years Later," *Prism*, March–April 1998, 8.
30. Emerson and Smith, *Divided by Faith*, 90, 112.
31. John Alexander, "Racism," *The Other Side*, March–April 1970, 33; "Chicago Declaration," 1; Collum, "Clear Signals," 6; Wallis, "America's Original Sin," 17.
32. "Can My Vote Be Biblical?" *ESA Update*, September–October 1984, 4; "Here We Stand: A Reaffirmation of ESA's Commitments," *ESA Update*, September–October 1984, 2 (emphasis added); Ronald J. Sider, "Mischief by Statute: How We Oppress the Poor," *Christianity Today*, July 16, 1976, 14; ibid., *Rich Christians in an Age of Hunger: A Biblical Study* (Downers Grove, IL: InterVarsity Press, 1977), 133; Jim Wallis, "An Agenda for Tomorrow," *The Other Side*, July–August 1975, 50.
33. John Alexander, "Reverse Racism: Why I'm for It and Why We've All Got to Work Harder to Practice It," *The Other Side*, March 1978, 12–13; Jim Wallis, "The 'Equality' of the Hard-Hearted," *Sojourners*, August 1978, 4–5.
34. Van Temple, "Affirmative Action is Good Business," *ESA Advocate*, December 1991, 12; Jim Wallis, "Is Affirmative Action Obsolete? Or Just in Need of Repair?" *Sojourners*, July–August 1998, 12; Barbara Reynolds, "Playing the Race Card," *Sojourners*, May–June 1995, 10–11; Timothy Tseng, "Affirmative Action: Scapegoat or Sacred Cow?" *Prism*, January–February 1996, 12.
35. Emerson and Smith, *Divided by Faith*, 80.
36. Fred Alexander, "White Pastor, Black Church," *The Other Side*, November–December 1969, 22–23; ibid., "The American Dream," *The Other Side*, November–December 1970, 29; Mark Olson, "John Alexander: Taking Jesus Seriously," *The Other Side*, October 1985, 10.

37. Jim Wallis, *Revive Us Again: A Sojourner's Story* (Nashville, TN: Abingdon Press, 1983), 45; Sider, quoted in Jeffrey McClain Jones, "Ronald Sider and Radical Evangelical Political Theology," (Ph.D. diss., Northwestern University and Garrett-Evangelical Theological Seminary, 1990), 406; Kathleen Hayes, "Ron Sider: Working for Kingdom Values," *The Other Side*, October 1986, 11.
38. William H. Bentley, *The National Black Evangelical Association: Reflections on the Evolution of a Concept of Ministry* (Chicago: William Bentley, 1979), 104; Danny Collum, "Filling Out the Vision," *Sojourners*, October 1984, 3; Michael McKinley, "Telling the Truth," *Prism*, May–June 2000, 12–15.
39. Jim Wallis, *The Soul of Politics: A Practical and Prophetic Vision for Change* (New York: New Press, 1994), 87, 91.
40. Emerson and Smith, *Divided by Faith*, 171, 172.

4
"Buttcheek to Buttcheek in the Pew": Interracial Relationalism in a Mennonite Congregation, 1957–2010

Tobin Miller Shearer

ON THE SOUTH side of Chicago in the late 1950s, a congregation erupted. Ron Krehbiel, the first pastor of Community Mennonite Church (CMC) in Markham, Illinois, had turned his pulpit over to Vincent Harding, an African American Mennonite pastor, historian, and civil rights activist. Krehbiel's white congregants, many of whom hailed from the South, cried foul saying, "If this ever happens again, we cannot come to your church anymore." Within hours Krehbiel called a meeting. That very night, following intense deliberation, lay leaders declared that the church would accept all people regardless of race. Said one charter member, "Our point was there was no such thing as segregation in heaven, so why should we have it here? God wasn't going to create two heavens, one for the blacks and one for the whites, so we better deal with it right now, which we did." In response, a third of the congregation left.[1]

Only a few years after the crisis initiated by Harding's visit the white members at Community had to decide whether they meant what they said. The historical narrative of the journey that followed from segregation to integration and beyond complicates the sociological frame employed in *Divided by Faith* and challenges one of its basic findings. As Community Mennonite's story makes plain, relationalism, far from being a universal block to anti-racist efforts, has effectively undermined racial supremacy and subordination when born of crisis, formed by service, and grounded in identity.

Michael Emerson and Christian Smith have challenged the white evangelical community to examine the structural nature of racism in the United States. In *Divided by Faith,* they argued persuasively that a focus on individualism, relationalism, and anti-structuralism has undermined evangelicals' stated interest in righting racial wrongs. Rather than close the gap between racial groups, white evangelicals' emphasis on relationships, refusal to examine social forces, tendency to blame victims of racism, and penchant for simplistic solutions actually makes things worse. Although other scholars have critiqued Emerson and Smith for failing to recognize how "individualistic ideals and negative attitudes toward African Americans are ... intertwined and mutually reinforcing" of white identity and privilege, the majority of critics have confirmed the authors' claim that individualized racial notions counter the stated interracial commitments of the white evangelical community.[2]

Emerson and Smith nonetheless completed their book with a problematic prescription. To counter white evangelical myopia, they suggested a program of "serious reflection on race-relations issues." The scholarship on which this educational program would naturally rely—critical race theory, whiteness studies, and sociology of race—does indeed open up necessary and insightful conversations about the legacy of race-based institutional oppression and systemic privilege. In many instances, however, these scholarly sources and the popularized texts that they inspire fall short at the point of application. In light of pervasive systemic injustice, race-focused scholars frequently end with grim determination to oppose white privilege, calls for deliberate withdrawal into racially separate communities, or the occasional encouragement to move outside of one's "comfort zone." In their well-intentioned support of systemic analysis, however, these authors, along with Emerson and Smith, too quickly dismiss the potential of relationships to transgress oppressive racial norms.[3]

The racial reflection they call for is further compromised by an analysis frequently uprooted from historical context. To be fair, the authors of *Divided by Faith* are sociologists and thus attend first to the dynamics of groups and trends across time. They did not set out to write a history of the white evangelical movement. Even so, they offer a serviceable overview of evangelicalism and the charismatic figures who figured prominently in that movement such as nineteenth-century revivalist Charles Finney and twentieth-century evangelist Billy Graham. Their historical account does not, however, offer context to the specific white evangelical congregations that they study. Although the period from the Great Awakening to the present has seen some recurring racial trends, those patterns vary greatly by region and decade as well as by denomination and congregation. A Baptist church in mid-nineteenth-century San Francisco approached racial issues differently than an Assemblies of God church in mid-twentieth-century Philadelphia.[4]

The account offered in *Divided by Faith* likewise underplays the importance of congregationally based narratives. The stories that a church tells about itself are as important as the larger trends into which they may or may not fit. As Emerson and Smith pointed out, the white evangelical community has consistently avoided systemic analysis of white privilege and racial inequity. Yet that larger pattern should not be allowed to obscure the particular stories of congregations who have had frank conversations about race. A congregation like Community Mennonite, for example, used its own narrative of racial integration to disrupt the traditional white evangelical pattern of avoiding systemic analysis. The narrative itself over time encouraged white church members to evaluate their participation in and benefit from a racialized society and support new polity, outreach, and mission initiated by African American leaders.[5]

A brief history of Community Mennonite in Markham thus highlights a group that used a relational framework to deepen systemic analysis of racism rather than detract from it. That shift toward a structuralist reading of racial inequity came about through a particular kind of relational framework, one that incorporated a story of crisis into its motivational architecture, found relief and sustenance in interracial gatherings, and supported a range of social service initiatives requiring commitment and contribution across racial lines. In turn, Community Mennonite's commitment to relationship fostered an identity that called for the systemic and interpersonal to be held constantly in tension. Those who worshipped at Community Mennonite between 1957 and 2010 embraced each other even as they grappled with a society that tried to tear them apart.

The story of Community Mennonite does not then so much contradict *Divided by Faith* as much as it expands the scope of Emerson and Smith's original study. As the authors noted, given racial demographics in the United States and the composition of the evangelical community in America, most white evangelical congregations will not become integrated.

Rather than contradict this finding, Community Mennonite's story simply expands upon one of the "exceptions" that Emerson and Smith note in passing. Such an examination of an integrated congregation suggests that relationalism may not be as uniformly detrimental as the authors suggest and points to a few decisions that at least one congregation has made to ameliorate the negative effects of relationalism.[6]

The method employed to research the story of Community Mennonite requires brief explanation. In addition to structured oral history interviews, examination of existing secondary sources, and archival research into church records, photographs, and correspondence, the author of this chapter drew upon personal experience as a member of the congregation and regular attendee from 2002 until 2008. Although no longer a participant, the author maintains formal church membership at Community as of this writing. As such, all the particular pitfalls of accounts arising from participant/observer status need to be named and identified—affection for the subjects, contribution to decisions made in the period of attendance, and involvement in discussions about race with pastors and other church members. Thus, while not having written an entirely detached and objective history, the author has aimed to narrate the story in the fullness of its humanity and in the best tradition of other participant/observer accounts.[7]

The Mennonites whom the author joined in worship sit precariously within the evangelical community. Originally born of the sixteenth-century Radical Reformation in Europe, Mennonites emerged from the larger Anabaptist—literally rebaptizers—movement under the leadership of Menno Simons, a former Dutch Catholic priest. They migrated to the United States and Canada in the late seventeenth and early eighteen centuries and quickly became known for mutual aid, emphasis on discipleship, their refusal to bear arms, and commitment to separating from a society that they deemed sinful. In many communities, members marked their separation through men's distinctive collarless plain coats and women's white prayer caps and form-hiding cape dresses. Although separatist dress patterns became less distinct in the twentieth century and generally nonexistent at Community Mennonite by the 1950s, many Mennonite communities maintained a conflicted relationship with the broader society in general and the larger evangelical community in particular.

The source of Mennonites' unease with and attraction to evangelicalism springs from service. On the one hand, Mennonites had a deep affinity with evangelicalism. The language of rebirth, evangelism, sin, and salvation could be heard frequently in Mennonite congregations during the period of this study. Mennonites joined the National Association of Evangelicals, attended Billy Graham "crusades," and went to evangelical schools like Wheaton College and Fuller Theological Seminary. Community was no exception. With some variation over time, members at Community regularly listened to sermons on the necessity of conversion and the dangers of sin. On the other hand, Mennonites cared deeply about meeting human need. A quote attributed to Menno Simons captures the importance of service to the community: "True evangelical faith cannot lie dormant. It clothes the naked, it feeds the hungry, it comforts the sorrowful, it shelters the destitute, it serves those that harm it, it binds up that which is wounded, it has become all things to all people." Thus, where a commitment to the traditional confessions of evangelical theology prompted ministry to spiritual needs, a commitment to service prompted ministry to physical needs. At Community Mennonite both impulses influenced the church for the half-century span covered here.[8]

Nevertheless Community Mennonite's founders first sought to serve those inside the community rather than those without. In 1955, the pastor of another Mennonite church in the Chicago area, John T. Neufeld, noticed that a number of white Mennonite families had begun to leave the inner city of Chicago for the surrounding suburbs. Although other church leaders in Chicago at the time expressed uncertainty about how to respond to white flight, Neufeld helped purchase property for a new congregation, a sale that included a restrictive covenant barring use of the land by anyone "who is not a Caucasian." The Supreme Court had ruled such racially discriminatory covenants illegal in 1948, but Neufeld and others involved in the 1956 real estate negotiations seemed unaware of the ruling, even going so far as to inform the broker that the covenant would "cause no difficulty." Representing a denomination that promoted racial equality but had little practical experience reaching across racial lines, the founders of the group that would claim by 1959 to be "a friendly church that makes visitors feel at home" had a vision to welcome some but not all of those who would come inside to worship.[9]

As negotiations progressed on the purchase of the church property, Ron Krehbiel agreed to begin meeting with residents of the rapidly developing suburb in Markham. A seminary student at the time, Krehbiel first began visiting residents in the area in the fall of 1955. By December of that year he had begun to lead informal services and continued on as the group's first pastor after they officially organized on March 10, 1957. While members worked to construct their new church building, Krehbiel led services in the local Lion's Club hall. The original group of eighteen founding members included a number of former congregants from Neufeld's congregation, Grace Mennonite, as well as First Mennonite in Chicago, but Krehbiel soon discovered that he garnered most interest from those who had moved into the Kedzie Avenue neighborhood surrounding the new church building. As the relocated Mennonites began to meet in the red brick sanctuary, dedicated by the fledgling group in 1959, white residents of Markham joined them. The newcomers had no previous experience with Mennonites and had themselves relocated within a generation from the South.[10]

The congregation faced its first and most foundational race relations crisis soon after the dedication service. Although the congregation, which, by 1959, was an all-white group, had sent its children to participate in a Mennonite-run rural hosting program focused on providing "an experience of inter-racial living" to "promote goodwill and prevent prejudice," members at Community had far less experience in relating across racial lines in the context of Sunday morning worship. Krehbiel assumed at the time that his congregants would welcome a black preacher as warmly as had members of his father's rural Mennonite congregation when Krehbiel was a boy. And so with little trepidation, Krehbiel invited Vincent Harding to speak one Sunday morning.[11]

Krehbiel welcomed into his church a formidable presence. In the late 1950s, Harding and his wife Rosemarie worshipped and helped provide leadership at the nearby Woodlawn Mennonite congregation in southeast Chicago. Harding, at that time a doctoral student in American History at the University of Chicago, also served as a Mennonite minister. Although he would later go on to an illustrious career as a historian of African American history, in the late 1950s he had already become known throughout the Mennonite community as a prophetic voice for racial justice. Around the time of his sermon at Community, Harding challenged his white co-believers to give up their "quiet, pleasant, secluded farm and small town lives" to "bear [the] burdens" of "Negro boys and girls whose welfare is endangered and whose educational freedom is being stifled." Such passion and willingness to challenge white Mennonites impressed Krehbiel, and he gladly received both Harding and his wife Rosemarie when they arrived in Markham.[12]

The ensuing crisis thus caught Krehbiel by surprise. After listening to Harding give what he thought was an "outstanding message," Krehbiel began to notice "disturbed" looks on the faces of many of his congregants as they left church. Those who had moved up from the South appeared particularly distressed. He thought little of it until, after the Hardings returned to Woodlawn following lunch with Krehbiel and his family, his phone began to ring. Congregants expressed displeasure and threatened to leave immediately should he insist on inviting an African American to preach again. In response, Krehbiel called a congregational meeting.[13]

Given that the congregation numbered no more than sixty at the time, Krehbiel was able to contact the entire church body in what remained of the afternoon. People responded in full and repeated their earlier comments: if it happened again, they would leave. After an airing of perspectives, Krehbiel announced that the members of the church council would stay behind, make a decision, and then inform the rest of the congregation. In addition to declaring that they would not create a segregated church on earth when there would be none in heaven, council members decided after prayer and further deliberation that they wanted "to have an open door policy. Any one and everyone." Notably the unanimous vote in favor of full acceptance did not represent any of the southern participants who, although church attendees, had not yet become full members and as a result could not serve on Community's leadership council.[14]

The response left Krehbiel and the rest of the congregation reeling. Krehbiel flew out the next morning on a previously scheduled trip to Kansas City uncertain as to how much of a congregation he would have left upon his return. He was right to be concerned. Immediately, a third of the congregation departed, most of them the same members who had earlier threatened to leave. Good friendships frayed. One member's boss told him that he would "go to hell" for staying in a congregation that might become integrated. In the heat of the moment, the member responded that his boss would end up in the same place for leaving. Nearly a half a century later, charter members recalled the crisis with great clarity. Although uncertain about the future and destabilized by the exodus, to a number those who remained behind "felt very good about the decision" they had made.[15]

The contentious response arose in part from changing demographics in Markham. At the time of Harding's visit, Markham was growing faster than any other suburb in southern Cook County with an average growth rate of 325.1% between 1950 and 1960. During the same period, the nonwhite population increased from 2.4% in 1950 to 21.6% in 1960. White residents who had left Chicago's inner city for the supposed racial haven of the suburbs suddenly found that African Americans had followed them there. The reactivity and displeasure present among those who terminated their relationship with Community so abruptly reflected similar feelings among the white populace of Markham. As the controversy at Community indicated, the emotional intensity of the time made even the prospect of an integrated church—let alone its realization—a grave threat to the racially homogenous enclave many white residents had envisioned.[16]

The next pastor ushered the church into a new kind of relationship with African Americans. In December of 1960, Larry Voth began his pastorate in Markham. Although still a student at the Mennonite seminary in Elkhart, Indiana, Voth worked part time until he finished his degree and then relocated with his family to Markham. As he picked up full-time pastoral responsibilities in 1961, he served within a denomination that still had little experience working with African Americans in any capacity other than objects of service and charitable missions. The General Conference denomination, one of the two largest Mennonite groups in the United States and the primary sponsor of Community, supported several urban and rural missions to African Americans but rarely counted African Americans as full church members. Other than the nearby Woodlawn Mennonite Church where Vincent Harding served as associate pastor, Voth came into a denomination and church that frequently spoke of its racially egalitarian commitments but had much less experience in making them practical.[17]

Voth quickly learned that the decision to implement an open-door policy would initiate a crisis as significant as the original decision to open the church's doors. Upon his arrival, Voth began visiting the church's neighbors. In light of the demographic shifts underway in Markham, this process meant he spent significant time in the living rooms of African American families. On one Sunday in 1961, three African American women—Faye Mitchell, Ola Mae Smith, and Johnetta Wooden—decided to accept Voth's invitation to visit Community. Dissatisfied with their black Baptist congregation, they had come seeking a "different type of involvement with Christian life." As the three women entered and sat down, some congregants stared, some wondered whether a civil rights organization had sent them to test the congregation, others remembered not even noticing that the visitors "were black people." Most, however, did notice and wondered, "How do we deal with this now?" Once again, a crisis erupted.[18]

Yet the church leadership did not waiver at this juncture. Soon after the women's visit, Voth again called a congregational meeting. Again, members voiced sentiments in favor of and opposed to integration. In a decision unusual for a church destabilized by the white flight of the 1960s, the congregation "went on record to say that Negroes are welcome and if they accept Jesus Christ as their Lord and Savior and wish to unite with our local church they will be accepted." Despite ongoing discussion and debate, Voth and the congregation's leadership council remained steadfast in their decision to welcome all those who wanted to worship with them. Some who objected to the practice of racial integration left, although not on the same scale as following Harding's visit. Like his predecessor, Voth wondered if he would have a congregation in the ensuing weeks and even approached two charter members to query, "You guys going to leave me, too?" To Voth's great relief, they responded, "No, we're committed. We're going to stick it out and make it work." The church leadership stood by Voth, as did the new visitors who, in turn, invited more visitors. Within a year, Willie Smith, husband to one of the first three African American visitors, had joined and thereby integrated the church board. The congregation seemed well on its way to full integration.[19]

A Christmas pageant two years later demonstrated that even those in favor of integration balked when interracial romance became a possibility. By 1963, African American members not only served on the church board but also taught Sunday school, participated in the women's fellowship, attended the youth group, and filled the position of head usher. The process of integration had not been without its missteps. Some youth got into fights. A few white parents complained that new African American Sunday school teachers were unqualified. Other white congregants criticized Voth for moving too quickly toward integration and suggested that he should "move at a slower pace" so that members would "be able to better handle it." In the midst of the integrated church board meetings, racial tensions emerged when a white member made unthinking use of a racially charged rhyme. Tensions erupted in full when those responsible for the Christmas celebration cast a white girl to play Mary and an African American boy to play Joseph. Evidencing the volatility of one of the most deep-set and controversial racial topics of the first seven decades of the twentieth century, several white members accused church leaders of promoting "intermarriage" and voiced new objections to integration.[20]

The intensity of the discussion prompted Voth to invite denominational leaders to help resolve the crisis. On February 15, 1964, Community's church board convened and welcomed to the table Walter Gering, the president of the General Conference Mennonite Church. At a meeting of the board the previous month, Al Levreau, the church board chairperson, had abruptly resigned in protest of what he believed to be the church's support of "intermarriage." Although Levreau had been a strong advocate for the church's open-door policy, the recent influx of African Americans had changed his perspective as he became concerned that his daughters might become romantically involved with African American men. In response to the crisis initiated by Levreau's departure, President Gering assured the board that the denomination did support racial integration but had never encouraged intermarriage. Furthermore, he queried Willie Smith, the lone African American member of the church board, as to whether black members wanted to become interracially involved. In response, "Smith said no." Three weeks later, the board met again to discuss the issue and, evidently growing weary of the debate, declared the "racial issue [to] be closed as of this meeting," vowed that it would "not be discussed again at any future meeting," and restated their "official position" that "the church body welcomes continued growth on a racially integrated basis." As for Levreau and his family, they began attending a white Baptist church where the pastor assured them it was "sin to mix the races."[21]

The Community congregation continued to grow on an integrated basis and became immersed in the life of the rapidly shifting Markham neighborhood. The same year that the congregation weathered the storm brought about by the racially integrated holy couple, they also started a church day care that in turn brought in new African American members. By that point, the Markham African American population had grown to just under 30% of the total community. To respond to other needs in the area, the church under Voth's leadership started a voluntary service program in which young Mennonites served one- to two-year terms in a variety of social service agencies. Riding the wave of youthful optimism and activism then present on both religious and secular college campuses, Voth successfully recruited recent graduates from Mennonite colleges to move to Markham, get jobs in the public schools, and support the congregation's mission when not teaching. The bulk of the volunteer and teaching posts, like the bulk of the church leadership positions, continued to be filled by white people. Nonetheless, African Americans joined the church, in part attracted by Voth's increasingly high profile role in the community. In 1965, for example, Voth served on the town's human relations committee and signed a memo protesting discriminatory housing policies on the part of the Veteran's Affairs.[22]

A substantive increase in African American church membership by 1969 began to make a difference in the internal life of the congregation. By that time, the congregation had an eight-year history of worshipping and working together as an integrated community. Those who opposed integration had long since found other places to worship or changed their perspectives. Those drawn to the separatist ideas of Black Power then rocking many denominations ignored the little church on Kedzie Avenue. Some members marched with Martin Luther King in his controversial efforts to overcome race-based housing and economic inequities in Chicago. In early 1969, the white volunteers in the church's service unit also received copies of James Forman's "Black Manifesto" and were encouraged by national staff to discuss his demands for reparations from white Christian churches. In general, however, Black nationalism remained at a distance for a congregation where thirty-three of the seventy-nine official church members were African Americans. Sunday school classes likewise were often more than half black. The group had long left behind the tipping point of 20% African American membership that social scientists assert is the portion at which a minority group begins to affect substantively the life of the majority. By 1969, even worship and outreach—often the most difficult elements of congregational life to change—had begun to look different.[23]

One African American member's experience traces the manner in which worship patterns shifted. Mertis Odom came to the congregation in the first several years after African Americans began attending Community. In September 1967, she and her husband bought a house a few blocks away from the church. Due to her husband's work schedule, she was often left alone with her children on Sunday morning. Although she noticed that it seemed to be mostly white people who entered the red-brick building, she decided to give it a try. By Tuesday of the week after she first attended, Larry Voth had been to her house to visit. In addition, despite a few less than welcoming looks, she found the people there to be "very, very warm." She noted that when she first arrived, "It was only hymns and one would not dare sit in the back and say, 'Amen.'" If someone would utter a "Praise God," Odom continued, "They would say, 'What is this?'" to express their disapproval. Over time, however, Odom began to see changes as worship leaders responded to the expressed desire of African Americans to clap their hands, use instruments, gesture with their hands, and have the "freedom to express" their emotions. As the church changed, so did Odom's feeling about the congregation. Over time, she came to "love my church" and "talk about my church all the time." When those who confused the Mennonites with their more conservative religious cousins asked, "Is that [church] Amish? Are those white people?" Odom learned to reply, "Yeah, some of them are. It's not a big deal." Because the congregation responded to the concerns expressed by Odom and others about worship, she made the church her home despite the racial and religious differences.[24]

Voth continued to practice a high profile, politically focused ministry within the Markham community that drew more residents like Odom to the church. In 1971 the congregation began yet another service ministry, Southwest Community Services, a sheltered care workshop for adults with mental and emotional disabilities. His vision for ministry brought the Sunday morning worship service together with local and, inevitably, political involvement. Through his service on the Markham Human Relations Commission and various community involvements, Voth made many connections with civic leaders, noting as he did, "Relations between the church and political figures should also be close, and they should work as a team." Although foreign to many white Mennonites at the time, especially to those from the more conservative (Old) Mennonite community who eschewed political involvement of any kind, Voth's forays into government made perfect sense to African American members of the congregation who had come from traditions where pastors routinely made political endorsements from the pulpit or ran for office themselves. The unique blend of traditional Mennonite church-based service and traditional African American church-based politics appealed to a broad spectrum of the integrated group that filled the sanctuary every Sunday.[25]

Yet integration of service and politics proved to be easier to achieve than integration of ministry and leadership. In 1973, Larry Voth moved back to his home community to begin his new job as a fundraiser for Bethel College, a Mennonite school in Newton, Kansas. At a time when Mennonite seminaries saw few African American students, the congregation welcomed another white minister, Ed Springer, to the church with little evidence of fanfare or controversy. The following year, the most powerful leadership posts of the women's fellowship remained in white hands despite active participation by African American women. Although a racially integrated lay ministry team did serve the congregation from 1976 through 1978 under the leadership of African American member Orell Mitchell, the church chose to return to a paid ministry team upon discovering that the lay model left "significant needs . . . unmet" and exposed the "frailty" of the church "as a bi-racial congregation." Following the ministry of white co-pastors Menno and Margaretha Ediger from 1978 through 1984, the congregation again hired a white, male Mennonite minister, David Ewert.[26]

Nonetheless a decade's worth of white-dominated leadership at the ministerial level did not erode the congregation's integrated base in part due to ongoing service activities. In addition to the early learning center, youth committee, and sheltered care workshop, members of the congregation initiated new ministries to low-income families, the visually impaired, and senior citizens. Furthermore, in a highly political move rarely taken by African American congregations, Community Mennonite declared itself a sanctuary for Central American refugees in 1983, a decision that brought them into long-term contact with refugee families and, at least for a short while, complicated the black–white binary at the center of the congregation's life.[27]

Social activities and the resulting friendships also kept African American and white members in the church. Photos from the 1980s and 1990s show black and white members in close personal contact while cooking benefit suppers, organizing charity craft sales, celebrating birthdays, and sharing jokes. In particular, women from the congregation enjoyed each other's company. They learned to "act a little silly and have a little fun" and, in so doing, developed a reputation at the annual retreats for Mennonite women in the area. Already a novelty due to their integrated status, the women's group gained further notoriety by sneaking off camp property to buy "pies and cakes and cheese" and then returning to hold their own party. In the process, African American members noted that the "traditional Mennonites" had "really loosened up." In this case, attention to relationships increased the likelihood of long-term integrated activity rather than decreased the same.[28]

Sustainable interracial partnerships proved more difficult to realize at the leadership level. Thirteen years elapsed from the congregation's first attempt at an integrated ministry team in 1976 until Les Tolbert, an African American man, joined David Ewert, a white man, as paid pastoral staff in 1989. Ewert deliberately cut back to a half-time position to make the change possible. After two and a half years Tolbert stepped down from pastoral leadership for personal reasons, and Ewert continued in his role. Two more years lapsed until the congregation called another African American, Brent Foster, to join Ewert in 1994. Ewert then retired from active ministry in 1996 so that Foster could serve as lead pastor. That same year Bonnie and Chuck Neufeld, a white couple who had returned to Markham after serving in church administration in Kansas, joined the pastoral team under Foster's leadership. This partnership also did not last long. A year after the Neufelds arrived, Foster abruptly announced his resignation. He moved with his wife and family back to Peoria, Illinois, in an effort to maintain marital harmony. Once again the congregation had tried and failed to sustain interracial ministry at the leadership level.[29]

Foster's departure in particular left the congregation reeling. In 1997, the church's leadership body consisted of an equal number of black and white elders. This leadership team responded to the crisis of Foster's leaving by inviting congregants to share their "dreams, visions, fears, hurts, disappointments, gratitude" over the Fosters' departure. The subsequent five-month "listening process" culminated in a report that highlighted the congregation's commitment to fostering a "racially mixed congregation" even while asking why "black pastors continue[d] to leave" and registering "anxiety regarding future black leadership." Reflecting a value then beginning to gain prominence in the broader evangelical community, by early 1998, the congregational chairperson noted that "multiracial leadership" was still important to the church, but that they did not have "clarity as to who or when or how" they would again achieve that goal. In the interim, congregants affirmed the Neufelds in their pastoral roles. The couple in turn called the congregation "to make sure the pastoral team reflects the racial make-up of the congregation and surrounding community."[30]

This period of discovering the fragility of interracial ministry teams did not curtail the congregation's commitment to service. In 1986 the church founded a program to refurbish homes in the community while other members helped start and give ongoing leadership to the Chicago Mennonite Learning Center, a school designed to provide a low-cost alternative to the often substandard public schools in the area. These activities would be followed in subsequent years by support for and involvement in ministries to youth, the homeless, and people with substance dependency. Although the evangelical language of individual rebirth and salvation continued to be preached from the pulpit and peppered throughout members' testimonies, the congregation also remained active in their ministry to social needs. As one member proclaimed, "I think [a church] should serve the area it is in."[31]

The Neufelds continued to share pastoral leadership without an African American team member for three years until 2000 when Horace McMillon joined the church. A mattress salesman and manager by day,

McMillon served as associate pastor on the weekends and evenings. For a half-decade, the interracial team provided stability and integrity to a church that continued to claim and promote its interracial profile. McMillon preached and led worship alongside the Neufelds and provided a visible symbol that racial integration could be achieved at all levels of congregational life. In particular, the team excelled in generating an atmosphere of "generous hospitality and nurture." That welcoming spirit in turn invited new members to join. As one member noted, the congregation attracted people because "respect" typified "how we treat one another, how we treat strangers, how we fellowship."[32]

The congregation once again found itself in a crisis in 2005 for reasons that had become all too familiar. Pastor McMillon announced that he and his family were moving to Jackson, Mississippi, where he would manage regional mattress sales and serve as pastor at Open Door Mennonite Church, another small congregation with a long history of racially integrated ministry. Community Mennonite sent the McMillons to Jackson, Mississippi, without the trauma involved in previous departures of African American ministers, but members nonetheless felt a strong urgency to reinstate an integrated ministry team. At a time when their sponsoring denomination had claimed antiracism as one of its top four priorities, long-time African American member and congregational leader Mertis Odom expressed a sentiment common among members when she said, "I don't think we need to start looking next week, but I also don't think we should lay back and say that God will send us somebody. We need to say that we need somebody." African American historian and activist Vincent Harding wrote to Chuck Neufeld in the summer of 2007 that the congregation evinced a "steady and increasing resolve" to "realize [their] best possibilities" as an integrated fellowship. At a time when the congregation again found themselves at a crossroads, Neufeld posted Harding's epistle on the church website as a word of encouragement from the same man who had precipitated the congregation's first race-related crisis back in the 1950s.[33]

That sense of crisis did not dissipate until the congregation called an African American woman to the ministry team. With the assistance of staff at Associated Mennonite Biblical Seminary where Cyneatha Millsaps was then pursuing a degree, in 2006 the Neufelds invited Millsaps and her husband Steve to visit Markham, a town that by that time had become 80% African American with 40% of its household making less than $35,000 on an annual basis. Although not raised in a Mennonite home,

Millsaps had first encountered Mennonites during her youth when a group of seminarians moved into her neighborhood in Elkhart, Indiana, and provided food and financial resources for her family after "her parents divorced, an uncle died and her mother became a paranoid schizophrenic." Her intention had not been to pursue a pastoral role but rather continue as CEO of a social service agency in Elkhart. The relationship between the two couples quickly grew, however, and in 2007 Millsaps joined the pastoral team to be part of a congregation where, she noted, the "young and old, the haves and have-nots, whites and blacks . . . love each other. . . . You can feel it and it's nothing phony, nothing fake."[34]

The congregation took another step to demonstrate their commitment to integrated leadership the following year. In June of 2008, church members "voted to call Cyneatha to serve full-time as Lead Pastor, beginning January 1, 2009." As part of the decision, the Neufelds "publicly committed to working under Cyneatha's leadership" in a bid to "to intentionally step back" from their long-held leadership roles. In keeping with previous turning points in the congregation's history of supporting an integrated ministry team, the story of Millsaps's journey to Markham quickly became one repeated both within the congregation and throughout a denomination eager for such narratives of integrated ministry. National church publications reported on the racially integrated team, and Millsaps gained church-wide attention through a series of high-profile speaking engagements at denominational and regional conferences. The story of racial integration at Community had, to a degree, become the story of the Mennonite church as a whole.[35]

The experience of CMC between 1957 and 2010 suggests that *Divided by Faith*'s critique misses the complexity of relationalism within integrated congregations. Rather than dismiss the role of friendships and relationships among evangelicals seeking to build racially integrated congregations, Community's narrative suggests that a relational approach fostered by crisis, service, and identity can challenge white racial hegemony and nourish racial integration. Although the historical particularity of a fifty-year span in the life of one church does not provide adequate evidence for establishing universal principles, the ability of a group to sustain racial integration through more than half a century deserves further exploration.

Crisis proved more central to sustaining a racially integrated congregation than any other element of this church's experience. In worship, public presentation, and informal storytelling, members of the congregation supported each other through difficult times by recalling past turning points. Although some of the earlier crises—in particular the controversies surrounding Harding's late 1950s visit and the subsequent arrival of African American women in 1961—had become conflated in the minds of founding members; time and again members used the past crises as implicit rationale for moving forward. When discussing the departure of one of the African American pastors, members referred to the decision to open the congregation's doors as a reason also to open the leadership team's doors. By the 2000s, members regularly noted that they had been through similar crises before and that they would get through them again. In some ways, the experience of weathering crises born of the contradiction between stated commitments and unrealized action kept congregants within the church. One member noted, "I put a lot of blood and sweat in this church and I ain't ever going to leave." Because he had struggled through crises in the past and yet maintained relationships across racial lines, he—along with many others—was determined to stay.[36]

The ability to deal with crisis and continue as an integrated community sprung at least in part from a collective willingness to jettison some relationships to sustain others. After Harding's visit, Krehbiel and his lay leadership team accepted that a third of the congregation might leave when they decided to open their doors to all comers. Many of those same lay leaders lost close white friends when they reaffirmed their decision in 1961. Although they gained new friendships with African Americans who joined the church, they did so at the cost of existing relationships. When church chairperson Al Levreau left in protest over the integrated nativity play, the remaining leaders jettisoned their relationship with Levreau to invest in those who remained. As other crises through the years prompted additional members to leave, those who stayed behind chose repeatedly to build new relationships even as old ones ended.

The racial dynamics of managing repeated racial crises influenced all involved but especially shaped white members of the congregation. As Emerson and Smith correctly note, white evangelicals tend to "minimize and individualize the race problem" rather than analyze the systemic elements of the issue. The cycle of crisis and departure present in Community's history pulled long-term white members into deeper, sustained relationships with African Americans, and through that process the white members took on some of their co-believers' perspectives about race in society. Although not complete or uniform—a few continued to insist that racial issues could be solved at the individual level—the recurring racial crises did counter the tendency of white evangelicals to downplay structural racism.[37]

The multiple crises and relationships that emerged also interacted with a strong service ethic at Community Mennonite. Most notably, service initiatives at Community consistently countered a common pattern among evangelical congregations wherein white people gave and people of color received. Congregational initiatives such as the early learning center, sheltered care workshop, homeless program, and low-income ministry positioned white and African American members in the role of servers. Although the congregation did host a service group of white Mennonite youth from rural Iowa every other year in the 1990s and 2000s, in 2009 a group of African American youth from Community travelled to rural Iowa to do service in the white youth's hometown. By upending the usual racial arrangement of server and served, the congregation challenged rather than confirmed white racial superiority and provided yet another context in which interracial relationships could thrive and develop.[38]

More robust research into service across racial lines would enrich scholarship on integrated congregations like Community. Given the popularity of short-term service projects among evangelical communities in the latter half of the twentieth century and the predominance of those service ventures within communities of color, attention to service ventures is all the more necessary. At a minimum, service ventures have supported the kind of individualized, simplistic, relationally focused solutions that *Divided by Faith* exposes. A more complete analysis of evangelical involvement with short-term service ventures—and especially those that venture across racial lines—would provide an opportunity for examining whether the role of service at Community was as anomalous as a comparison with evidence provided in *Divided by Faith* suggests.[39]

A set of more mundane but no less significant factors also served to sustain Community as an integrated congregation. Although it took them repeated tries to achieve it, the congregation knew that developing an interracial leadership team was crucial to their life as an integrated community. They displayed a collective tenacity that served them well. Other congregations might have given up after the third African American pastor in a row left his position abruptly. The leadership at Community chose not to do so. This tenacity also saw them through "personally difficult times, trying to understand and accept our cultural differences." Those internal conflicts emerged most consistently around worship, a not uncommon dynamic in any congregation. Over time, the congregation adopted a style that by the 2000s was as likely to include southern gospel tunes as four-part a cappella hymns. That worship style welcomed a broad array of worshippers from a diversity of racial backgrounds, a welcome that congregational members extended further by offering financial assistance to members going through "rough" economic times. The combination of integrated leadership, personal tenacity, adapted worship, and financial support encouraged members to struggle through the difficulties of maintaining a racially integrated congregation.[40]

This record of integrated struggle still left racial taboos intact. Despite working together across racial lines for several decades, African American members in particular identified certain topics "you cannot talk about." Long-time member Mary Ann Woods noted, "You can't come up and say, well, these white people, I'm about tired of them today. Whites can't say, well, you know, these negroes are really acting up." Likewise, during the seven years that the author spent at the congregation from 2002 through 2008, congregants seldom addressed in open forum the lack of an African American treasurer, for example, even though a white pastor had commented on this pattern already in 1993. Although pastors and elders discussed such issues of leadership composition in closed session, they avoided addressing them in front of the entire congregation.[41]

Yet congregants broke the silence on racially sensitive issues when their relationships demanded it. One Sunday morning in the early 2000s, worship leaders invited congregants to smudge the original title deed to the church property with oil and ashes as a sign of mourning. The congregation together lamented the inclusion of a racially restrictive covenant that "excluded all but whites from ever owning, leasing or even occupying the church building." On another Sunday, Mertis Odom, an African American member, and Paul Mares, a white member, countered another congregant's call for color blindness by telling a story from when Odom taught Mares in her Sunday School class. In response to Mares's comment as a boy that he did not notice Odom's skin color, Odom told him, "Don't ever forget I'm black. That's part of whom I am as much as anything else." In addition to observing this exchange, the author also witnessed an African American pastor inviting African Americans in the church to lay hands on their white co-believers to commission them to challenge racial oppression in society. Informal conversations about racial politics in Markham and the Mennonite church also suffused the congregation. In every instance, those involved referred to interracial relationships prompting them to take action. White members in particular noted that they spoke up because they knew their African American co-congregants would correct them if they did not respond in some way.[42]

Amid racial taboos and their trespass, members of Community Mennonite testified to the possibility of a relationally based integrated congregation. Sociologist Korie Edwards notes that such interracial faith communities remain "elusive" because "whites are accustomed to their cultural practices and ideologies being the norm and being structurally dominant in nearly every social institution" and thereby require people of color—whether African Americans or other racially marginalized communities—"to sacrifice their preferences" and accept "the dominant culture and whites' privileged status." Although many of Edwards's assertions held true at Community for much of the period under study, her claims did not always apply. White members of this congregation opened their doors to African Americans in a neighborhood experiencing white flight, reconfirmed their decision in times of crisis, built interracial relationships through service to their community, and refused to give up on the possibility of interracial leadership even after black pastors kept leaving. Amid the particularities of their historical circumstance, the congregation created a fragile space where the prevailing patterns of white domination did not hold true at every turn.[43]

The experience of Community Mennonite is not in the end exceptional. In *Divided by Faith*, the authors concede that "under the condition of extensive cross-race networks, white evangelicals modified . . . their racial understandings, so much so that their understandings began to resemble those of African Americans." Emerson and Smith describe such instances of white racial transformation, however, as "exceptions." Given the formative role that crisis-birthed relationships played in sustaining an interracial congregation like Community, such interracial friendships appear as likely to develop transformative attitudes and involvements as to detract from them. Rather than simply explain such instances as exceptions, a more nuanced approach examines how interracial relationships form, analyzes the period in which they develop, and explores the racial demographics in which they are situated. One can easily imagine a different past at Community in which relationships failed to foster frank discussion about systemic racism because leaders undercut racially integrated leadership or kept their doors closed to African Americans in interest of congregational harmony. In actuality, relationships opened productive dialogue because the demographic changes, geographical situation, and theological commitments at Community set up frequent crises that prompted the congregation to make conscious choices to stay integrated. As their experience suggests, a relational framework can transform white evangelicals' racial outlook as much as it can limit the same. Relationalism may be less of a problem for white evangelicals than an impulse to decontextualize interracial relationships from the neighborhoods, crises, and historical circumstances in which they have thrived.[44]

The history of Community Mennonite's repeated struggle to stay integrated offers a few other practical lessons. In the case of *Divided by Faith*, Emerson and Smith echo Swedish sociologist Gunnar Myrdal's 1944 *An American Dilemma* by calling, as he did, for extensive and widespread educational initiatives. While the authors' suggestion avoids the often paternalistic and artificial relationally based solutions offered by groups like the Promise Keepers men's movement, their approach suggests that formal academic education will counter the racial myopia present within the white evangelical community. In the case of Community Mennonite, insight gained from scholarship had far less to do with the congregation's record of racial integration than did knowledge gained from relationships. Former pastor Chuck Neufeld has noted, "We gained more from sitting buttcheek to buttcheek in the pew than from studying any book on race relations." Although most white evangelicals can learn much from seminars and articles written by academics, they may also gain insight from listening to members of congregations like Community who have been educated through crisis, struggle, and practical experience.[45]

One lesson does arise from Community's narrative. Over time the church shifted the primary question they asked of themselves. Rather than query, "How can we as a congregation stay integrated?" by the 1990s they began to ask, "How can we as a congregation resist racism among ourselves and in our community?" As their congregational claim declared in 2010, "We see it as part of our mission to actively resist racism where we find it, dismantle it where we can, and name the dynamics of white power and privilege as they occur." The congregation's faith statement had previously referred only to overcoming stereotypes and separation to be a "multi-ethnic, anabaptist community of faith." White evangelical congregations can also learn from this shift. Rather than ask how they can become integrated, a more productive and realistic question may be to query how they too can "name the dynamics of white power and privilege as they occur." This second question may, in the end, hold the most promise for unifying those in an evangelical community still divided by faith.[46]

Notes

1. Ronald Krehbiel, interview with author, April 25, 2007; Gerald Mares and Dolores Mares, interview with author, September 17, 2006.
2. Michael O. Emerson and Christian Smith, *Divided by Faith: Evangelical Religion and the Problem of Race in America* (New York: Oxford University Press, 2000), ix, 76, 119, 70; Antony W. Alumkal, "American Evangelicalism in the Post-Civil Rights Era: A Racial Formation Theory Analysis," *Sociology of Religion* 65, no. 3 (2004): 195–213; Penny Edgell and Eric Tranby, "Religious Influences on Understandings of Racial Inequality in the United States," *Social Problems* 54, no. 2 (2007): 263–288; Curtis J. Evans, "White Evangelical Protestant Responses to the Civil Rights Movement," *Harvard Theological Review* 102, no. 2 (2009): 245–273; D. Michael Lindsay, "Social Networks within American Evangelicalism," *Sociology of Religion* 67, no. 3 (2006): 207–227; Eric Tranby and Douglas Hartmann, "Critical Whiteness Theories and the Evangelical 'Race Problem': Extending Emerson and Smith's 'Divided by Faith,'" *Journal for the Scientific Study of Religion* 47, no. 3 (2008): 341–359; R. Stephen Warner, "2007 Presidential Address: Singing and Solidarity," *Journal for the Scientific Study of Religion* 47, no. 2 (2008): 175–90.
3. Emerson and Smith, 171. For scholarship on race theory, whiteness studies, and sociology of race, see, for example, Anthea Butler, "In the Absence of the Theoretical: Positing a Direction for African American Religious History," paper presented at the American Academy of Religion (Montreal, Quebec, 2009); Anthony E. Cook, "Beyond Critical Legal Studies: The Reconstructive Theology of Dr. Martin Luther King, Jr.," in *Critical Race Theory: The Key Writings That Formed the Movement*, eds. Kimberlé Crenshaw, NeilCotanda, Gary Peller, and Kendall Thomas (New York: New Press, 1995), 85–102; Eric L. Goldstein, *The Price of Whiteness: Jews, Race, and American Identity* (Princeton, NJ: Princeton University Press, 2006); Grace Elizabeth Hale, *Making Whiteness: The Culture of Segregation in the South, 1890–1940* (New York: Vintage Books, 1999); Matthew Frye Jacobson, *Whiteness of a Different Color: European Immigrants and the Alchemy of Race* (Cambridge, MA: Harvard University Press, 1998); William Hamilton, "The Whiteness of God: The Unintended Theological Legacy of James Baldwin," in *Religion in a Secular City: Essays in Honor of Harvey Cox*, ed. Arvind Sharma (Harrisburg, PA: Trinity Press International, 2001), 78–90; Cheryl I. Harris, "Whiteness as Property," in *Critical Race Theory: The Key Writings That Formed the Movement*, eds. Kimberlé Crenshaw et al. (New York: New Press, 1995), 276–291; Victoria C. Hattam, "Whiteness: Theorizing Race, Eliding Ethnicity," *International Labor and Working-Class History*, no. 60 (2001): 61–68; Peter Kolchin, "Whiteness Studies: The New History of Race in America," *The Journal of American History* 89, no. 1 (2002), 154–173; Ian F. Haney López, *White by Law: The Legal Construction of Race* (New York: New York University Press, 1996). For

evidence of grim determination in race scholarship, see Paula Harris and Doug Schaupp, *Being White: Finding Our Place in a Multiethnic World* (Downers Grove, IL: InterVarsity Press, 2004), 19. See also Louise Derman-Sparks and Carol Brunson Phillips, *Teaching/Learning Anti-Racism: A Developmental Approach* (New York: Teachers College Press, 1997); Gary R. Howard, *We Can't Teach What We Don't Know: White Teachers, Multiracial Schools* (New York: Teachers College Press, 1999); Paul Kivel, *Uprooting Racism: How White People Can Work for Racial Justice* (Gabriola Island, BC: New Society Publishers, 2002); Douglas R. Sharp, *No Partiality: The Idolatry of Race and the New Humanity* (Downers Grove, IL: InterVarsity Press, 2002).

4. Emerson and Smith, 21–49.
5. Ibid., 130.
6. Ibid., 122, 132.
7. See, for example, Courtney Bender, *Heaven's Kitchen: Living Religion at God's Love We Deliver* (Chicago: University of Chicago Press, 2003); Lynn Davidman, *Tradition in a Rootless World: Women Turn to Orthodox Judaism* (Los Angeles: University of California Press, 1991); R. Stephen Warner, *New Wine in Old Wineskins: Evangelicals and Liberals in a Small-Town Church* (Berkeley: University of California Press, 1988); Phil Zuckerman, *Strife in the Sanctuary: Religious Schism in a Jewish Community* (Walnut Creek, CA: AltaMira Press, 1999).
8. Dennis P. Hollinger, "Evangelicalism," Global Anabaptist Mennonite Encyclopedia Online, 1989, accessed November 22, 2010, http://www.gameo.org/encyclopedia/contents/E938ME.html; Menno Simons, "Why I Do Not Cease Teaching and Writing (Elkhart, IN: John F. Funk, 1871; originally published 1539).
9. Memorandum by Marlene Suter, "Church History Notes," November 3, 2001, CMC pastor's office: 2nd file cabinet: 3rd drawer marked "Admin": Folder—Church History; John T. Neufeld, "The Grace Mennonite Church," *Mennonite Life*, April 1953, 65–66; Andrew R. Shelly, "This Is Chicago," *Mennonite Life*, April 1953, 52–55; Memorandum, "Preliminary Report on Title Guarantee Policy Application Number 45-59-339," August 3, 1956, CMC pastor's office: 2nd file cabinet: 3rd drawer marked "Admin": Folder—Building, CMC, Tax, Deeds, Titles, etc; John T. Neufeld to Chicago Title & Trust Co., September 24, 1956, CMC pastor's office: 2nd file cabinet: 3rd drawer marked "Admin": Folder—Building, CMC, Tax, Deeds, Titles, etc; memorandum, "Dedication," August 2, 1959, CMC pastor's office: 2nd file cabinet: 3rd drawer marked "Admin": Folder—Building, CMC, Tax, Deeds, Titles, etc; John T. Neufeld to Paul J. Saengert, July 9, 1956, CMC pastor's office: 2nd file cabinet: 3rd drawer marked "Admin": Folder—Building, CMC, Tax, Deeds, Titles, etc.; Donald Burklow, CMC Photo (Markham, IL: Community Mennonite Church, c. 1959), framed photo from CMC displayed at church.
10. S. F. Pannabecker, *Faith in Ferment: A History of the Central District Conference* (Newton, KS: Faith and Life Press, 1968), 278–279; Suter, "Church History

Notes"; Pannabecker, 278–279; memorandum, "CMC 1959 Dedication"; Krehbiel, interview with author.

11. Delton Franz to Parents of Chicago Children and to the Host Parents, 1959, Mennonite Library & Archives, Bethel, Kansas: MLA.VII.R GC Voluntary Service, Series 11 Gulfport VS Unit, Box 1, Folder 4, Correspondence—General Conf. 1960.

12. Vincent Harding, "To My Fellow Christians: An Open Letter to Mennonites," *The Mennonite*, September 30, 1958, 597–598; Neither existing records nor oral histories pinpoint the date of the Harding's sermon. In the author's estimation, the visit took place toward the end of 1959 or the beginning of 1960.

13. Krehbiel, interview with author.

14. Ibid.

15. Ibid.; Interview with anonymous member of CMC, 2005; Krehbiel, interview with author.

16. Memorandum by Karen Daigl, "Markham: Integration Worked Here," 1970, CMC pastor's office: 2nd file cabinet: 3rd drawer marked "Admin": Folder—Markham—Race—Village—Issues—General; Andrew Wiese, *Places of Their Own: African American Suburbanization in the Twentieth Century*, Historical Studies of Urban America (Chicago: University of Chicago Press, 2004), 121–22.

17. Memorandum by Lawrence Voth, "Markham Introduction," May 19, 1964, CMC Second Floor Storage Area, Box "Church Bulletins 1970–73: Missions CCM Reports 1974, 1975, 1976: Church Board Records Thru 1974," Binder: "Board Records 1961–64"; Suter, "Church History Notes"; Lois Barrett, *The Vision and the Reality: The Story of Home Missions in the General Conference Mennonite Church*, Mennonite Historical Series (Newton, KS: Faith and Life Press, 1983), 244.

18. Suter, "Church History Notes," 2; Memorandum by Lawrence Voth, "The Story of the Markham Day Care Center," July 22, 1969, 1, Marlene Suter's personal file; Suter, "Church History Notes," 2; Don Burklow and Grace Burklow, interview with author, April 15, 2005; Mares and Mares, interview with author.

19. Lawrence Voth, "Markham and the Race Revolution," *The Mennonite Church in the City*, November 15, 1963, 5–6; Voth, "Markham Introduction"; Mares and Mares, interview with author; Memorandum, "Community Mennonite Church Church Board Meeting," December 15, 1962, CMC Second Floor Storage Area, Box "Church Bulletins 1970–73: Missions CCM Reports 1974, 1975, 1976: Church Board Records Thru 1974," Binder: "Board Records 1961–64."

20. Voth, "Markham and the Race Revolution"; Burklow and Burklow, interview with author; Memorandum, "Community Mennonite Church Mission Board Meeting," July 26, 1963, 1, CMC Second Floor Storage Area, Box "Church Bulletins 1970–73: Missions CCM Reports 1974, 1975, 1976: Church Board Records Thru 1974," Binder: "Board Records 1961–64"; memorandum by Peter J. Ediger, "Report on an Informal Meeting at Markham, Illinois, September 24, 1963," CMC pastor's office: 2nd file cabinet: 3rd drawer marked "Admin":

Folder—Markham—Race—Village—Issues—General; Mares and Mares, interview with author. Memorandum, "Community Mennonite Church Church Board Meeting," February 15, 1964, 1, CMC Second Floor Storage Area, Box "Church Bulletins 1970–73: Missions CCM Reports 1974, 1975, 1976: Church Board Records Thru 1974," Binder: "Board Records 1961–64." For discussion of the history of interracial marriage, see Fay Botham, *Almighty God Created the Races: Christianity, Interracial Marriage, and American Law* (Chapel Hill: University of North Carolina Press, 2009); Aaron Gullickson, "Black/White Interracial Marriage Trends, 1850–2000," *Journal of Family History* 31, no. 3 (2006): 289–312; Charles F. Robinson, *Dangerous Liaisons: Sex and Love in the Segregated South* (Fayetteville: University of Arkansas Press, 2003); Renee Christine Romano, *Race Mixing: Black–White Marriage in Postwar America* (Cambridge, MA: Harvard University Press, 2003); Sherelyn Whittum Yancey, "Interracial Sexual Relations in Early American History," in *Just Don't Marry One: Interracial Dating, Marriage, and Parenting*, eds. George A. Yancey and Sherelyn Whittum Yancey (Valley Forge, PA: Judson Press, 2002), 70–89.

21. "Community Mennonite Church Church Board Meeting," 1; Ibid.; Memorandum by Lawrence Voth, Andrew F. Taylor, and Duane Zehr, "Visit with Alfred Levreau Family," March, 1964, CMC Second Floor Storage Area, Box "Church Bulletins 1970–73: Missions CCM Reports 1974, 1975, 1976: Church Board Records Thru 1974," Binder: "Board Records 1961–64"; Krehbiel, interview with author; "Community Mennonite Church Church Board Meeting," 2; Memorandum by M. Carr, "Community Mennonite Church Board Meeting," March 7, 1964, CMC Second Floor Storage Area, Box "Church Bulletins 1970–73: Missions CCM Reports 1974, 1975, 1976: Church Board Records Thru 1974," Binder: "Board Records 1961–64"; Voth, "The Story of the Markham Day Care Center," 1.

22. Mertis Odom, interview with author, July 3, 2005; Mary Ann Woods, interview with author, April 29, 2005; Voth, "Markham Introduction," 2–3; Barrett, *The Vision and the Reality*, 246–247; Pannabecker, *Faith in Ferment*, 279; Memorandum by Madelyn Bonsignore, Louis Freeman, Richard Henneberger, William Moyer, George Strein, Lawrence Voth, Helen Zimmerman, "Veteran's Administration Policy with Regards to Race in Its Repossessed Housing Program in the South Suburbs," March 1, 1965, CMC pastor's office: 2nd file cabinet: 3rd drawer marked "Admin": Folder—Markham—Race—Village—Issues—General.

23. Jane Voth to author, December, 2006, author's personal files; Lois Rensberger, "A Weekend in Chicago," *The Mennonite/Central District Reporter*, June 17, 1969, A-3-5, A-12-14; Memorandum, "Community Mennonite Church Directory," October 6, 1969, Marlene Suter's personal file; Voth, "The Story of the Markham Day Care Center," 1; Brad Christerson, Korie L. Edwards, and Michael O. Emerson, *Against All Odds: The Struggle for Racial Integration in Religious Organizations* (New York: New York University Press, 2005), 185.

24. Odom, interview with author.

25. Memorandum by David Ewert, "Twenty-Five Years: A Presence with a Difference," 1982, Marlene Suter's personal file; Willard H. Smith, *Mennonites in Illinois* (Scottdale, PA: Herald Press, 1983), 385; Barbara Dianne Savage, *Your Spirits Walk Beside Us: The Politics of Black Religion* (Cambridge, MA: Harvard University Press, 2008), 6–7.
26. Memorandum by David Ewert, "The Story of Community Mennonite Church," December, 1990, CMC pastor's office: 2nd file cabinet: 3rd drawer marked "Admin": Folder—Church History; "Womens Fellowship 1974," 1974; Ewert, "CMC Story."
27. Chuck Neufeld, "History of CMC: Founded in 1957," CMC, accessed November 29, 2010, http://communitymennonite.us/History.html; Ewert, "CMC Story."
28. Bill Ridder, Fixin' Dinner; Mike Voss, Holly Bell, and Mertis Odom . . . (*The Star Tribune*, 1983, 2); Photo of Community Mennonite Group Party (1988); Photo of Mertis Odom and Bonnie Neufled on Retreat; Photo of Mertis Odom, Bonnie Neufeld and Other Women on Retreat. Photos in author's personal collection supplied by Mertis Odom; Odom, interview with author; Woods, interview with author; Ibid., interview with author.
29. Jody Miller Shearer, *Enter the River: Healing Steps from White Privilege Toward Racial Reconciliation* (Scottdale, PA: Herald Press, 1994), 134–135; Neufeld, "History of CMC: Founded in 1957."
30. Memorandum by Chuck Neufeld, "Listening to the Congregation During This Time of Transition," September 7, 1997, CMC pastor's office: 2nd file cabinet: 3rd drawer marked "Admin": Folder—Listening Process 1997; Ibid; Memorandum by Grace Showalter, "Listening Process Summary," January 11, 1998, CMC pastor's office: 2nd file cabinet: 3rd drawer marked "Admin": Folder—Listening Process 1997; Memorandum by Norma Devine, "Listening Process Report," January 11, 1998, CMC pastor's office: 2nd file cabinet: 3rd drawer marked "Admin": Folder—Listening Process 1997; Neufeld, "History of CMC: Founded in 1957."
31. Ibid.; Woods, interview with author.
32. Neufeld, "History of CMC: Founded in 1957"; Odom, interview with author.
33. "Reconciled in Christ!" Open Door Mennonite Church, accessed December 1, 2010, http://www.churchoftheweb.org/Open%20Door.html; Odom, interview with author; "Our Shared Vision," Mennonite Church USA, accessed July 15, 2013, http://peace.mennolink.org/articles/purposestmt.html; Neufeld, "History of CMC."
34. Celeste Kennel-Shank, "Pastors Reflect Diversity of Churches: Churches in Illinois and California Find Blessings, Challenges in Bridging Cultures," *Mennonite Weekly Review*, October 19, 2009, accessed December 1, 2010, http://www.mennoworld.org/2009/10/19/pastors-reflect-diversity-their-congregations/?page=1; Anna Groff and Heidi Martin, "Youth Worship and Are Filled," *The Mennonite*, July 21, 2009, accessed December 1, 2010, http://www.themennonite.org/issues/12-14/articles/Youth_worship_and_are_filled; Ryan Miller, "Prayer, Discernment and Divine Coincidence Lead Millsaps to Markham," *The*

Mennonite, May 17, 2007, accessed December 1, 2010, http://www.themennonite.org/public_press_releases/Prayer_discernment_and_divine_coincidence_lead_Millsaps_to_Markham.

35. "Pastor Cyneatha & Steve Millsaps!" CMC, accessed December 1, 2010, http://communitymennonite.us/Cyneatha_1_1_09.html; Kennel-Shank, "Pastors Reflect Diversity of Churches"; Groff and Martin, "Youth Worship and Are Filled"; Cyneatha Millsaps, "Help Me Save My People," Mennonite Church USA, accessed December 1, 2010, http://www.mennoniteusa.org/2011/10/05/embracing-the-challenges-an-interview-with-pastor-cyneatha-millsaps/; Mary E. Klassen, "Pastors Week 2010: Pastors Read the Bible and Let the Bible 'Read Them' at Pastors Week," Associate Mennonite Biblical Seminary, February 9, 2010, accessed December 1, 2010, http://www.ambs.ca/news-and-publications/news/pastor-week-2010; Melanie Zuercher, "Urban Pastor Shares Vision with Bethel Students," *Mennonite World Review*, November 23, 2009, accessed December 1, 2010, http://www.mennoworld.org/2009/11/23/urban-pastor-shares-vision-bethel-students/.

36. Burklow and Burklow, interview with author.

37. Emerson and Smith, *Divided by Faith*, 170; Mares and Mares, interview with author.

38. As an example of the proliferation of white-dominated service ventures, see Jenell Williams Paris and Kristin Schoon, "Antiracism, Pedagogy, and the Development of Affirmative White Identities Among Evangelical College Students," *Christian Scholar's Review* 36, no. 3 (2007): 285–301; "City Meets Country—Exchange Visit," Iowa Mennonite School, October 19, 2009, accessed December 3, 2010, http://www.iowamennonite.org/2009/10/19/city-meets-country-exchange-visit/.

39. Jenny Trinitapoli and Stephen Vaisey, "The Transformative Role of Religious Experience: The Case of Short-Term Missions," *Social Forces* 88, no. 1 (2009): 121–146; Robert Wuthnow and Stephen Offutt, "Transnational Religious Connections," *Sociology of Religion* 69, no. 2 (2008): 209–232; David A. Livermore, *Serving with Eyes Wide Open: Doing Short-Term Missions with Cultural Intelligence* (Grand Rapids, MI: Baker Books, 2006); G. Jeffrey MacDonald, "Rise of Sunshine Samaritans: On a Mission or Holiday?" *Christian Science Monitor*, May 25, 2006, accessed December 8, 2010, http://www.csmonitor.com/2006/0525/p01s01-ussc.html.

40. Marlene Suter to author, November 10, 2006; George W. Bullard, Jr., *Every Congregation Needs a Little Conflict* (Danvers, MA: Chalice Press, 2008); David B. Lott, ed., *Conflict Management in Congregation* (Herndon, VA: Alban Institute, 2001); Woods, interview with author.

41. Ibid.; Shearer, *Enter the River*, 134–35.

42. Neufeld, "History of CMC." In most social movements that counter prevailing norms, as was the case at Community, personal relationships prompt more

action than any other single factor. For example, see Doug McAdam, "Recruitment to High-Risk Activism: The Case of Freedom Summer," *American Journal of Sociology* 92, no. 1 (1986): 64–90.

43. Korie L. Edwards, *The Elusive Dream: The Power of Race in Interracial Churches* (New York: Oxford University Press, 2008), 139–140.
44. Emerson and Smith, *Divided by Faith*, 132.
45. Ibid., 171; Gunnar Myrdal, *An American Dilemma: The Negro Problem and Modern Democracy*, 3rd ed. (New Brunswick, NJ: Transaction Publishers, 1996), 556; For discussion of racial reconciliation from a sympathetic insiders' perspective in the Promise Keepers movement see John P. Bartkowski, *The Promise Keepers: Servants, Soldiers, and Godly Men* (New Brunswick, NJ: Rutgers University Press, 2004); Conversations with the author.
46. "What We Believe," CMC, accessed December 7, 2010, http://communitymennonite.us/We_believe.html; Memorandum, "Community Mennonite Church Color Brochure," CMC pastor's office: 2nd file cabinet: 3rd drawer marked "Admin": Folder—Listening Process 1997.

5

Still Divided By Faith? Evangelical Religion and the Problem of Race in America, 1977–2010

Ryon J. Cobb

WITHIN CONTEMPORARY AMERICAN evangelicalism, noted movements and thinkers have achieved a measure of notoriety for promoting awareness about the problem of race and calling for heartfelt, genuine reconciliation. Consider three such examples from the past twenty years. Promise Keepers issued the imperative that a "promise keeper" engage in practices that might lead to racial unity. Longtime evangelical activist John Perkins's recognizable three Rs—relocation, reconciliation, redistribution—reminded fellow Christians that the call for justice must have follow-up actions. And prominent Dallas minister Tony Evans—a rare example of a black pastor who has the ear and respect of a wide swath of conservative white evangelicals—recently proclaimed that black and white Christians need to embrace "oneness" to bridge racial and ethnic division. Despite the increasing attention that evangelicals have given to the problem of race in America—epitomized by these three well-known examples—has change in evangelicals' attitudes toward race actually occurred?

This chapter examines how white racial attitudes have changed or remained stable over the past thirty years and how religious culture plays a salient role in attenuating those attitudes. It draws on insights from cultural sociology and the sociology of religion by examining the effect and influence of what Emerson and Smith called a "white evangelical toolkit" on white American attitudes regarding racial inequality between blacks and whites. The "white evangelical toolkit" emphasizes individual responsibility, personal relationships, and individual accountability over social structures in assessing social problems. This chapter reveals that, even after we account for the influence of sociodemographic factors typically associated with explaining inequality attitudes, white evangelical Protestants continue to stand apart from all other whites in strongly holding to an anti-structural and individualistic perspective on racial inequality. Despite a greater intellectual awareness about racial problems that began to grow in the evangelical community after the publication of *Divided by Faith* and more strident activity to eliminate prejudice—noted in the examples of Promise Keepers, John Perkins, and Tony Evans—white racial attitudes have remained largely the same: an individual's perceived lack of prejudice or an individual's attention to issues of personal race relations *always* trumps the structural. Hearts often matter more than bodies and certainly more than systemic problems.

Put in recent historical perspective, the gradual emergence of white evangelicalism into mainstream American culture has successfully turned this embattled religious movement from a marginal minority to a leading cultural constituency among white Americans. This shift carries significant implications for American social life in the twenty-first century and warrants further understanding of how the white evangelical toolkit shapes racial attitudes and support for structural solutions to racialized social inequities.[1]

Religion and Racial Attitudes

The core thesis of religious influence on racial inequality attitudes rests with the concept of the cultural toolkit. Swidler defined culture as the "symbolic vehicles of meaning, including beliefs, ritual practices, art forms and ceremonies, as well as informal cultural practices such as language, gossip, stories and rituals of daily life." Through beliefs, symbols, and practices, Swidler argued, culture shapes a person's understanding of pressing issues and also provides tools that individuals draw on to respond to these pressing concerns. In relationship to racial inequality attitudes, Winant[2] has argued that culture is at the core of racial processes because culture provides the tools for individuals to assess the causes of racial inequality in America.[3]

Over the past decade, scholars have given particular attention to the theologically conservative Protestants—evangelicals—who make up roughly 25% to 35% of America's population. Emerson and Smith[4] were the first to draw on Swidler's understanding of culture in exploring evangelicalism's influence on whites' racial attitudes. They contended that evangelical religious culture derives from a racialized social context. Over time, residue from this context becomes ingrained in the three important religious cultural tools that white evangelicals draw on to shape their approach to racial inequality: (i) accountable freewill individualism, that is, an ontological perspective in which individuals are independent of social structures and are individually accountable for their life outcomes; (ii) anti-structuralism, or eschewing the role of social structures; and (iii) relationalism, defined as an emphasis on the centrality of interpersonal relationships as the root of social problems. Although American culture in general is highly individualistic, Emerson and Smith suggested that this freewill individualism, buttressed by theology and combined with the rejection of structural explanations, makes white evangelicals more individualistic than other white Americans.[5]

Drawing on this view of race, religion, and culture, Emerson and Smith hypothesized that evangelicalism would reinforce anti-structural and individualist explanations for black/white inequality among evangelical white Americans. To test this claim, Emerson and Smith used data from the 1996 General Social Survey (GSS), as well as in-depth interviews with hundreds of white evangelicals across the United States. Their findings revealed that evangelicalism polarizes white Americans in the explanations that they offer for the black/white socioeconomic gap. For example, when asked whether structural explanations—for instance, discrimination and education—contribute to socioeconomic gaps between black and white Americans, evangelicals were less likely than other whites to respond *yes* to both the discrimination and education options. Evangelicals were also more likely than other whites to hold individualistic racial attitudes indicating their belief that inequality is attributable to personal failings among African Americans (e.g., blacks lack the motivation/will power to succeed in America). In sum, Emerson and Smith found that evangelicalism accounted for differences in whites' racial attitudes and that on average white evangelicals are more anti-structural and individualist than their nonevangelical white counterparts. The data therefore suggest that in comparison to nonevangelical white Americans, white evangelicals will be more anti-structural and more individualist in their interpretations of racial inequality.

Few studies explore the consistency of evangelicalism to account for differences in white racial attitudes over time. For instance, as a part of their larger study on religion's role in shaping Americans' social attitudes, Putnam and Campbell[6] explored changes in religious influences on white racial attitudes over time using thirty-four years of data from a subsample of non-Hispanic whites in the GSS (1970–2004). Across all years, they found that white evangelicals express higher levels of opposition to interracial marriage in comparison to Catholics, mainline Protestants, and religiously nonaffiliated Americans. They also found that white evangelicals are more likely than nonevangelical whites to believe that blacks are biologically inferior. Finally, they found that evangelicals are less likely to report strong opposition to laws that allow for racial discrimination in home sales. Thus, it appears that differences between white evangelicals and white nonevangelicals in racial inequality attitudes remain relatively consistent over time.

Social Location and American Christian Toolkits: Alternative Explanations of White Racial Inequality Attitudes

Over the past decade, scholars have tested alternative explanations for Emerson and Smith's findings on the effect of evangelicalism on racial attitudes. However, methodological limitations preclude these studies from directly countering Emerson and Smith's conclusions. A related study by Edgell and Tranby explored the possibility that social location (e.g., education) as well as religious involvement mediated evangelical influences on white racial attitudes. Edgell and Tranby's findings revealed that white evangelicals did not differ from other white Americans in the explanations that they offer for the black/white socioeconomic gap when controlling for education and religious involvement. However, their study does not include tests to show the mediating effect of education on evangelicalism. Further, by including a measure for Catholicism as a control, they created a reference group comprised of Americans from various types of religious traditions, which made determination of differences between evangelicals and other white Americans difficult to understand. Finally, because they use cross-sectional data, we do not know whether these effects persist over time.[7]

Taylor and Merino's[8] research suggests that it is American Christianity more broadly, and not evangelicalism in particular, that accounts for differences in racial inequality attitudes among white Americans. Using pooled data from the GSS (1996–2006), they found no differences between evangelicals and other Christian or non-Christian white Americans in the explanations they offered for black/white inequality, holding all else constant. These findings suggest future researchers should only explore Christian and non-Christian differences in racial attitudes rather than one toolkit specific to evangelical Protestants. Three issues prevent them from effectively challenging previous claims of evangelical differences in white racial attitudes. First, Taylor and Merino did not control for church attendance and political party identification, which also shape white racial attitudes. Second, collapsing the discrimination and education option into one measure prevents researchers from understanding differences in the effect of evangelicalism on different types of structuralist explanations. Third, although they relied on data from multiple years, they did not make any claims about the consistency of evangelicalism to shape racial inequality attitudes over time.

Results

Table 5.1 shows the percentage of the sample of non-Hispanic whites in each religious category that responded *yes* to each of the four explanations for the black/white socioeconomic gap within each religious tradition. Across religious traditions, evangelicals were least likely to view discrimination as a source for the racial economic gaps (29% compared to 34–45%

Table 5.1 Percentage of Non-Hispanic Whites by Religious Group Saying *Yes* to Explanations for the Black/White Socioeconomic Gap for Selected Years (General Social Survey, 1977–2010), N = 13,750

	Evangelical	Mainline Protestant	Catholic	Jewish	Other Faith	Non-affiliated
	Model 1	Model 2	Model 3	Model 4	Model 5	Model 6
Discrimination	29.02	35.40	34.42	45.30	41.71	43.20
Education	38.40	52.37	48.88	65.84	57.53	55.67
Motivation	64.45	56.44	54.95	43.07	45.41	41.41
Ability	17.38	16.14	16.21	11.39	9.31	7.46

of other groups). Similarly, evangelicals were least likely than all other groups to respond *yes* to education as a determinant of the black/white socioeconomic gap in America (38% relative to 49–66% of other groups). Accordingly, greater percentages of evangelicals responded *yes* to "motivation" as well as "ability" as an explanation for the racial economic gaps in America (65% relative to 41–56% in the former, and 17% compared to 7–16% in the latter).

When controlling for relevant variables, the hypotheses that evangelicals are more likely to reject structuralist explanations and accept individualist explanations find support. Table 5.2 shows odds ratios for the independent effects of each religious group, with evangelicals as the reference category. Members of every religious group are more likely than evangelicals to attribute the socioeconomic gap between whites and blacks to structuralist explanations, discrimination, and education (Models 1 and 2). Those who are nonaffiliated show the greatest difference from evangelicals in this regard—the odds of responding *yes* to discrimination and education as a reason for inequality among the nonaffiliated are 98% and 83% higher, respectively, than evangelicals.

Among whites, evangelicals are more likely than all other groups to believe that motivation explains the black/white gap (Model 3 in Table 5.2). The odds of other groups responding *yes* to this item are 22% to 46% less likely than evangelicals. Interestingly, evangelicals do not differ from other religiously affiliated groups in their support for biological racism. In comparison to evangelicals, I see no differences in support for the claim that blacks' ability accounts for the black/white gap. However, nonaffiliated whites were 33% less likely to respond *yes* to this claim. This result supports other research that finds that Americans have generally decreased their support for biological explanations for racial inequality over the past thirty years.[9]

To determine whether the difference between evangelicals and other religious groups are consistent over time, I also tested the interaction effect of religious affiliation and year. Although the coefficients for the interaction effects are not statistically significant, they indicate that the relationship between evangelicals and the propensity to explain black/white inequality with individualist rather than structuralist explanations did not change between 1977 to 2010 (Table 5.3). The only exception is the effect of Catholic views on inborn ability. Model 4 of Table 5.3 indicates that the difference between white evangelicals and Catholics in the propensity to believe blacks' ability mainly determines the black/white

Table 5.2 Estimated Odds Ratios of Seven Modes of Explanation for the Black/White Socioeconomic Gap (General Social Survey, 1977–2010), N = 13,750

	Structuralist		Individualist	
	Discrimination	Education	Motivation	Ability
	Model 1	Model 2	Model 3	Model 4
Mainline Protestant	1.25***	1.44***	0.78***	1.01
	(4.64)	(8.05)	(−5.28)	(0.12)
Catholic	1.21***	1.33***	0.77***	1.11
	(4.17)	(6.51)	(−5.93)	(1.76)
Jewish	1.72***	1.93***	0.65***	0.97
	(4.96)	(5.79)	(−3.88)	(−0.15)
Other faith	1.45***	1.67***	0.64***	0.79
	(4.52)	(6.38)	(−5.53)	(−1.67)
Nonaffiliated	1.82***	1.83***	0.54***	0.67***
	(9.71)	(10.02)	(−10.09)	(−3.82)
Century	0.98***	0.98***	0.98***	0.96***
	(−10.75)	(−11.31)	(−10.95)	(−15.84)
Income	1.00***	1.00	1.00	1.00***
	(−9.03)	(1.39)	(−0.07)	(−3.64)
Education	1.05***	1.14***	0.87***	0.85***
	(7.43)	(20.00)	(−21.47)	(−17.62)
Female	1.31***	1.29***	0.81***	0.78***
	(7.72)	(7.73)	(−6.19)	(−5.21)
West	1.43***	1.30***	0.73***	0.59***
	(8.56)	(6.36)	(−7.51)	(−7.42)
Church attendance	1.00	1.00	1.00	0.98
	(−0.04)	(−0.09)	(−0.51)	(−1.91)
Democrat	1.39***	1.24***	0.83***	1.03
	(9.05)	(5.95)	(−4.97)	(0.56)
Age (logged)	1.00	1.00***	1.01***	1.03***
	(0.49)	(3.95)	(13.11)	(19.45)
Ll	−10,181.6	−10,738.3	−10,405.3	−5,886.0
chi-squared	626.0	1,019.6	1,502.3	1,801.4

t-statistics are in parentheses. *** p<0.001.

Table 5.3 Estimated Odds Ratios of Seven Modes of Explanation for the Black/White SES Gap (General Social Survey 1977–2008 GSS) N = 13,750

	Structuralist		Individualist	
	Discrimination	Education	Motivation	Ability
	Model 1	Model 2	Model 3	Model 4
Mainline Protestants * New century	0.86 (−1.50)	1.00 (0.00)	1.05 (0.53)	1.25 (1.44)
Catholic * New century	0.97 (−0.31)	0.97 (−0.38)	1.04 (0.42)	1.56** (3.11)
Jewish * New century	1.31 (1.17)	1.51 (1.72)	1.11 (0.46)	1.69 (1.34)
Other Faith * New century	1.27 (1.38)	0.76 (−1.61)	0.80 (−1.25)	1.10 (0.29)
Nonaffiliates * New century	1.10 (0.84)	1.03 (0.28)	1.01 (0.05)	1.53* (2.04)
New Century	1.33*** (5.19)	1.48*** (7.31)	0.79*** (−4.20)	1.02 (0.30)
Mainline Protestants	1.23*** (3.83)	1.35*** (5.79)	0.77*** (−4.93)	1.03 (0.36)
Catholics	1.61*** (3.66)	1.72*** (4.00)	0.64*** (−3.32)	0.91 (−0.48)
Jewish	1.35** (3.06)	1.83*** (6.16)	0.68*** (−3.90)	0.78 (−1.63)
Other faith	1.71*** (6.90)	1.78*** (7.40)	0.53*** (−8.00)	0.58*** (−4.32)
Nonaffiliates	0.74*** (−4.56)	0.74*** (−5.03)	0.74*** (−4.92)	0.42*** (−9.06)
Income	1.00*** (−8.96)	1.00 (1.47)	1.00 (−0.05)	1.00*** (−3.57)
Education	1.04*** (6.51)	1.13*** (19.16)	0.86*** (−22.61)	0.83*** (−19.49)
Female	1.30*** (7.52)	1.28*** (7.56)	0.81*** (−6.36)	0.77*** (−5.50)
West	1.44*** (8.72)	1.31*** (6.46)	0.73*** (−7.42)	0.60*** (−7.18)

(continued)

Table 5.3 (continued)

	Structuralist		Individualist	
	Discrimination	Education	Motivation	Ability
	Model 1	Model 2	Model 3	Model 4
Church Attendance	1.00 (0.29)	1.00 (0.19)	1.00 (-0.17)	0.99 (-1.22)
Democrat	1.41*** (9.41)	1.26*** (6.39)	0.85*** (-4.54)	1.07 (1.37)
Age	1.00 (-0.05)	1.00*** (3.37)	1.01*** (12.46)	1.03*** (18.36)
LI	-8,057	-4,397	-8,287	-8,508
chi-squared	445.5	456.3	442.4	657.2

t-statistics are in parentheses. ***p<0.001. **p<0.01. *p<0.05.

socioeconomic gap increases over time. Further, the effect of evangelicalism on racial attitudes persists even when controlling for individual demographic characteristics, religious service attendance, region, or political affiliation.

Discussion and Conclusions

In this chapter, measures of religious affiliation, particularly the effect of evangelicalism, reveal persistent significant differences in racial attitudes among non-Hispanic whites in America. This study attempts to address several methodological weaknesses in previous work by providing an analysis that takes into account change in public opinion over time as well as potentially conflating factors such as gender, political affiliation, and education. Contrary to recent research I find that social location does not eliminate the effect of white evangelical affiliation on racial inequality attitudes. In addition, the persistent difference between white evangelical views on racial inequality and other religious groups and the nonaffiliated does not support recent work arguing for a broader American Christian toolkit. I extend Emerson and Smith's contention that a unique white evangelical cultural toolkit that emphasizes personal accountability and freewill individualism drives evangelicals' views about racial inequality in America. Moreover, the absence of change over time suggests that this individualism is a deeply ingrained application of this cultural theology.

As this study shows, structural explanations for inequality among non-Hispanic whites tend to be rejected in favor of beliefs concerning blacks' personal motivation to achieve socioeconomic parity with whites. Although few Americans actually favor biological explanations for the socioeconomic gap between blacks and whites, evangelicals and other white conservative Protestants still hold blacks accountable for the persistent socioeconomic gap, attributing it to a lack of motivation. Evangelicalism can therefore be considered an important "cultural root" for white opposition to government efforts to address racial inequality, which may contribute to the perpetuation of a racialized society. Among white evangelicals, notions of racial difference are drawn from deeply held beliefs about sin, individual accountability, and free will, along with the transformative power of individual conversion that characterizes American evangelicalism.[10]

These results provide further evidence for Emerson and Smith's thesis that the theologically informed individualist orientation among white non-Hispanic evangelicals shapes their attitudes toward blacks and their explanations for racial inequality. The research suggests that studies on race should take into account the effect of religion, and in particular American evangelicalism, to understand the persistence of racial inequality. The fact that evangelicals have continued to reject structural explanations in favor of individualist explanations over a period of 30 years shows the enduring effect of evangelicalism on racial attitudes among whites. Evangelicalism remains divided by faith and efforts to change this fact appear to have achieved very little.

Appendix

The GSS has been conducted by the National Opinion Research Center in most years since 1972 and is designed to yield a nationally representative sample of adults 18 years and older living in noninstitutionalized settings within the United States. Although the specific wording of some questions varies from year to year, the cumulative GSS data file has been refined for across-survey consistency and represents a valuable source for examining trends in Americans' social attitudes. Using a subsample of non-Hispanic white Americans from the GSS between 1977 and 2010 allows this chapter's thesis to be tested. The response rate varies between

74% and 82% and the sample size of non-Hispanic whites is 16,243 across all thirty-three years of the survey.

Dependent variables

Attitudes about racial inequality were measured using four modes of explanation applied to the black/white socioeconomic gap in the United States. The dependent variables are based on the following question within the GSS: On average, blacks have worse jobs, income, and housing than white people do. Do you think these differences are . . .

A. Mainly due to discrimination.
B. Because most blacks have less inborn ability to learn.
C. Because most blacks don't have the chance for education that it takes to rise out of poverty.
D. Because most blacks just don't have the motivation or will power to pull themselves out of poverty.

In line with previous research, structurally oriented racial attitudes attribute economic gaps between blacks and whites to systemic deficiencies within social structures and institutions.[11] Therefore, structural explanations for racial inequality are option A (mainly due to discrimination) or option C (lack of educational opportunities). Individualist explanations for racial inequality are that blacks' personal choices (e.g., government dependency) or innate inferiority contributed to persistent racial economic inequality. Consequently, individuals who hold individualist/"person-centered" views of racial inequality are those who responded *yes* to option B (inborn ability) or option D (motivation).

Independent Variables

Emerson and Smith (2000) used the evangelical self-identification measure in the GSS, but that variable was only available for six years. To provide a consistent and comparable religious affiliation measure across all thirty-three years, this chapter employs the RELTRAD scheme developed by Brian Steensland and colleagues.[12] The RELTRAD classification scheme places individuals into one of seven categories based on their denominational preference: evangelical Protestant, mainline Protestant, black Protestant, Catholic, Jewish, other faith, or none.

Control Variables

This chapter's trend variable derives from the GSS variable YEAR. This dummy variable is coded so that the new century (e.g., 2000 and beyond) equals 1 and the twentieth century equals zero. The measure for income derives from the GSS variables CONINC, which is a continuous measure for household income, and education, which is measured in terms of years spent in school. To control for the effect of region, I created a dummy variable for each of the four regions. I allocated those from regions other than the West Coast as the reference group. Gender is a dummy variable that equals 1 for men and zero for women. Political affiliation is a dummy variable that equals 1 for individuals who are Democrats, and otherwise zero. Church attendance is a dummy variable that equals 1 for individuals who attend religious services at least once a month or more; and zero for individuals who did not attend services at this rate. Age measured in years is a logged variable that captures all respondents from age 18 to 89. I also created six interaction variables among each of the focal predictors and the trend variable.

Analytic Strategy

The analysis begins by exploring the bivariate relationships between religious affiliation and the modes of explanations that white Americans offer for the black/white socioeconomic gap. Next, I analyze evangelical differences on each of the seven dependent variables, controlling for demographic and other characteristics that shape Americans' racial attitudes, such as political (party) identification. Finally, I create interaction terms for religious traditions and year to test whether evangelical differences in racial attitudes persist over time. Because all dependent variables are dichotomous, I use logistic regression and present the results in odds ratios.

Notes

1. Christian Smith, *American Evangelicalism: Embattled and Thriving* (Chicago: University of Chicago Press, 1998).
2. Howard Winant, "Race and Race Theory," *Annual Review of Sociology* 26 (2000): 169–185.
3. Ann Swidler, "Culture in Action: Symbols and Strategies," *American Sociological Review* 51 (1986): 273–286.

4. Michael O. Emerson, and Christian Smith, *Divided by Faith: Evangelical Religion and the Problem of Race in America* (New York: Oxford University Press, 2000).
5. Andrew Greeley and Michael Hout, *The Truth About Conservative Christians: What They Think and What They Believe* (Chicago: University of Chicago Press, 2006).
6. Robert D. Putnam and David E. Campbell, *American Grace: How Religion Divides and Unites Us* (New York: Simon & Schuster, 2010).
7. Penny Edgell and Eric Granby, "Religious Influences on Understandings of Racial Inequality in the United States," *Social Problems* 54 (2007): 263–288.
8. Marylee Taylor and Steven M. Merino, "Race, Religion, and Beliefs About Racial Inequality," *Annals of Political and Social Science* 634, no. 1 (2011): 60–77.
9. Putnam and Campbell, *American Grace*.
10. Michael O. Emerson, Christian Smith, and David Sikkink, "Equal in Christ, But Not in the World: White Conservative Protestants and Explanations for Black White Inequality," *Social Problems* 46 (1999): 398–417.
11. Matthew O. Hunt, "Race/Ethnicity and Beliefs about Wealth and Poverty," *Social Science Quarterly* 85 (2007): 827–853.
12. Steensland, Brian, Jerry Z. Park, Mark D. Regnerus, Lynn D. Robinson, W. Bradford Wilcox, and Robert D. Woodberry, "The Measure of American Religion: Toward Improving the State of the Art," *Social Forces* 79 (2000): 291–318.

SECTION TWO

Looking Forward – Possibilities for Overcoming the Color Line

6

Worshipping to Stay the Same: Avoiding the Local to Maintain Solidarity

Mark T. Mulder

IN *DIVIDED BY Faith*, Michael Emerson and Christian Smith explored the particular anxiety that white evangelicals exhibit toward race in the United States. More explicitly, they found that white evangelicals, because of their cultural toolkit, tended to do more to perpetuate the racialized society than to mitigate it. Moreover, Emerson and Smith contended that the conflagration within US religion of homogeneous ingroups and the segmented market buttressed the racialized society. In other words, congregations have trended more and more toward affinity groups and niche identities and that has resulted in fewer instances of attenders worshipping with folks who might be different from them in various social categories (especially race). Because American religion functions as such a segmented market, it fragments the prophetic voice of churches and actually reinforces the status quo. The availability of numerous other congregational options inhibits the ability of a church to ask attenders to sacrifice for the cause of a greater good. Doing so, according to Emerson and Smith, will likely lead to ghettoization—that church will be marginalized and see a decline in attendance. Thus congregations and church leaders tend to emphasize discourse that nurtures group cohesion at the expense of a prophetic voice.[1]

Eight years after the publication of *Divided by Faith*, and in the heat of a tremendously divisive presidential election, Bill Bishop argued that the segmenting of people in the United States continued to ever more extreme levels during the first decade of the twenty-first century. In an echo of Emerson and Smith, Bishop noted in a chapter about religion that churches in the United States are "more culturally and politically segregated than our neighborhoods."[2] That intense religious structuring finds some impetus in the fact that people simply like to worship in like-minded congregations. However, Bishop also contends that church growth proponents who pushed the "homogeneous unit principle" (i.e., like attracts like: people will be attracted to congregations full of attenders who look and think mostly like they do) also bear some responsibility. These same advocates found that "the method worked so well that now these techniques for creating group cohesion through like-mindedness are employed by most churches."[3] Bishop concludes that "the goal of church in other times was to transfigure the social tenets of those who came through the door. Now people go to a church not for how it might change their beliefs, but for how their precepts will be reconfirmed."[4] More recently, Robert Putnam and David Campbell note that the extreme sorting of religious networks function to create churches that act as echo chambers.[5] In the end, the racial segregation and market segmentation of congregations that Emerson and Smith delineated a decade ago shows little sign of amelioration. Considering Bishop's evidence, it seems that church segregation has continued to only grow more extreme in its forms. The following case study considers how worship figures into the maintenance of ever more extreme patterns of segregation.

Context

On a quiet residential street in a medium-sized city in the Great Lakes region of the United States sits a Roman Catholic Church. Or does it? Upon further inspection, the main entrance for parishioners attending mass certainly does face that aforementioned street. However, for those utilizing the food and clothing pantry run by the church, there exists an entirely different entrance. Instead of the grand flight of steps up to beautiful wooden doors under a canopy of matured trees, folks patronizing the pantry use what has to be considered the alternative entrance on the backside of the building. Immediately off the sidewalk on an arterial street that cuts east and west through the entire city, the pantry entrance leading to the basement of the church is utilitarian: a nondescript steel door, no windows, and paint chipping. In short, visiting the building for worship or for social service directly affects an individual's perception of the church and its location within the city.

That visual disconnect between entrances also manifests in worship. Put simply, despite the fact that the church has involvement in the community, the neighborhood and related local issues rarely find voice during worship. Moreover, within this case study of six congregations, the dearth of local references was not unique to this Roman Catholic Church. Based on interviews with attenders, the churches all clearly had notions that they wanted to offer something to the people that inhabit the surrounding area. However, the evidence (worship service transcripts) demonstrates that worship does not function as a venue where such concepts are nurtured and cultivated. Interviewees indicated that discussion of the local had no place in worship because it threatened to be too political and, thus, too divisive. With that in mind, it seems that worship functions as a forum for group cohesion rather than operating as a venue for transformation. Knowing that contemporary congregations already have more to do with affinity groups than geography, the disregard of the local during worship seemed to have a role in nurturing a perceived unity. That is, people already congregate to worship with other people who they think and look like—not people who they live by. Moreover, inhibiting references to local issues during worship works to preempt the manifestation of fissures within the congregation and nurtures a perceived internal similarity.[6]

Literature Review

Worship is a term that has been accorded a multitude of definitions. Sociologically, worship tends to refer to the average 70 minutes per week that a person of faith spends with his or her community of believers, or congregation.[7] These 70 minutes offer a rich variety of stimulations for a person's senses—the visual arrangement of the pulpit, altar, and communion table at the front of a sanctuary; the sound and lyrics of a singing choir; and even the smell of so-called "sanctuary musk" all elicit a particular understanding of his or her location in space, time, and the social arena.

Worship remains a salient feature of American social life. It is estimated that every week over 100 million North Americans attend worship services. The spaces in which these services occur range from storefronts to malls to cars (at drive-in churches) to ornate cathedrals to simple rural churches. As is obvious by the places they inhabit, the styles of worship also vary dramatically. Worship practices include praying, reading the

Bible, preaching, celebrating communion, confession, altar calls, laying on of hands, foot washing, and even drinking coffee. No matter what the particular tradition, public worship services remain a significant and common religious practice in America. "Going to church," for many people, simply means attending a worship service, and worship style is a key (possibly the dominant) variable individuals and families employ in making their decisions about where and with whom they will worship. Accordingly, worship has become central to the identity of most congregations. In his case study of an African Methodist Episcopal congregation, Tim Nelson finds that worship style trumped other variables such as denominational affiliation or doctrine as a method for attenders to identify the distinctive of their church. Mark Chaves describes worship the "primary output" of congregations and contends that without worship, congregations would cease to be congregations. Beyond that, Robert Wuthnow contends that the music and art that occur during weekly worship in the United States have been crucial in cultivating the consistently high level of religious practice among Americans.[8]

Tracing the study of worship in particular neighborhoods, Michael Ducey's *Sunday Morning: Aspects of Urban Ritual* examined four white middle class churches in the Lincoln Park area of Chicago during the socially turbulent late 1960s–early1970s. Employing participant observation, Ducey studied whether, in a parallel to larger social transformations, these four congregations transitioned in their worship from mass ritual (i.e., emphasis on tradition and clear distinctions between clergy and laity) to interaction ritual (i.e., use of more contemporary language/music and more ambiguous distinctions between clergy and laity). Perhaps most germane to this study, Ducey vividly detailed how it was the context of the neighborhood, Lincoln Park, that affected the worship rituals of these four congregations. The late 1960s context of urban renewal and civil unrest made for a potentially anomic situation. Ducey contended that in some instances the neighborhood context of conflict and chaos had dramatic effects that manifested in altered worship rituals.[9]

Continuing in that vein of investigating the content of worship, Marsha Witten examined forty-seven sermons that considered the New Testament story of the prodigal son (Luke 15:11–32). The collected sermons came from congregations from the Southern Baptist Convention and Presbyterian Church (U.S.A.). Despite denominational regional differences, Witten found "accommodative speech" (adaptation to the norms of secular culture) dominant throughout the sermons. Moreover, the notion of sin has been denuded: it is deflected to outsiders and those sins of insiders are mitigated. Witten concluded that her study of an aspect of worship demonstrated how preaching could be utilized to create boundaries of identification between insiders and outsiders.[10]

In addition to the aforementioned examinations of congregations and worship, some sociological studies have referred more explicitly to place in their discussion of congregations. Roozen et al. created a typology for the manners in which congregations participated in their respective communities. Based on their study of ten congregations in Hartford, Connecticut, the authors asserted that the "presence" of a church (i.e., its missional, or contextually focused, orientation) could be positioned within one of four categories: (i) activist—congregations that are interested in actively establishing God's Kingdom in the present age; (ii) civic—similar to activist in manifestation, but more comfortable working within the parameters of dominant political and economic structures; (iii) sanctuary—congregations that are focused on the hereafter in which all concerns from this world will be overcome; and (iv) evangelistic—similar to sanctuary in a focus on a future world but differ in that these congregations encourage participation in public life in an effort to share the message of salvation. In the end, the authors found that within their ten-church case study congregations appeared to have significant difficulty relating to their respective neighborhoods: no matter the type of presence, because the congregations drew from such wide areas, geographic location was marginalized.[11]

More recently, Omar McRoberts, in his study of churches in the Four Corners district of Boston, found an "exilic" sensibility among the congregations; that is, they felt that although they were located in a particular neighborhood, they were not necessarily "of" that neighborhood. Because of their niche identities, the congregations drew commuters from a wide radius beyond Four Corners. In addition, "bouncing" (church mobility) tended to inhibit churches' attachments to the neighborhood. In other words, because the congregations did not rely on the Four Corners for attenders, McRoberts found that most of the churches saw no impetus to focus mission activities at their neighborhood (to the point that a number of the clergy failed even to identify their neighborhood accurately). In the end, McRoberts concluded that the congregations of Four Corners fostered little to no neighborhood cohesion. Instead, they tended to nurture cohesion among affinity groups: "the churches were communities in themselves that happened to be located within the geographic bounds of Four

Corners; they were not nodes in a network of neighborhood residents."[12] Because of mobility and niche identities, these churches tended to have low levels of neighborhood attachment—they were not connected to place. Witmer Sinha et al. found similar patterns in their study of resident, city commuter, and suburban commuter congregations in Philadelphia. The authors wrote that "people are willing to commute longer distances to worship with co-ethnics."[13] They also argued that "three types of congregations are likely to be distinguished by the neighborhoods in which they are located."[14] That is, the neighborhood demographics had significant impact on the categorization of the congregations in the study.

Continuing the theme of congregations and relationship to neighborhood, Elfriede Wedam and Susan K. Gallagher have both published studies that articulate the significance of place for Christian congregations. In her consideration of three "high-status, commuter-based" Indianapolis congregations, Wedam concluded that the churches' locations in the "religious district" of Meridian Street shaped material and cultural factors to create a sense of centrality that contributed significantly to those congregations' identities. Wedam asserted that "place . . . is a salient, contributing factor toward the creation of the subculture that this high status religious district constitutes."[15]

Gallagher similarly conducted a qualitative study of three diverse congregations in the Pacific Northwest and concluded that the unique characteristics of each congregation related to space, ritual, and community were the most important to identity formation, even more so than denominational identity. Perhaps most interesting, in light of this research is Gallagher's argument that worship style actually impacted the sense of community in each congregation. Regarding the Baptist and Presbyterian churches she studied, she wrote, "The energy and action of worship move between auditorium and stage. . . . Worship generally takes place in the front as a performance to be observed."[16] In contrast, she described St. Andrew's ritual-oriented Orthodox worship:

> More than performance *for* the congregation, worship is performance *with* the congregation. During most of the service the entire body of worshipers faces forward. The liturgy itself moves the congregation forward, drawing attenders from "this world" into participation in the next. The open doors of the iconostasis invite this movement, as does the music coming from behind, as sound flowing forward toward the sanctuary. Rather than worship happening

between the priest and the congregation, the movement of the service is toward the front, drawing attention toward the iconostasis, through the open doors flanked by icons of Jesus as an infant and Jesus the final Judge, into the altar and beyond to the kingdom of God.[17]

While the Orthodox Church "shifts the locus of religious authority away from the individual alone," Valley Baptist and First Presbyterian focus on more individually driven approaches to faith. Gallagher also asserted that the buildings housing each congregation are indicative of the social class of their members—an observation which, if generalizable, is likely to have implications for congregants' understanding of place along with their location in the social world. She concluded that facets of these churches' buildings and worship "all embody and speak into the future distinctive sets of beliefs about what it means to be a person, connecting to others and to God."[18]

The implications of class and social location have been especially important features in research on congregations. The social homogeneity and "niche" mentality of many American congregations prove to be some of the most salient of such characteristics. In *Congregation and Community* Nancy Ammerman examined how urban congregations changed as a result of the demographic transition of the 1960s and 1970s. Ammerman found that churches chiefly adapted by either relocating themselves along with the members of their congregation or by adopting a marketing strategy that aimed their services at a particular, scattered clientele. She contended more recently, "Rather than identifying with a particular neighborhood, urban middle-class residents may more readily identify with the cultural slice of life-style that binds the institutions with which they are affiliated."[19] In short, attenders may be more drawn to a church because of the kinds of people who attend it than its geographic location. Similarly, Susan Gallagher quoted the pastor of the upper-middle class Presbyterian congregation whom she studied: "People don't come because we're Presbyterian.... People aren't looking for doctrine, they're looking for people like them."[20]

The homogeneity of church congregations carries significance because other scholars have argued that worship and its impact on worshipers are heavily influenced by the makeup of the worshiping congregation. Chaves noted how social characteristics of a congregation influence the way in which worship is conducted, proposing that certain elements of worship, like speaking in tongues and hand-raising, are linked specifically because of the social homogeneity of the members in a congregation. He elaborated, "Since congregations tend toward social homogeneity, individual worship practices attractive to people in a particular region of sociodemographic space will tend to co-occur in the same worship services." Chaves uses congregational reading and the use of written programs as an example: if the "better educated" favor these practices, they will tend to be found together in worship services that contain a high percentage of "better educated" worshipers.[21]

In addition, religious scholar Douglas Davies argues that worship can also reinforce people's differences: "Shared worship can help bind people together into a unified group but it can also help keep them apart from others whose way of worship, even within the overall world of Christianity, is different from their own. . . . Worship can serve as the focus for wider religious differences that divide people."[22] In essence, the rituals of worship have been found by numerous sociological studies to have almost polarizing properties: tightly bonding those in-group members who appreciate similar worship styles and elements and further distancing individuals who practice differing rituals.

Similarly, a 2009 study by Kevin Dougherty and Mark Mulder examined how fourteen fairly homogeneous congregations from the same white ethnic denomination in the same city had adapted to neighborhood change. The authors found that even though the congregations had much in common in terms of doctrine and polity, the combination of their neighborhoods and the identity that they forged (or failed to forge in some cases) played significant roles in the overall health and vitality of the institutions. A key component for many of these congregations was worship—especially the style for which they were known. A number of these congregations existed in neighborhoods that experienced significant social change, but that modification in environment had very little effect on worship. Those congregations tended to see declining attendance numbers. However, some congregations in the study that demonstrated flexibility in a number of areas—including worship—based on contextual change tended to see steady or increasing attendance.[23]

While that study focused at least partially on how local environment had affected congregations, other recent research has attempted to decipher the interplay between both congregation and neighborhood. A 2006 study by Nancy Kinney and William Winter examined how congregations affect neighborhood stability. The authors, to their surprise, found that storefront churches in high poverty urban neighborhoods tended to have "significant, if modest, contributions to neighborhood stability."[24] In addition, they found that freestanding churches contributed little to property values or residential longevity in a neighborhood.

More recently a number of scholars have examined how or whether congregations contribute to their respective communities. While debating the overall contribution related to secular and government entities, these studies have found a significant amount of monetary and social service impact are generated at the local congregational level. In short, congregations contribute to their communities with everything from food pantries to financial counseling to bike repair.[25]

In the end, studies consistently indicate that context matters: (i) the location and neighborhood of congregation has tremendous impact on the life of a church, and (ii) congregations tend to offer some manner of outreach to their respective neighborhoods. In other words, congregations play a widespread and significant role in the civic life of their respective communities. How are these two aforementioned issues approached in worship? Our interest here is a better understanding of how the central practice of congregations, worship, actually fosters homogeneity. In other words, is there a coherent rhetoric in worship that either mitigates or nurtures congregational bonds? If not, what does that reveal about worship related to church practice as a whole?

Methodology

Six congregations within a transect of a Midwestern metropolitan region participated in the study. The six congregations were chosen based on denominational affiliation (Baptist, Catholic, and United Methodist) and location (urban and suburban). Specifically, the study includes the following eight congregational types: urban Catholic, suburban Catholic, urban Baptist, suburban Baptist, urban United Methodist, and suburban United Methodist. All three suburban congregations were located in the same suburb (and same census tract). The three urban congregations were located in the same quadrant of the core city and included three census tracts. All six congregations agreed to record the morning worship service that occurred during the second week of the month for one year (for a total of twelve recordings from each congregation). These recordings were then transcribed and analyzed. Beyond that, at least one participant observation was conducted at each church. Finally, we conducted five to six semi-structured interviews with attenders from each congregation. These interviews were transcribed, coded, and analyzed.

Findings: Worship Services

Based on this case study of six congregations in a Great Lakes metropolitan region, little attention seems to be given to the church's locality within the context of worship. In fact, for these six congregations, they might be best described as practicing a largely decontextualized worship. That is, so few references exist to the local that these services could be taking place in almost any community in the United States. In fact, in these congregations the worship included much more time focused on global mission projects.

At the urban Baptist congregation, the worship services contained almost weekly references to global missionary work. These included prayers for a youth mission trip to Brazil, prayer for a college student headed to Peru for the same reason, references to Sudan in a sermon, an announcement concerning missionaries in Indonesia (multiple Sundays), a presentation concerning the Gideons' work in 181 countries, and discussion of a church trip to Israel. In comparison, during the twelve recorded worship services we found very limited references to anything local. The most distinct reference to anything local related to an announcement concerning the church's Vacation Bible School (VBS). However, it should be noted that the person speaking states that although there will be VBS preschool available, that "it's just for the [VBS] leaders' kids. This year we're not going to allow any of the neighborhood kids to come to preschool." The speaker seems to indicate a clear distinction between "neighborhood kids" and "church kids."

In the transcript of the final recorded worship service, the speakers discussed "sense of community"—it seemed to function as a theme for the service. However, explicitly in the sermon, the minister discussed community in terms of "church family" and the fact that this particular congregation was "very family oriented." The sermon also included references to reconciliation. Again, however, reconciliation seems to have an explicitly internal focus: the minister broaches the subject in terms of "church families" and "church fights." In the end, the twelve worship services examined demonstrated an acute cognizance of global priorities but betrayed very few clues as to church's neighborhood and its identity.

interviewees indicated that such subjects could be "too political" to be a part of worship. After analysis of the transcripts, it becomes apparent that the congregations have different relationships and attitudes toward their respective localities, but these seem to be more about geography and denominational proclivities than anything that arises in worship.

In all, the urban United Methodist interviewees seemed to have the strongest sense that local issues could plausibly be a part of worship. Of course, that might also have to do with the church's high profile on the edge of the central business district and bordering another area of the city known for its high population of homeless people—thus, being located in a high-need area functioned as an aspect of congregational identity. Just as the worship service transcripts indicated that the neighborhood needed the church to offer services, those interviewed consistently demonstrated an ability to discuss how the church interacted with the neighborhood (one interviewee even listed fourteen different programs). The interviews also elicited the fact that forty years ago the congregation considered relocating but instead recommitted to the current neighborhood. Interviewees indicated that that history led the congregation to a "sharply focused emphasis on feeding the hungry, comforting the people, and helping them." With that in mind, another interviewee stated that people in the neighborhood saw the church "as a great resource, a tremendous resource, especially poor people." Such sentiments would be consistent with the "lighthouse lexicon" that repeatedly appeared during worship services. More than respondents from the other congregations, those interviewed from the urban United Methodist church discussed issues of homelessness and poverty being of part of the worship discourse. However, it should also be noted that despite the focus on helping in the neighborhood, when interviewees responded to questions about local issues arising during worship, one person interpreted that as concerning politics: "No, worship is never allowed to politicize."

That theme of "local" or "neighborhood" having political connotations also appeared in interviews with suburban United Methodist attenders. One interviewee noted:

> We don't get into social issues during the worship. We don't get into social or committee issues—it's pretty much a sermon based on the Bible and scripture and I would say that's the main focus. The other social issues are really incidental.... But [the minister] really is not preaching social issues. I really don't know whether [the minister] is, for example, a Republican or a Democrat.

Previous to that remark the same interviewee noted that the minister did occasionally address homosexuality. In other words, local issues were seen as taboo in worship but clearly not social issues in their entirety. However, that did not mean that the congregation was disconnected from the community. Multiple interviewees again listed numerous efforts on the part of the church for the surrounding community.

In that same suburb, the interviewees from the Catholic church seemed less articulate about activities that the congregation engaged in locally (perhaps because the United Methodist church was located in older residential neighborhood while the Catholic church was set back on a busy highway with very few neighbors in close proximity). Again, however, when the interview turned to community issues, the respondents interpreted that as political. For instance, one man noted that "[the church has] people taking action, but it's not authorized by the congregation or parish; so we haven't had anything local, I guess, that would have been addressed at worship. . . . Those things do bring tension because with local issues there are probably people on both sides in your congregation." Another man from the suburban Catholic church voiced something similar about community issues in worship: "There's a reluctance to address a lot of the issues specifically because there might be the thought that it fringes on the political." In short, the interviews again demonstrated a sense among attenders that worship services included few local references because they could be interpreted as polarizing or offensive.

Interviews from the Baptist congregation in the same suburb yielded similar results. When prompted by questions about neighborhood or community issues, the respondents tended to interpret those as political and, therefore, potentially divisive. One woman stated that when it came to local issues, "Sunday morning isn't a time to, I guess, address specific items." In a similar manner, interviewees from the urban Baptist church also viewed worship as an inappropriate venue for community matters. A woman from the congregation responded to a question about whether a recent rash of violence in the city would be addressed during worship: "It would maybe come up as an example. It wouldn't be something we need to focus on. The one thing that would come up as something we need to do something about is abortion, and it comes up with some frequency." It should be noted that the two Baptist congregations included in this case study had radically different neighborhood contexts, but the interviewees from both also repeatedly stated that larger issues like abortion were permissible during worship; local issues (which were interpreted as politically charged) were not.

Finally, the interviews from attenders of the urban Catholic church maintained the same theme. Although interviewees described the church as "tuned in" to the neighborhood and demonstrated impressive knowledge of congregational involvement in the neighborhood in manner much different than either of the Baptist churches, they still tended to respond to questions about "local" or "community" in terms of political. For instance when asked about "local happenings" or "local issues" being mentioned during worship, one woman asked, "Political?" When the interviewer responded perhaps "political, but perhaps not," the woman stated, "[The priests] usually say that they're careful there. They will tell you to vote your conscience, but vote." Again, the respondents from the urban Catholic church, in a fashion similar to the other five congregations, understood a question about local issues as having political connotations.

Beyond that, and as seen throughout the interview transcripts, attenders noted that community issues were too potentially divisive to be a part of worship. The congregations, however, were involved in their communities. They had different environments, diverse emphases in programming, and various rationales for reaching out to their respective locales, but all had some level of involvement. Despite that involvement, the interviewees consistently noted that local issues had to be avoided so as not to politicize worship. It seems that for many, "political" was synonymous with "divisive" and, therefore, had no place in the context of worship.

Conclusion

The congregations within this case study did not use worship as a medium for communicating about local issues. Rather, the worship services clearly demonstrated that Sunday mornings in these churches consistently referenced global issues much more frequently. And yet, this dichotomy typically did not lead to an absence of local engagement or an exclusive focus on national and international issues. This finding raises some interesting questions about worship and what actually occurs during those 70 minutes on Sunday mornings. Why is "place" not located in worship? What does this tell us about worship related to church as a whole?

Although there are certainly variable levels of discourse concerning the congregations' respective neighborhoods, it is also quite clear that it does not approach the frequency of national and international events or issues. Those interviewed for this study seemed not to notice or lacked concern about this discrepancy. Moreover, numerous interviewees indicated that it was not proper to locate discourse about local issues within the context of a worship service. In essence, there seemed to be misgivings about addressing local or neighborhood issues for fear of offense. At the opposite end of the spectrum, both the worship service transcripts and the interviews demonstrated much more latitude in discourse about events or issues on national and international scales.

Perhaps nonlocal issues are seen as proper for worship while local is, at times at least, taboo for worship because the local has more immediate and threatening possibilities. National or international issues are more vague and thus neutered by distance. Such a dynamic would echo Witten's findings on sermons that projected sin on outsiders while absolving insiders. In any case, by excluding local issues from worship, congregations maintain a persistent unity and a perceived homogeneity in social viewpoints—perhaps an echo of Emile Durkheim's "mechanical solidarity"; that is, a homogeneous experience lends to social cohesion. Whereas national and international issues function as a staple within worship because they do not impinge on the day-to-day lives of attenders, local issues are avoided during worship because of the threat of discord. In this way, worship serves to cement the "lifestyle enclave" status of congregations. Because local issues might engender disharmony, they tend to be avoided.

If this is the case, the examination of worship content perhaps lends new insights as to why congregations persist as homogeneous institutions and how niche identities can become so deeply entrenched. It seems that worship functions to highlight the "exilic" (as McRoberts describes it) tendencies of congregations in regard to their neighborhoods. Moreover, it reveals a bit more about the sources of the organizational inertia that strikes so many congregations as they fail to adapt to changing social environments. Finally, it raises questions about the coherence of community development or local charity work in which almost congregations engage. Worship seemed to have limited transformative possibilities. Attenders were not interrogated. Instead, by avoiding local issues, the culture of worship service prohibits revealing fissures within the congregation and precludes any acknowledgement of involvement/culpability in local problems by attenders. This case study demonstrates a linchpin role that worship plays in nurturing the market segmentation, homogeneous ingroups, and racial exclusivity in American religion by evading the local. In the end, worship—so crucial to the identity of congregations—must be considered as a key variable in understanding a congregation's persistent homogeneity.

With that in mind, it may be incumbent upon congregations to consider how certain taken-for-granted worship practices might actually foster exclusion and segregation. Studies are emerging that indicate some of the problematic ways in which congregations attempt to alter worship practices in the pursuit of racial integration.[26] However, based on the evidence of this case study, it seems that congregations maintain homogeneity in ways they do not even recognize. For churches hoping to pursue the dream of becoming multiracial, it seems that explicit reflection on not just the style but also the substance of worship is necessary. Without it, the status quo of cultural and racial homogeneity becomes further entrenched and more intractable.

Notes

1. Michael Emerson and Christian Smith, *Divided By Faith: Evangelical Religion and the Problem of Race in America* (New York: Oxford University Press, 2000). The author thanks the Calvin Institute of Christian Worship at Calvin College and the Lilly Endowment for providing generous funds to support the research that appears in this chapter.
2. Bill Bishop, *The Big Sort: How the Clustering of Like Minded America Is Tearing Us Apart* (New York: Houghton Mifflin, 2008), 159.
3. Ibid.
4. Ibid., 180.
5. Robert D. Putnam and David E. Campbell, *American Grace: How Religion Divides and Unites Us* (New York: Simon and Schuster, 2010).
6. See especially Nancy Ammerman, *Congregation and Community* (New Brunswick, NJ: Rutgers University Press, 1997); and Omar McRoberts, *Streets of Glory: Church and Community in a Black Urban Neighborhood* (Chicago: University of Chicago Press, 2003).
7. Mark Chavez, *How Do We Worship?* (Bethesda, MD: Alban Institute, 1999).
8. Tim Nelson, "Sacrifice of Praise: Emotion and Collective Participation in an African American Worship Service," *Sociology of Religion* 57, no. 4 (1996): 379–396; Mark Chavez, *Congregations in America* (Cambridge, MA: Harvard University Press, 2004); and Robert Wuthnow, *All in Sync: How Music and Art Are Revitalizing American Religion* (Berkeley: University of California Press, 2003).
9. Michael H. Ducey, *Sunday Morning: Aspects of Urban Ritual* (New York: Free Press, 1977).
10. Marsha Witten, *All Is Forgiven: The Secular Message in American Protestantism* (Princeton, NJ: Princeton University Press, 1993).
11. David A. Roozen, William McKinney, and Jackson W. Carroll, *Varieties of Religious Presence: Mission in Public Life* (New York: Pilgrim Press, 1984).

12. McRoberts, *Streets of Glory*, 128.
13. Jill Witmer Sinha, Amy Hiller, Ram A. Cnaan, and Charlene C. McGrew, "Proximity Matters: Exploring Relationships Among Nieghborhoods, Congregations, and the Residential Patterns of Members," *Journal for the Scientific Study of Religion* 46, no. 2 (2007): 258.
14. Ibid., 257.
15. Elfriede Wedam, "The 'Religious District' of Elite Congregations: Reproducing Spatial Centrality and Redefining Mission," *Review of Religious Research* 64, no. 1 (2003): 56.
16. Sally K. Gallagher, "Building Traditions: Comparing Space, Ritual, and Community in Three Congregations," *Review of Religious Research* 47, no. 1 (2005): 84.
17. Ibid., emphasis in the original.
18. Ibid., 82, 84.
19. Ammerman, *Congregations and Community*, 35.
20. Gallagher, "Building Traditions," 74.
21. Chavez, *Congregations in America*, 138–39.
22. Douglas Davies, "Christianity," in *Worship*, ed. Jean Holm and John Bowker (London: Pinter, 1994), 60.
23. Kevin D. Dougherty and Mark T. Mulder, "Congregational Response to Growing Urban Diversity in a White Ethnic Denomination," *Social Problems* 56, no. 2 (2009): 335–356.
24. Nancy T. Kinney and William E. Winter, "Places of Worship and Neighborhood Stability," *Journal of Urban Affairs* 28, no. 4 (2006): 348.
25. See especially Robert Wuthnow, *The Linkages Between Churches and Faith Based Nonprofits* (Washington DC: Aspen Institute, 2000), Ram Cnaan, *The Newer Deal: Social Work and Religion in Partnership* (New York: Columbia University Press, 1999); and Edwin Hernandez and Neil Carlson, *Gatherings of Hope: How Religious Congregations Contribute to the Quality of Life in Kent County* (Grand Rapids, MI: Calvin College Center for Social Research, 2008). Hernandez and Carlson estimate a replacement value between $95.5 and $118.7 million annually from Kent County congregations.
26. See especially Gerardo Marti, *Worship Across the Racial Divide: Religious Music and the Multiracial Congregation* (Oxford: Oxford University Press, 2012). Marti finds that many congregations' attempts at integrated worship actually reinforce mistaken notions of racial essentialism. That is, these churches promulgate the notion that African Americans are just "better worshippers."

7

Beyond Body Counts: Sex, Individualism, and the Segregated Shape of Twentieth-Century Evangelicalism

Edward J. Blum

AT THE BEGINNING of the twentieth century, the muckraking journalist Ray Stannard Baker traveled throughout the United States to chronicle the places of African Americans in American society. He published his racial odyssey in a fascinating book, *Following the Color Line* (1908). What he found at Protestant churches shocked and confused him. There, as in many other venues, he observed racism and segregation. "One would think that the last harbour of prejudice would be the churches," Baker wrote, "and yet I found strange things in Boston. There are, and have been for a long time, numerous coloured churches in Boston, but many Negroes, especially those of the old families, have belonged to the white churches." The complexions of congregations were changing, and changing rapidly. "In the last two years increased Negro attendance, especially at the Episcopal churches, has become a serious problem. A quarter of the congregation of the Church of the Ascension is coloured and the vicar has had to refuse any further coloured attendance at the Sunday School." The Church of the Ascension was going to try something new for them, but something that had been done by other churches and missionary groups many times before. It was going to create "Negro mission" churches where blacks could worship separate from whites. Allegedly "separate but equal" public facilities had been the legal and social order of the day, especially since the Supreme Court had declared them constitutional in 1896.

The church plan didn't please everyone. As Baker reported, it caused "bitterness" among many local blacks. One white pastor threw his hands up in exasperation: "What *shall* we do with these Negroes! I for one would like to have them stay. I believe it is in accordance with the doctrine of Christ." But the pastor had to consider much more than the doctrine of Christ or the decisions of individuals. This matter was a corporate affair. He observed that when the number of blacks increased, the number of whites decreased. Strangers and new white residents avoided the church. And local African Americans did not contribute as much as the local whites. "Think about it yourself," the minister rationalized to Baker, "What shall we do?"[1]

Baker's work on the state of race and religion in the early twentieth century was telling.[2] Much of his account fits with what sociologists Michael Emerson and Christian Smith detail in *Divided by Faith: Evangelical Religion and the Problem of Race in America*: churches were at times places of interracial interaction; white Protestants oftentimes capitulated to racial segregation when they could have stood courageously against white supremacy; some African Americans wished to be part of biracial or integrated churches only to be turned away; and whites thought separate facilities would be proper equivalents.[3]

But there is much in Baker's narrative that fails to align with our general thinking about race and religion. Why did Baker refer to this as a "strange" circumstance since church racial segregation seemed to be so common? Why did Baker assume that white Christians would be less racially prejudiced and discriminatory than others? Why was the Boston pastor surprised by the unfolding events? Why too was the pastor willing to sacrifice his religious ideology—the explicit belief that it was wrong to turn away African Americans—for racial practicality—the desire to have a church harmonious and comfortable for whites even though it upset black congregants? And why did he blame blacks for the crisis?

Baker found the whole ordeal perplexing because there were so many factors at play. The complications were personal, communal, and historical, and they brought attitudes, ideas, finances, social relations, race, and faith together. *Following the Color Line* was published at a distinct moment in American history when new connections between race and religion were being created. The old structure of slavery had given way to a new one of segregation, but the new edifice was built on sandy ground. Total racial segregation was never the goal. Whites always wanted black laborers and domestic servants. And complete racial separation was never the all-encompassing reality. Whites and blacks interacted so often and in so many venues that segregation laws were often necessary because of the lack of separation, not the realities of it.[4] Another reason religious segregation seemed strange to Baker, perhaps, was because there were so many religious voices and actors in favor of racial integration—either that it was desirable, or that it was happening, or that it was possible. Christ, metaphorically and literally, crossed the color line in a number of guises. All in all, Baker rendered this happening a strange occurrence because the links between race and religion throughout the twentieth century were complicated, contradictory, and often changing shape. They beg for further, deeper, and more thoughtful consideration, not just so we can better know our religious history but also so that we can think in new and innovative ways about creating viable interracial congregations today and in the future.[5]

Baker's exposé allows us to appreciate and complicate Emerson and Smith's *Divided by Faith*. What happened at the Church of the Ascension exemplified some of Emerson and Smith's main points. Through the process of segregation, racial animosity trumped religious commonalities. The ideologies of individualism and individual choice made it virtually impossible for evangelical Christians to unsegregate their churches in any meaningful way. For Emerson and Smith, the individualistic ethos of evangelicalism has been imperative. Individualism has bound evangelicalism to segregated churches and blinded them from the structural problems of American society.

Yet Baker's work—what he examined and what he and Emerson and Smith failed to examine—offers new directions to explore. Black and white Christians attended the same churches in part because they shared so many religious sentiments. Even as they physically separated, these black and white congregants held many traditions, songs, and spiritual experiences in common. What the church wanted to segregate wasn't just people but physical bodies. Neither Baker nor Emerson and Smith have detailed why bodies had to be separated. Moreover, individualism has a complicated racial history. At times, individualism has been used to attack racial structures like slavery or segregation. At other times, it has been used to oppose dominant trends within society. Individualism and its relationship to religious viewpoints and racial structures have histories, and by looking at the shifts we can see why separating bodies mattered so much in the early twentieth century and therefore better understand its legacies.

This essay traces some of the intersections among race and religion in twentieth century evangelicalism. It first examines the numerous ways Protestantism crossed the color line through music and medium, image and imagination. It shows the ways evangelical individualism and its missionary focus could paradoxically work on behalf of interracial activity and hinder it as well. Evangelical individualism, however, ultimately fails to provide a full rationale for how and why racial segregation developed in twentieth century evangelicalism.

The second portion of the essay turns from the individual to the corporate. Rather than just count the bodies being segregated, this section takes seriously why particular bodies—both white and black—were segregated. At this point, issues of sex and marriage take center stage in justifying evangelical segregation. By turning to family units, evangelicals cast aside their individualism in favor of notions of group purity. God's plan was not just for saved individuals but also for particular family units.

This essay concludes by suggesting that sociologists, historians, ethicists, and theologians interested in church integration may wish to turn their attention from individual bodies to corporate bodies—such as families and familial networks. If churches were segregated, in part, to maintain sexual segregation, then perhaps integrated churches could come from sexual integration. Perhaps new multiracial churches in the twenty-first century could be built upon multiracial family units.

In their aggregate, all three sections of this chapter show that when we look beyond body counts we find a myth of white evangelical individualism. Never for white evangelicals was individual choice or individualistic thinking the only reason for racial segregation. At certain historical junctures, individualism could actually work against racial discrimination, while at other times—especially when it came to sex and marriage—arguments about community, the social good, and God's purposes for groups trumped individualism. This history not only offers a new perspective on the creation of church segregation but also provides a key to dismantling it. If white evangelicals in the twentieth century could think in corporate terms when it came to family and community, perhaps those in the twenty-first century could think in those terms when it comes to the entire family of God and the entire community around them. Already integrated at a variety of levels, multiracial families may be a key to successfully challenging church segregation in the future.

What and How They Shared

Ray Stannard Baker may have been surprised to find racial segregation on the rise in churches because for all of their differences, white and black Protestants shared a great deal socially and culturally. These similarities were binding ties and provided avenues for interracial interaction. Denominational specificities were one clear arena of similarity for many whites and blacks. Black Methodists and white Methodists shared a love for the Wesley brothers, an Arminian theology, and an inclination toward notions of holiness. Black Baptists and white Baptists prized their independent church structures and democracies. Black Presbyterians and white Presbyterians shared an admiration for the Westminster catechism, a focus on the teachings of John Calvin, and an emphasis on ideas and thoughts. In all of these Protestant denominations—white and black—men dominated the pulpits while women dominated the pews. They read the same Bible and quoted the same stories.[6]

At formal and informal levels, interracial exchange was abundant from the late nineteenth century to the early twentieth century. During the Reconstruction of the United States after the Civil War, white Christian missionaries went to black Americans in the South, to Native Americans on the Plains, and to Chinese Americans in the West. The great commission and its emphasis to move beyond boundaries and borders drove missionaries from their communities to interact with others. Historians may dislike the messages that these missionaries taught or the cultural imperialism of their spiritual endeavors, but perhaps other than economic interests, religious callings were the primary motivation for interracial interaction. Oftentimes, these missionaries opposed racial discrimination and violence. During the age of Ku Klux Klan attacks in the South and anti-Chinese pogroms in the West, white missionaries often stood against the racial mayhem.[7] Missionaries applauded the federal government's attempts to destroy the Ku Klux Klan in the early 1870s, and in California during the 1870s and 1880s, Protestant missionary groups opposed arguments to ghettoize or eliminate the Chinese American populations. Christ's teaching to go and make disciples" was one taken seriously and one that often led to earnest opposition to racial violence.[8]

In this pre-Civil Rights era—when racial groups were explicitly treated differentially in American law and social organization—individualism could actually cut against racial particularism and discrimination. Although sociologists Michael Emerson and Christian Smith identify individualism as a central reason for evangelical acceptance of segregation (not just their acceptance and their unwillingness to do anything about it, but also their perpetuation of segregation more than other social organizations), the political and social outcomes of individualism could be very different in different historical situations.[9] During the late nineteenth and early twentieth centuries, individualism had a complicated relationship to racial activities. In this era, new state laws and federal actions hindered the rights of groups (such as racial disfranchisement in the South, immigration restrictions in the West, and detribalization of Native Americans). The Protestant ideology of individualism could work against racial segregation in this case. Take John Watson Foster as an example. A Presbyterian minister, he preached in 1899 that "Christ's civilization is a personal system both as respects its Author and its recipient." He went on further: "It is an appeal to the individual man." Foster's personal individualism led him to spend half of his life as a missionary. He lived in Russia and in Spain; he dined with Buddhists, Muslims, and a variety of different Christians. Through it all, his individualism led him to interact with peoples and groups different from his own middle-class, white background.[10] In the context of legal racism against particular groups, individualism, coupled with the Great Commission, led many white Protestants to make the personal choice to leave their social group behind and link up with other social groups. In the case of Gilded Age missionaries, individualism could render cross-racial and interracial interactions. Individual choices (although the missionaries were often funded by evangelical groups) made corporate interactions more possible.

At informal levels, as Paul Harvey has meticulously shown in his work on religion in the South from the Civil War to the end of the twentieth century, whites and blacks shared much in their religious cultures. They reveled in impassioned sermons that were based on biblical passages and themes; they sang the same hymns, had revival services and baptisms that looked similar, and even ate the same foods at church picnics and potlucks. Traveling evangelists, faith healers, and itinerant singers often attracted biracial crowds. Moreover, new Protestant faiths, such as Pentecostalism, had biracial origins and accepted—if not encouraged—religious identity to trump all other human differences. Music was shared and shaped by interracial interaction. New hymns from Ira Sankey were used equally by white and black Protestants. "Negro singers" were welcomed in white churches, universities, and organizations. Gospel music became a cultural tie that constituted a shared expressive form for many white, black, and Chinese Americans.[11]

The center of much of this singing was Christ—the center of evangelicalism itself. He too was shared—not just in belief but also across the color line in visions and material culture. As historian John Giggie has shown in his study of black religion in the Mississippi Delta, this period was the age of black church material growth. They were building more buildings, debating what kind of art to place in their churches, and publishing new newspapers and magazines. To represent Jesus, the vast majority of white and black Protestants used standard visual images of a white, brown-haired Jesus.[12] If black churches had stained glass windows—and usually only urban churches had these—Jesus was white. In the inexpensive Sunday School cards purchased by white and black Christians, Jesus too was white with short brown hair. The presence of white depictions of Christ in black churches was so upsetting to sociologist E. Franklin Frazier in the 1930s that he blamed them for tying whiteness to godliness in the minds of African Americans in general. The black "church contributes a great deal to the self-evaluation of lower-class Negroes," Frazier maintained, because some "of them accept literally the pictures of God and Christ given in Sunday school lessons."[13]

At the turn of the twentieth century, when African Americans imagined or explained Christ, they rendered him as a white man too. One preacher explained in an interview. "I saw the Lord in the east part of the world, and he looked like a white man. His hair was parted in the middle, and he looked like he had been dipped in snow, and he was talking to me." Another southern African American recounted the time when "Jesus came to me just as white as dripping snow, with his hair parted in the middle just as white as snow." In these cases, white men—"the Lord" and "Jesus"—crossed the color line not to dominate or exploit but to save and love.[14]

While white and black Americans shared a white Jesus in the late nineteenth and early twentieth centuries, a number of white and black Americans invoked Christ's spirit to denounce segregation. Christian ideas were foundational to anti-segregation arguments, and white and black civil rights activists drew upon the Bible to make their claims. In his study of the social gospel, historian Ralph Luker found white and black Protestants opposing segregation, lynching, and political disenfranchisement with similar biblical stories and interpretations. Oftentimes, they charged whites with placing race above faith. Even the pastor interviewed by Ray

Stannard Baker acknowledged that he believed Christ's teachings were against his church's actions. Several years later, leading black historian Carter Woodson similarly charged northern and southern white Protestants with worshiping at "the shrine of race prejudice" and "sacrificing the principles of Jesus."[15]

White and black Protestants shared and exchanged much in the late nineteenth and early twentieth centuries. They had similar church structures and theologies; they sang similar—and oftentimes the same—songs; they read and quoted the same Bible; they used similar material objects in their churches; and biblical texts and ideals were easily used to attack racial violence, discrimination, and segregation. Moreover, evangelical concepts of individualism and of missionary work compelled many to move beyond their particular racial groups and interact with other groups of people. White and black missionaries routinely crossed color and national lines, and white missionaries oftentimes opposed violence against racial minorities. All of this may have accounted for Ray Stannard Baker's surprise at the drive for racial segregation in that Boston church, but it was that drive that became one of the dominant features of twentieth-century American church life. It was that push toward segregation—not the various moments and expressions of integration—that became a chief storyline of modern evangelicalism. Why and how whites pushed for and sustained segregation in their church life was the central story, and it was a tale where bodies became crucial sites of power and control.

What and Why They Separated

For all of the religious integration and cross-racial sharing, the arc of the twentieth century was not of religious integration but segregation. Baker was struck not by the process of Christ crossing the color line or of religious similarity among white and black Protestants but of the color line being drawn in Christian churches. This storyline has been examined by numerous scholars, but never as richly as Emerson and Smith's *Divided By Faith*. They found that in the late twentieth and early twenty-first centuries the vast majority of American congregations were racially homogenous. In their sociological rendering, the tale of evangelical church life in the United States is one of racial separation, and the theology of evangelicals—especially their focus on individualism—has hindered and continues to hinder their ability to overcome their segregated past.[16]

For Emerson and Smith—as well as Ray Stannard Baker—body counts mattered more than religious culture, style, vision, or ideas. They were fixated on the physical location of individual bodies as the markers of church integration or segregation. For this reason, Emerson and Smith counted the numbers of white and black bodies in congregations to assess how integrated or segregated they are. Then Emerson and Smith—just as Ray Stannard Baker did— looked for explanations for how and why those bodies were and remain separated. At this point, they and the scholars who follow them turned to cultural, economic, ideological, theological, and social explanations.[17]

Back in the early twentieth century, the Boston minister that Baker interviewed explained the need for physical separation of bodies in two ways: general white racism and financial practicalities that black congregants didn't give enough proportionally. Clearly, however, there was much more going on than generic white racism or problems with church bank accounts. The church was happy to set up a separate church and to fund missionary activities—probably expecting to lose money in the ventures. Moreover, why would the presence of some blacks be acceptable but not more? Was there some kind of unwritten threshold that the congregation understood that the minister did not?

To explain church segregation simply as another variant of white racism conceals more than it exposes. Throughout American history, prejudice and discrimination against African Americans have been constants, and yet they have changed remarkably over time and have been expressed in remarkably different ways. Sharecropping wasn't chattel slavery; the desire to colonize black Americans was an effort to rid the nation of them, while the desire to force them into low-income jobs was a means to keep them in place and exploit them; the making of sundown towns (where African Americans had to leave the city limits by the time the sun went down) was distinct from charging higher mortgage rates for homes.

And in church relations, churches with racially segregated pews were created for different reasons than those churches that explicitly barred blacks from attending. When it comes to explaining racial segregation in churches, even when explaining it as moments from the past that were clearly drenched in white supremacy, we need to examine exactly how and why Protestants justified their actions. And when we look at the late nineteenth and early twentieth centuries, we find the new justifications for church segregation bending and molding evangelicalism in particular ways—ways that moved away from individualism and toward group identities. These particular ways also had much to do with perceptions of bodies and what people do with their bodies.

The centrality of bodies brings us to the physical nature of interracial church worship. Bodies that pray together may lie together. Through sexual integration, they may create literal new bodies, bodies in the form of children that defy typical American racial categories. Bodies that sing holy songs together may wish to participate in other holy ceremonies. Through marriage, they may create new family and social units. Religious theorist Anthony Pinn has recently called scholars of American religion to take bodies and embodiment seriously. Bodies, he contends, are "religiously vital and significant," and they draw attention to questions of race and racial representation, sex and sexuality, and the boundaries made and destroyed by religious values.[18] Physical interaction opens the door for interracial sex and marriage, while sheer cultural exchanges or shared religious concepts do not necessarily. The presence and problem of bodies was another feature of church life that Ray Stannard Baker failed to examine but may offer a key way to understand why so many churches have been and are divided by faith.

Baker's minister never referenced sex or marriage, but fears about interracial sexuality have run rampant throughout the United States well into the twentieth century. In the world after slavery, black sexuality was no longer controlled and exploited by white men. Suddenly black men and women, along with white women, had greater potential degrees of sexual and marital freedom. A new band of Protestant theologians, led by Charles Carroll, rendered interracial sexuality as the greatest sin known to man. They exclaimed that social integration was the reason for original sin and that interracial sex was "itself the most infamous and destructive crime known to the law of God."[19] Carroll characterized God's entire relationship with human history as one of anger over interracial sexuality. "The Bible is largely a history of the long, destructive conflict which has raged between God and man, because of man's social, political, and religious equality with this beast, and the amalgamation to which these crimes inevitably lead." The great flood of the book of Genesis resulted from amalgamation, Carroll continued, and so too did the Israelites' fall from grace. And now, in the United States, God's wrath may be coming, and it would alter everything in the nation. When amalgamation happens, "the nation's relation to God, its relation to the earth and the animals has completely changed."[20]

It is hard to assess how widely and deeply these sexualized and racialized religious sentiments went. The editor of the *South Atlantic Quarterly*, for instance, acknowledged that Carroll's *The Negro: A Beast?* "has had a wide sale and approval among the mass of the white people of the South." Minister and religious writer H. Paul Douglass likewise claimed in 1909 that Carroll's work "has become the Scripture of tens of thousands of poor whites, and its doctrine is maintained with an appalling stubbornness and persistence."[21] Several scholars have shown that these concepts worked their way into American novels, missionary literature, and political discourse of the time.[22]

Historian Jane Dailey uncovered that even though pro-segregationists had weak literal biblical arguments to support segregation in the middle of the twentieth century, they had powerful sexual appeals. In opposition to *Brown v. The Board of Education* (1954), which rendered school segregation unconstitutional, many southern whites claimed that segregation was necessary—in churches, schools, and throughout society—because it would patrol the boundaries of bodies. According to Dailey, it "was through sex that racial segregation in the South moved from being a local social practice to a part of the divine plan for the world." Ministers pronounced that humans would incur the "Judgment of Almighty God" for their "gross immorality and lawlessness." Even the Daughters of the American Revolution declared that "racial integrity" was a "fundamental Christian principle."[23]

Sex could even alter the precious and potent ideology of individualism. In American law and social mores, legal bans and political arguments against interracial sexuality were often filled with biblical readings and Christian sentiments. Individual rights were legislated against—with white Protestant backing—in the arena of marriage and sexuality. The Pennsylvania Supreme Court stated in an 1867 interracial marriage case, "Why the Creator made one white and the other black, we do not know; But the fact is apparent and the races are distinct. . . . The natural law which forbids their intermarriage and that amalgamation which leads to a corruption of the races, is as clearly divine as that which imparted to them different natures." Then in 1930, Alabama Senator James Thomas Heflin told his colleagues that "God intended that each of the four races should preserve its blood free from mixture with other races and preserve race integrity and prove itself true to the purpose that God had in mind for each of them when He brought them into being." Even Harry Truman—who actively supported civil rights—told a reporter that interracial marriage "ran counter to the teachings of the Bible."[24]

When considering bodies as sexual beings, even the most thoughtful and progressive-minded white southerners stood against racial integration. The case of Southern Baptist leader T. B. Maston is instructive. In the 1940s and 1950s, he was a lion who roared against biblical arguments for segregation. His 1959 work, *The Bible and Race*, demolished pro-segregation biblical interpretations. He declared unequivocally that all humans were made "in the image of God," that there "is no partiality with God," that God made all people "of one blood," that God was "no respecter of persons," that loving your neighbor meant loving all your neighbors, and that the "curse of Canaan" was not intended for African Americans in the twentieth century. He told his readers, "The race problem is, in a very real sense, 'American Christianity's test case.'"[25]

These were strong words from a white Texan Baptist. These were heroic words of opposition to the religious power of segregation. Yet when it came to issues of sexuality and marriage, Maston pulled out. Although an evangelical who prized the Bible and individualism, Maston turned to social conventions, traditions, and the importance of the community when speaking against interracial marriage. In his second chapter, titled "Of One," Maston revealed how sexual issues limited how far racial integration should go. He maintained that although whites and blacks should consider one another "brothers" and "sisters" who love one another in Christ, they should not become husbands and wives with one another in love under Christ. Maston admitted, "This emphasis on one 'Father' and one 'family' creates some very real problems or questions for some people. . . . 'How is all this related to intermarriage?' with the companion question, 'What about intermarriage—is it wise or unwise?'" Maston claimed that interracial marriage was not wise, that it violated community sentiments, and that it would hurt Christian missions. "Marriage, particularly for a child of God, is not exclusively a personal affair. Society and the institutions of society have a stake in his marriage. He should consider the effects of his marriage on his family, his community, his church, and the cause of Christ in general. If by entering into a particular marriage one would lose his opportunity to witness or to minister for Christ, or if his marriage would handicap and hurt the work of Christ, then the marriage would be not only unwise but positively wrong."[26] When it came to interracial marriage, strict readings of the Bible and the evangelical emphasis individualism fell by the wayside. What mattered more were community obligations and the overall mission of the church.

The voices of opposition to interracial sex and marriage stretched from sea to shining sea in the United States. A host of white senators and presidents, ministers and theologians, liberals and conservatives, northerners, southerners, and westerners agreed that either God created the races separate and therefore should not intermingle or that sexual integration hindered the work of the church. From all of these vantage points, individualism fell prey to collectivism and the importance of segregated churches hinged upon a broader focus on segregating particular bodies.

If we take bodies seriously, we find a new and disturbing reason for the presence and persistence of white evangelical segregation. Pushing aside individual choice or an individual call on one's conscience or emotions when it came to marriage, white evangelicals in the first two-thirds of the twentieth century took a corporate approach to race, faith, and marriage. They privileged group needs and the alleged good of the whole not only in social mores and theology but also in American law. Keeping bodies separated—because those bodies could make other bodies—was crucial to evangelical segregation.

This dark history may contain a ray of light, however. Within the history of sex-based church segregation may be an ideological, theological, and social answer to the problem of race in American evangelicalism. If white evangelicals could think and act in corporate ways when considering family units and when justifying segregation, perhaps they could turn those corporate worldviews about family units to embrace the rise of multiracial families—a twenty-first-century American phenomenon that may change the church radically.

Conclusion: From Individual to Family Bodies in the New Millennium

Bodies mattered in the story of church segregation and integration, not just as objects that could be counted but also as expressive beings that could love, marry, and bear new children. When it came to bodies as embodied, raced, and sexual, modern white Protestants turned against integration vigorously with all the powers they could muster. Even evangelicals who opposed segregation and prized individualism weighed in against sexual integration and did so by appealing to community norms and social standards.

Much has changed since the mid-twentieth century, however. First in the 1950s and then in the 1960s, the Supreme Court outlawed segregation in schools, public facilities, and marriage. From *Brown v. the Board of Education* (1954), which overturned segregated schooling, to *Loving v. Virginia* (1967), which nullified state laws against interracial marriage, the federal tide moved against the segregation of bodies and body parts.

In many instances, laws didn't change evangelical hearts, and there have been numerous tales of white and black evangelicals experiencing discrimination and family disdain for their love across the color line. In 1995, for instance, one "devout Christian" detailed how her parents encouraged her to "marry a Christian," but when the Christian she wanted to marry turned out to be black, she recalled: "My parents, although they have never met my boyfriend, are against our relationship." Her parents went so far as to claim that their romance "disgraces them and God." This young woman was stuck; she didn't want to disobey her parents, but she "found no evidence in the Bible to support their claim."[27]

Although anecdotal, this woman's experience reflected a sea change in white American thinking on interracial dating and marriage. While her parents opposed such activities, she did not. Recent surveys confirm this generational shift. They show that young Americans in the early twenty-first century are far more accepting of interracial dating and marriage than previous generations. In 2010, the Pew Center reported that an overwhelming number of Millennials (individuals born after 1981) accept interracial dating and marriage. In fact, roughly 90% of Millennials were "very supportive" of interracial marriage. By comparison, only 36% of white Americans over the age of 65 in 2010 said they would accept an interracial marriage within their families. Even more, another survey from earlier in the century revealed that one-half of Milliennals had interracially dated. The numbers suggest that a wave of interracial marriages may sweep across the United States in the next twenty years and may very well be followed by another wave in the decades after that.[28]

The new data suggest that evangelicalism must pay attention to multiracial families, for they may very well change the face of the United States itself. The new data on interracial dating and marriage could offer white evangelicals a new and exciting way to enact church integration. Traditionally, evangelicals know how to privilege the place of families and family life. They know how to approach family units as made by God. So if the number of interracial couples and families grow, new evangelical churches could arise by tailoring themselves to interracial family units (rather than individuals). If established as a spiritual place for interracial couples, these new churches could be set in place to reap the benefits of the shift in American thinking on interracial sex and marriage. They could be positioned for the way of interracial families and children that may very well transform the racial composition of the United States once again. This turn hinges on a number of factors—including a shift in thinking from the individual to the family. Thankfully for white evangelicals, they have long focused on families, and the shift from individual to family thinking is not a far leap for many evangelicals—even when it comes to the problems of race.

Notes

1. Ray Stannard Baker, *Following the Color Line: An Account of Negro Citizenship in the American Democracy* (New York: Doubleday, Page, and Company, 1908), 121–122; emphasis in the original.
2. Rayford W. Logan, *The Negro in America Life and Thought: The Nadir, 1877–1901* (New York: Dial Press, 1954). For more on this era, see Leon F. Litwack, *Trouble in Mind: Black Southerners in the Age of Jim Crow* (New York: Alfred A. Knopf, 1998); Matthew Frye Jacobson, *Barbarian Virtues: The United States Encounters Foreign Peoples at Home and Abroad, 1876–1917* (New York: Hill and Wang, 2000); Grace Elizabeth Hale, *Making Whiteness: The Culture of Segregation in the South* (New York: Pantheon Books, 1998); Ralph Luker, *The Social Gospel in Black and White: American Racial Reform, 1885–1912* (Chapel Hill: University of North Carolina Press, 1991); and Edward J. Blum, *Reforging the White Republic: Race, Religion, and American Nationalism, 1865–1898* (Baton Rouge: Louisiana State University Press, 2005).
3. Michael O. Emerson and Christian Smith, *Divided By Faith: Evangelical Religion and the Problem of Race in America* (New York: Oxford University Press, 2000), 21–49; Charles F. Irons, *The Origins of Proslavery Christianity: White and Black Evangelicals in Colonial and Antebellum Virginia* (Chapel Hill: University of North Carolina Press, 2008); Paul Harvey, *Freedom's Coming: Religious Culture and the Shaping of the South from the Civil War Through the Civil Rights Era* (Chapel Hill: University of North Carolina Press, 2005); Katharine L. Dvorak, *An African-American Exodus: The Segregation of the Southern Churches* (New York: Carlson Publishing, 1991); Paul Harvey, *Redeeming the South: Religious Cultures and Racial Identities among Southern Baptists, 1865–1925* (Chapel Hill: University of North Carolina Press, 1997); Reginald F. Hildebrand, *The Times were Strange and Stirring: Methodist Preachers and the Crisis of Emancipation* (Durham and London: Duke University Press, 1995).
4. Grace Elizabeth Hale, *Making Whiteness: The Culture of Segregation in the South, 1890–1940* (New York: Vintage, 1999); Leon F. Litwack, *Trouble in Mind: Black Southerners in the Age of Jim Crow* (New York: Alfred A. Knopf, 1998).

5. For more on the various links connecting race and religion, see Edward J. Blum, *W. E. B. Du Bois, American Prophet* (Philadelphia: University of Pennsylvania Press, 2007); Blum, *Reforging the White Republic*; Colin Kidd, *The Forging of the Races: Race and Scripture in the Protestant Atlantic World, 1600–2000* (Cambridge: Cambridge University Press, 2006).
6. Evelyn Brooks Higginbotham, *Righteous Discontent: The Women's Movement in the Black Baptist Church, 1880–1920* (Cambridge, MA: Harvard University Press, 1993); James Melvin Washington, *Frustrated Fellowship: The Black Baptist Quest for Social Power* (Macon, GA: Mercer University Press, 1991); Mark A. Noll, *America's God: From Jonathan Edwards to Abraham Lincoln* (New York: Oxford University Press, 2002); Gayraud S. Wilmore, *Black and Presbyterian: The Heritage and the Hope* (Louisville, KY: Witherspoon Press, 1998); William B. McLain, *Black People in the Methodist Church* (Nashville: Abingdon Press, 1990).
7. Blum, *Reforging the White Republic*, chapter 2.
8. Derek Chang, *Citizens of a Christian Nation: Evangelical Missions and the Problem of Race in the Nineteenth Century* (Philadelphia: University of Pennsylvania Press, 2010); Joshua Paddison, "Anti-Catholicism and Race in Post-Civil War San Francisco," *Pacific Historical Review* 78, no. 4 (2009): 505–544.
9. Emerson and Smith, *Divided By Faith*.
10. John Watson Foster, "The Civilization of Christ," delivered before the Presbyterian Ministerial Association, Witherspoon Building, Philadelphia; October 16, 1899. Special Collections, Presbyterian Historical Society, Philadelphia, Pennsylvania.
11. Paul Harvey, *Freedom's Coming*; Randall J. Stephens, *The Fire Spreads: Holiness and Pentecostalism in the American South* (Cambridge, MA: Harvard University Press, 2008); Chang, *Citizens of a Christian Nation*.
12. John M. Giggie, *After Redemption: Jim Crow and the Transformation of African American Religion in the Delta, 1875–1915* (New York: Oxford University Press, 2008).
13. Edward J. Blum and Paul Harvey, *The Color of Christ: The Son of God and the Saga of Race in America* (Chapel Hill: University of North Carolina Press, 2012); E. Franklin Frazier, *Negro Youth at the Crossways: Their Personality Development in the Middle States* (1940; reprint, New York: Schocken Books, 1967), 115.
14. Clifton H. Johnson, ed., *God Struck Me Dead: Voices of Ex-Slaves* (1969; reprint, Cleveland: Pilgrim Press, 1993), 74–75, 109; Edward J. Blum, "A Subversive Savior: Manhood and African American Images of Christ in the Early Twentieth-Century South," in *Southern Masculinity: Perspectives on Manhood in the South since Reconstruction*, ed. Craig Friend (Athens: University of Georgia Press, 2009), 150–173.
15. Ralph E. Luker, *The Social Gospel in Black and White: American Racial Reform, 1885–1912* (Chapel Hill: University of North Carolina Press, 1991); Carter Godwin Woodson, *The History of the Negro Church* (Washington, DC: Associated Publishers, 1921), 307.

16. Emerson and Smith, *Divided by Faith*.
17. Michael O. Emerson, *People of the Dream: Multiracial Congregations in the United States* (Princeton, NJ: Princeton University Press, 2006); Korie L. Edwards, *The Elusive Dream: The Power of Race in Interracial Churches* (New York: Oxford University Press, 2008). For important work from sociologists, see Gerardo Marti, *A Mosaic of Believers: Diversity and Innovation in a Multiethnic Church* (Bloomington: Indiana University Press, 2005); *Hollywood Faith: Holiness, Prosperity, and Ambition in a Los Angeles* (New Brunswick, NJ: Rutgers University Press, 2008); Kathleen Garces-Foley, *Crossing the Ethnic Divide: The Multiethnic Church* (New York: Oxford University Press, 2007); and Gerardo Marti, *Worship Across the Racial Divide: Religious Music and the Multiracial Congregation* (New York: Oxford University Press, 2012).
18. Anthony B. Pinn, *Embodiment and the New Shape of Black Theological Thought* (New York: New York University Press, 2010), xvii.
19. Charles Carroll, *The Tempter of Eve, or The Criminality of Man's Social, Political, and Religious Equality with the Negro, and the Amalgamation to Which These Crimes Inevitable Lead* (St. Louis: Adamic Publishing, 1902), 414, 402, 406. In *Anti-Black Thought, 1863–1925: "The Negro Problem"*, Vol. 6, ed. John David Smith (New York: Garland Publishing, 1993).
20. Ibid., 228, 457.
21. John Spencer Bassett, "Two Negro Leaders," *South Atlantic Quarterly* 2, no. 3 (July 1903): 272; H. Paul Douglass, *Christian Reconstruction in the South* (Boston, 1909), 114.
22. Blum, *W. E. B. Du Bois, American Prophet*, chapter 2; Mason Boyd Stokes, *The Color of Sex: Whiteness, Heterosexuality, and the Fictions of White Supremacy* (Durham: Duke University Press, 2001).
23. Jane Dailey, "Sex, Segregation, and the Sacred After Brown," *Journal of American History* 91, no. 1 (June 2004): 119–144.
24. These examples come from Fay Botham, *Almighty God Created the Races: Christianity, Interracial Marriage, and American Law* (Chapel Hill: University of North Carolina Press, 2009), 92, 108, 110.
25. T. B. Maston, *The Bible and Race* (Nashville: Broadman Press, 1959), 95.
26. Ibid., 29.
27. Barbara Pement, "Mixed Messages: Getting Personal About Interracial Marriage," *Cornerstone* 26, 111 (1997): 24–26, 28.
28. "Almost All Millennials Accept Interracial Dating and Marriage," Pew Research Center Publications, February 1, 2010, accessed May 3, 2012, http://pewresearch.org/pubs/1480/millennials-accept-interracial-dating-marriage-friends-different-race-generations; George Yancey, "Who Interracially Dates: An Examination of the Characteristics of Those Who Have Interracially Dated," *Journal of Comparative Family Studies* 33, no. 2 (2002): 177–190.

8

Color-Conscious Structure-Blind Assimilation: How Asian American Christians Can Unintentionally Maintain the Racial Divide

Jerry Z. Park

THE QUESTION OF diverse churches today is quite different from the era in which Dr. King stated his oft-quoted observation that eleven o'clock Sunday morning is the most segregated hour in America.[1] The segregation to which King referred historically implied a black and white divide. Michael Emerson and Christian Smith's groundbreaking book, *Divided by Faith* followed that historical trend, focusing exclusively on the separation of black and white conservative Protestants. Today, however, new considerations of Sunday morning segregation are warranted. For instance, what about Latino and Asian American Christians? Are they also segregated from one another and from blacks and whites? If so, should our efforts at racial unity not also include them?

This essay aims to unpack these questions by speaking to what sociologists call the social location and symbolic group position of Asian Americans and what these concepts imply for race relations among Christians in the United States. By *social location* I refer to the sociological position (e.g., working class or middle/upper-class, immigrants or second-generation) that different Asian Americans hold in American society. These different locations change their likelihood of being part of the multiracial church movement. In the following I argue that the incorporation of Asian Americans in discussions over multiracial churches refers to a highly select group among Asian Americans as a whole. The most likely candidates for multiracial church participation are second-generation, middle- and upper-class Asian American Christians who make up less than one-third of the today's 14 million Americans of Asian descent. This select group of Asian Americans also occupy the symbolic group position of "model minority" wherein their relative achievements are attributed to the aggregation of individuals' efforts with minimal attention to the unique background factors (such as immigrant parental patterns of migration and human capital) that gave them advantages from the start. Thus, I propose that when we account for social location and symbolic group positioning we will find a disproportional emphasis on *middle-class second-generation* Asian American Christians in multiracial congregations and in multiracial congregational research. Further I suggest that middle-class second-generation Asian Americans can unintentionally reinforce what I call *color-conscious structural-blindness*, a pattern of symbolically acknowledging ethnic cultural differences that simultaneously minimizes awareness of persistent systemic racism in American society. This situation is not merely a problem for white Christians but for any racial minority Christians who also worship alongside them.

American Integration Dilemmas: White (and Christian) Assimilation

When we teach our children about our national identity as Americans we commonly rely on two theories that explain the phrase *e pluribus unum* or "from the many, one," which aptly describes the diversity of people groups that form the United States. One theory describes us as diverse people groups that need to conform to the cultural norms and standards of the majority. At the start of the nation, those of English heritage were in the numerical and proportional majority. Understandably they also dominated the cultural centers of power. The language we use, the ideas of governance, economics, and civil life all had roots in English culture. Thus we characterized "from the many, one" as assimilation or Anglo-conformity. The second theory that appeared at the end of the nineteenth century promoted a different idea, popularly termed the melting pot and sometimes described as amalgamation. Rather than conforming to English culture, American identity under this alternative conception is thought of as a contribution of many groups. In this way the larger and more established groups understandably have a greater influence in defining American culture, but there remains room for inclusion of other groups and their norms as well. Over time, American identity becomes an ever-evolving hodgepodge of cultures and peoples who less resemble their peers from their countries of origin than they do one another.

These two theories of integration often left unexplained the inclusion of cultures and peoples who did not originate from Europe. Indeed, the most evident example of how assimilation and amalgamation worked was with the southern and eastern European immigrants. For a period of several decades, Italian, Jewish, and Russian arrivals were deemed unassimilable by experts.[2] Eventually however, racial proximity (specifically the degree to which an ethnic group could "pass" for white) became the measure by which assimilation and amalgamation might be estimated. Thus, the groups that were not part of the American identity would include those of African descent, Native American people groups, and those of Asian descent. Whereas their labor and services might be desirable, their cultures and their nonwhite appearance would not form part of American identity.

The definitions of American identity and of racial categories are important because they have implications for how Christian Americans think about diversity.[3] To the extent that white Christian Americans associate national identity with Christian identity, then Christian identity is linked with whiteness. Whether referring to assimilation or amalgamation, the end result is still conformity to the white majority. Because American culture has historically functioned under white norms and expectations, many (but not all) white Christians can arguably show that new groups incorporated into American society should conform to the Christianity of whites who house the roots of American culture.

But scholars and keen observers of social life have noted that this relationship among religion, race, and culture is not quite so simple, particularly after the 1960s. The victories of the civil rights movement provided greater protected opportunity for African Americans, particularly those in the South. This opportunity in turn raised new conversations over how American identity would be shaped. If American identity truly entails inclusion of different cultural groups, then those who have been historically marginalized and those who are newly arrived from non-European countries must be taken into account in our theories of integration. Attention turned more toward understanding diversity with these aims in mind. And from this new understanding emerged multiculturalism, an acknowledgment and celebration of cultural diversity. As an explanation of diversity, multiculturalism acknowledges that cultural domination is a historical reality and that this history creates a legacy of marginalization for groups that do not conform readily nor easily to the dominant group. Thus the disadvantages and "suboptimal outcomes" of racial minority groups, particularly for African Americans, can be explained in part by this history of exclusion.

This shift from Anglo conformity and the melting pot to multiculturalism has affected not only how we teach our children American identity but also how American Christians think about their faith. I suspect that for some white American Christians the change toward multiculturalism seems threatening because it presumes that the historic dominance of white Anglo Christianity was somehow less than ideal. Indeed, if Christianity, American identity, and whiteness are all linked together, then the roots of American identity have the imprint of their faith. Multiculturalism's critical eye toward the explicit and implicit marginalization of minorities becomes an accusation against Christianity to the extent that American identity and Christian identity are inextricably tied together.

These ideas play a significant role in how the multiracial church movement understands its aims and where Asian Americans fit in the process. For while multiracial churches promote racial unity, this aim occurs within a particular historical moment in which more Americans are encountering members of racial groups that are different from them. In the same decade that the Civil Rights Act guaranteed greater equal treatment for all Americans regardless of race, the Immigration and Nationality Act of 1965 (also known as the Hart–Cellar Act) radically altered the flow of new immigrants to the United States. With this law, anti-Asian legislation was ended and highly restrictive quotas on other immigrants were lifted. More significantly, new preferences for immigrants with specific skills needed in various employment sectors shifted the origins of newcomers from the western hemisphere to the eastern hemisphere. More middle-class white Americans then would see more persons of color with each passing year especially in many major metropolitan cities. By extension, more and more white Christians, to the extent that they were not sequestered in environments and webs of relationships that were exclusively white, would also encounter nonwhites.

As Emerson and Smith pointed out, sociologists have argued since the 1960s that merely encountering someone of a different race is insufficient in augmenting preconceptions of other groups. Through beliefs passed down within families, school lessons, and even churches and other civic institutions, white attitudes toward nonwhites were largely negative in tone. Instead, as Gordon Allport argued, intergroup contact would need to be frequent and on an equal status footing.[4] Members of one group must not be able to view the other group as socially inferior. To accomplish this task, especially after centuries of creating conditions of inequality, a society would need to restructure the environments of contact in a fairly radical manner. From the 1960s onward, federal and state legislation dismantled Jim Crow laws and made illegal the practices of segregation and unequal treatment in access to property and major institutions. Neighborhoods could not be blatantly inaccessible to minorities; job opportunities, medical care, and mixed-race juries would be equally available to all; and children of different racial backgrounds would now be in the same classrooms. Over the past several decades scholars have examined the ways in which racial diversity occurs in neighborhoods, workplaces, schools, and churches. By encouraging the organizations in these civic spaces to diversify, interracial contact ought to produce a weakening of prejudicial attitudes. On this point, churches, as Emerson and Smith noted, were the most segregated of all spaces in which Americans of different racial backgrounds might encounter one another.[5]

Racial diversity is more common in other social spaces than it is in American churches. But these other social spaces are more bundled together than might quickly be recognized. Neighborhoods contain homes with values attached to them. The value of those homes is often tied to local school quality. To afford those homes and enroll one's child in the local school, one must have a means to pay for that home. Thus, neighborhoods are tied to salaries, which are based on placement in the employment sector. Taken together, therefore, while racial diversity is more apparent in neighborhoods, schools, and workplaces, this diversity is at the same time closely bundled together with class. If we follow Allport's reasoning, social status similarity will help mitigate prejudicial attitudes. If no relationship between race and class existed, we would expect that our schools, neighborhoods, and jobs would roughly fall along the lines of our national demography where white non-Hispanics form 65%, followed by Latinos (14%), African Americans (12%), and Asian Americans (5%), mixed race (3%), and Native Americans (1%).

In the United States, however, race and class have a definite corresponding relationship. Not surprisingly, therefore, given the legacy of unequal treatment toward different minority groups, the presence of whites and nonwhites in schools, jobs, and neighborhood varies based on the social strata. In high status environments African Americans and Latinos are disproportionally lower in representation. That is, in neighborhoods containing high-valued homes, where taxes go toward the most resourced schools, which are therefore funded by higher paying workers, whites will be overrepresented and blacks and Latinos will be underrepresented. Numerous studies continue to point out that, despite legislation discouraging the marginalization of minorities, blacks and Latinos on average are paid lower wages, accumulate less wealth, and therefore live in lower valued neighborhoods and attend lower resourced schools.[6]

Asian American Demography and Its Implications for Race Relations

What about Asian Americans? Theirs is a complex story. Similar to other immigrant groups, Asian American low-wage labor was instrumental in industrializing America in the nineteenth century. The embodiment of that labor was eventually deemed a threat and racially discriminatory policies were instituted to prevent the growth of Chinese and Japanese immigrant communities.[7] These groups did not experience the natural population growth of other groups due to these policies, which barred Asian men and women from immigration and barred Asian American men from interracial relationships.[8] These laws continued through the first half of the twentieth century, effectively slowing Asian population growth below the rate of other groups. The change in immigration legislation in 1965, therefore, created a seismic increase in the Asian population in the United States. The new approach was based on quota systems that reunited family members and, more important, favored selective hiring for much-needed labor in service, medicine, and technology.[9] This change resulted in an immigration shift away from Europe and toward Asia and Latin America and produced an influx of nurses, engineers, teachers, and information specialists from China, India, Japan, Korea, and the Philippines.

While Asian Americans have long been part of the American social landscape, their numbers had remained quite small with less than 1 million Americans reporting any Asian heritage prior to the 1970 census.[10] Further, what constituted "Asian" largely referred to only three nationalities: Chinese, Filipino, and Japanese.[11] But since the 1970s, the US Census Bureau and various agencies that document immigration (e.g., Immigration and Naturalization Services, the Department of Homeland Security) have revealed a significant uptick in the number and variety of Asian immigrants coming to the United States. Forty years later, as of 2010, all Asian ethnic groups combined totaled just over 17 million in the United States.[12] This total includes significant numbers of Asian Indian, Korean, and Vietnamese who together with the Chinese, Filipino and Japanese constitute about 85% of all Asian Americans.[13] Moreover, political scientists Janelle Wong, S. Karthick Ramakrishnan, Taeku Lee, and Jane Junn have estimated that 67% of Asian Americans in 2008 were foreign born.[14]

In short, then, when one refers to Asian Americans, one is referring to several important characteristics that could have significant implications for multiracial churches today. Asian Americans are a largely immigrant class of people due to exclusionary practices that prevented earlier generations from growing. New Asian immigrants (those who migrated after 1965) constitute two-thirds of Asian Americans today and have expanded the variety of origins that make up the people constituted under this pan-ethnic label. Notably too, unlike Latinos, not one of these groups dominates this racial designation. In fact, the Chinese, the largest Asian ethnic group take up less than 25% of all Asian Americans. Importantly, of the millions of Asian immigrants in the United States today, many migrated with specific human capital skills sought by numerous businesses and institutions.

The implications of these characteristics of Asian Americans for multiracial churches are twofold. First, multiracial churches might face the significant challenge of being inclusive of so many different ethnic cultural norms and languages. Second, multiracial churches can mistake what appear to be cultural preferences for certain kinds of work by not knowing that many Asian immigrants were selected because of their particular work skills. They are unlike other minorities who may show a wider range of work interests because their group has been in the United States much longer and many did not migrate exclusively for work reasons.

Given the changes in immigration to an importation of specific kinds of labor, the older image of the penniless but hardworking immigrant who struggles to rise from the working class to middle class has been replaced by two types of immigrants. The first type continues to follow the traditional image of the low-resourced working-class immigrant. These immigrants are new Americans who are more often found in agricultural, manual, and service sector employment. Depending on their relative success, some immigrant small business entrepreneurs also fit here, and depending on their lack of success some highly educated professionals might also be found here. Asian American immigrants in this class include local Chinese restaurant and Vietnamese nail salon workers, Indian convenience store and Korean dry cleaner owners, and Sikh cab drivers in New York. Like other service sector workers, the hours are long, the pay is very low, and vulnerability to injury, disease, or random acts of violence is much higher. For the many Asian Americans who have limited English-speaking ability, these jobs are within reach because they demand less in terms of communication skills apart from a brief exchange in their place of work with their manager or with customers.

The second type of immigrant includes those middle-class workers mentioned earlier, highly educated Chinese, Filipino, Indian, and Korean immigrant nurses, engineers, medical technicians, computer programmers, and some highly successful entrepreneurs who start at the lower to middle range of the middle class. Many of these workers are hired due to their willingness to accept lower wages for what their skills should be valued. Sociologists describe this as "returns on education." Compared to other racial groups, the returns on education are lower for highly educated and skilled Asian Americans who often accept less pay for their labor.[15] Even still, some Asian Americans are able gain access to affluent neighborhoods and higher resourced schools for their children. Many live with nonnuclear family members and pool their resources to gain access to these communities with greater wealth. Judging by the higher average household incomes of Asian Americans (due to the higher than average number of adults workers), it is fair to say that many can be found in this strata of society.

The bifurcated flow of Asian Americans into education-intensive and service sector employment has implications for multiracial church formation. As discussed, the composition of our social surroundings is organized by class, which in the United States is tied to race. To the extent that multiracial churches are built on relationships emerging from social contact in same-status (i.e., social location) environments such as one's neighborhood, school, and workplace, those churches will have different racial group compositions based on social location. In other words, because the working class is proportionally more racially diverse, we would expect more multiracial churches populated by working-class whites, blacks, Asians, and Latinos, although arguably fewer in the latter two categories due to the higher proportion of nonnative English speakers.

Recall that working-class labor usually demands less fluency in English apart from brief exchanges with managers and customers. Latinos and Asian Americans in these social environments are more likely immigrant and not fluent enough in English to understand the experience of multiracial Christian worship and church life. Therefore nonblack minorities, to the extent that they are more often of the immigrant generation (such as many working-class Asian Americans) would be minimally motivated to participate in a religious community that demands that they must translate their experience of the sacred on a regular basis.

This scenario brings us to the Asian Americans of the middle and upper classes. As previously mentioned, the Asian American population is composed much more of the immigrant generation than subsequent generations, and much of the immigrant generation is specifically highly educated due to the selective need for their highly skilled labor. Therefore these Asian Americans are more likely fluent in English such that communication is not a barrier to participation in multiracial churches. And after forty or more years of immigration, their children and many of the children of working-class Asian Americans are emerging as highly educated native speakers who might also participate in such congregations. From this perspective we should not be surprised that Asian Americans might be more evident in middle- and upper-class multiracial congregations.

The Prevalence of Asian American Christians

One additional variable warrants consideration. How many Asian Americans are Christian? Scholars have pointed out that immigrants to the United States usually bring with them their religious practices partly because religion is a way to house the essence of one's ethnic values and practices[16] and because the experience of leaving one's family and familiar surroundings is so alienating.[17] This importation of religious affiliation is particularly significant because the United States is well known for its stated religious tolerance in the Bill of Rights (although American religious history suggests that public tolerance of non-Protestants has been fairly negative or uneven at best).[18]

Immigration research has also shown that not only are immigrants generally religious but also that they are more likely to be Christian.[19] Because the US Census is not required to ask Americans about their religion, we have had to rely on surveys to learn more about our nation's religious beliefs and behaviors. But when it comes to Asian Americans, we have some significant barriers. Given that they constitute only 5% of the country as of 2010, a typical survey of 1,500 identifies an insufficient number of Asian American respondents to make any kind of reliable estimates on their cultural beliefs and social or political attitudes. In addition, the vast majority of surveys are conducted exclusively in English and only a handful are translated; even fewer are translated into the major native tongues of immigrant Asian Americans.[20] To understand religion among Asian Americans requires a unique survey that not only is sensitive to cultural and religious diversity but also to language diversity. Such a survey was made public in late 2011: the 2008 National Asian American Survey (NAAS), the largest Asian American survey to date. With a sample of over 5,000 respondents and with multiple translations available, we now have a unique snapshot of this important part of the new American mosaic. Further we have new survey information on the state of Christianity around the globe from the Pew Research Centers. Although the data from these two reports differ in time, we have no reason to believe that significant shifts in religious affiliation have occurred between the two time points of 2008 and 2010.

Pro-Christian Migration and the Asian American Christian Minority

Table 8.1 shows that the NAAS is sufficiently large so that we can divide the respondents into the largest six Asian ethnic groups and view the religious preferences for members of these groups. I focus only on those who selected Christian backgrounds and then analyze the figures for the Christian portion of the same Asian nations from the Pew survey. To gain some nuance, I further subdivide the figures between Catholic and non-Catholic groups. Readers who wish to know how Asian Americans are represented in specific Protestant denominations will understandably find this delineation frustrating. A close look at the data reveal that only 5.4% of respondents selected a Protestant denomination; the most popular label selected among Asian American non-Catholic Christians was simply Christian (17.2% of the entire sample). That aside, let's turn our attention first to the Christian presence in the Asian-Pacific region of the world. The Pew Research Centers estimate that 285 million of the 4 billion people living in the AsiaPacific region are Christian.[21] To put that finding into context, the US population in 2010 was just over 300 million;

Table 8.1. Christian Distribution Within Asian Ethnic Groups in the United States (2008) and Asia (2010)

Ethnicity	Pew Global Christianity Survey 2010: Asia Pacific Region					National Asian American Survey 2008			
	Christian population (est.)	Catholic (% of nation)	Protestant (% of nation)	Christian (% of nation)	Asian Christians (%)	Catholic (%)	Non-Catholic (%)	Total Christian (%)	US ethnic composition (%)
Asian Indian	31,850,000	0.90	1.70	2.60	11.2	1.9	3.2	5.1	22.3
Chinese	69,200,000	0.69	4.35	5.04	24.3	2.2	21.8	24.0	26.2
Filipino	86,790,000	81.40	11.70	93.10	30.4	73.1	17.9	91.0	11.7
Japanese	1,900,000	0.30	1.20	1.50	0.7	3.5	26.2	29.7	10.5
Korean	14,100,000	10.90	18.40	29.30	4.9	13.2	67.6	80.8	11.9
Vietnamese	7,030,000	6.40	1.60	8.00	2.5	34.2	4.5	38.7	13.9
Total	210,870,000				74.0	14.8	27.4	42.2	3.5
Other Asian	7,425,0000	16.8	20.9	37.7	26.0				
Asian Pacific Christian population (est.):	285,120,000	Asian Pacific Christians in Asian population (%):			7.00				

in other words, there are almost as many Christians in Asia as there are people in the United States. However, 285 million constitutes only 7% of the Asia-Pacific population. One well-established pattern regarding religion and immigration is pro-Christian migration: Christian immigrants form the largest share of the Asian-Pacific population that migrate to the United States.[22] Because two-thirds of the Asian American population are immigrants, average figures usually reflect the immigrant population. That said, Table 8.1 shows that, for all major Asian ethnic groups in the United States, the proportion of Christians in the United States is high compared to the proportion in the country of origin (with the exception of Filipinos, where 91% of Filipinos in the United States are Christian compared to 93% in the Philippines). The NAAS survey shows that 5% of US Asian Indians are Christian whereas 2.6% of India is Christian. Most Asian nations are not dominated by Christianity; the Philippines is the only nation with a Christian majority (Catholic). If there was no pro-Christian migration, we would expect that Asian Americans are generally less Christian compared to the rest of the nation. Indeed the NAAS findings bear out this expectation to some extent. While Christians are disproportionally represented among Asian American immigrants, they are not the majority of Asian America: only about 38% of Asian Americans are Christian.[23] By contrast, 78% of the US population is Christian, including 85% of African Americans[24] and 84% of Latinos.[25] Put together, Asian Americans are more Christian than their counterparts in Asia, but they are much less Christian than their counterparts in the United States. In terms of religion they exhibit an in-between-ness, fitting neither religious composition very well.

Table 8.1 also implies that when we talk about inclusion of Asian Americans in the conversation over multiracial churches we are discussing certain Asian ethnic groups more so than others. Specifically, Filipino and Korean Americans are actually more like the general population and non-Asian minority groups in their rates of adherence to Christianity. About 90% and 80% of these ethnic groups, respectively, claim Christian affiliation, the former is more heavily Catholic (73%) and the latter, more Protestant (68%). From the racial lens, less than 40% of the other Asian ethnic groups identify themselves as Christian.[26] And because Christians are still distinctly Catholic and non-Catholic (even among those who are involved in multiracial congregation formation), these ethnic–Christian distinctions are further complicated.

Table 8.2. Christian Composition by Asian American Ethnic Groups (National Asian American Survey, 2008)

Ethnicity	Catholic (%)	Non-Catholic (%)	Total Christian (%)
Asian Indian	2.5	3.3	5.8
Chinese	3.5	27.3	30.8
Filipino	50.9	10.0	60.9
Japanese	2.2	13.2	15.4
Korean	9.4	38.5	47.9
Vietnamese	28.4	3.0	31.4
Other Asian	3.1	4.6	7.7
Total	100.00	100.00	

Table 8.2 shows that 78% of Asian American Catholics come from only two groups: Filipinos (51%) and Vietnamese (28%). Among non-Catholic Asian Americans, 81% come from only three groups: Korean (39%), Chinese (27%), and Japanese (13%). Thus Catholic multiracial churches will likely be comprised of different Asian Americans compared to Protestant multiracial churches.

In sum, for several sociological reasons Asian American immigrants seem unlikely to participate in the conversation over multiracial worship and community. Less than one-half of all Asian Americans identify as Christian, and by extension far fewer have access to Christian communities without someone or some group reaching them. Among those that are self-identified as Christian, more Filipinos and Vietnamese are found among Catholics while more Koreans, Chinese, and Japanese appear among non-Catholic Christians. This finding means that even a well-resourced outreach to "Asians" requires cultural awareness and perhaps linguistic capacity of a large variety of groups. This finding is even more pertinent for those Asian Americans in the working class. For those in the middle and upper class, many would prefer to spend time in community with others who are familiar with the world that they left behind. While they are fluent in English, they may nevertheless prefer to speak in their native tongue in matters of spiritual worship and community. These findings are some of main cultural and structural barriers that work against Asian American immigrant Christian participation.

The Social Location and Ethnic and Religious Identities of the Asian American Second-Generation

Given the limited role that we might expect of the immigrant generation of Asian Americans, we turn to the roughly one-third of Asian Americans, the English-preferred-speaking children of immigrants, or the second generation. As noted earlier, immigrants have arrived in larger numbers from the 1970s and with them their children, whether raised or born here. The first wave of the second generation were raised in the context of the 1980s and 1990s as the American economy continued to exhibit a bifurcation of jobs—ones that favored the highly educated and ones that required fairly minimal education.[27] Many Asian Americans immigrated precisely to fill the need for educated labor including nursing, engineering, and computer-related jobs. These immigrants had high levels of what sociologists call human capital, thus making them more employable and more likely to obtain higher paying jobs.[28] Access to higher paying jobs allows for other ancillary benefits such as better housing options and better schooling districts for their children. The children of these highly skilled and highly educated immigrants then were often raised in environments of relative privilege that did not follow the classic impression of the nineteenth-century penniless immigrant who made ends meet through long labor in dangerous manual work and found rest in disheveled and unsanitary housing. For the children of many contemporary Asian immigrants, home was in the suburbs, and they shared in the advantages experienced by millions of mostly suburban white youth.[29]

Spiritually, home for many of the second-generation was in the congregations of their parents but segregated into an English-speaking peer community typically defined as a youth group. This pattern of religious cultivation (which is fairly compulsory) is significant for many reasons, but the main issue is one of identity. As young people raised in the United States with parents whose cultures originate from outside the United States, their sense of self is one of constant negotiation: Which part of me is like that of my parents and which part of me is not? Is the culture of my parents also a part of being American? For many, the practice of ethnic church involvement is simultaneously a process of socialization into the Christian faith and a cultivation of ethnic attachment. This involvement might occur through a language and culture class or participating in activities that celebrate important moments in the life of the church. And because racial Asian-ness sets apart Asian Americans from whites, blacks, and Latinos, simply being around a critical mass of others who are physically similar also helps second-generation Asian Americans to develop a sense of ethnic awareness. This problem of self-definition is a challenge whether one is socially located in the working class or the middle and upper classes. For second-generation Asian Americans the resolution of their identities as American, ethnic, and religious individuals continues when they enter college. Judging by the statistics on Asian American college attainment rates, most will spend part of their early adulthood in this institution.

Christian Tiger Mom's Kids at Harvard

Sociologist Rebecca Kim insightfully pointed out that at places like UCLA, where Asian Americans took up well over one-third of the undergraduate student body, Christians faced a unique opportunity to participate in multiracial worship.[30] No longer influenced by their parents and the immigrant ethnic church, second-generation Asian Americans could well participate in multiracial campus groups where they could encounter believers of different backgrounds. But, as it turns out, many, perhaps most, did not. As Kim points out, the pressures of performance and the myth of the model minority were acutely felt by these young men and women, many of whom understandably sought support from others they felt could empathize with their peculiar place in the drama of twenty-first century America. For many in the second generation, the turn was to community with Christians, but particularly other second-generation Asian American Christians.[31]

Indeed, reports by the national leadership of groups like InterVarsity Christian Fellowship and Campus Crusade for Christ clearly acknowledged the astounding numerical presence of second-generation Asian Americans and the challenges of creating student groups that accommodate their particular needs as well as the needs of white, black, and Latino students.[32] These leaders, the staff who work on campuses, and scholars have all acknowledged that what has happened on these college campuses is not a utopic multicultural evangelical community that one might imagine for young optimistic, bright, and open-minded coeds. Instead they witnessed racial segregation. As second-generation Asian Americans grew in number at campus meetings, white students left and joined newly created multiracial evangelical student groups on the same campus. What few African American and Latino evangelical students there were have not been discussed much.

The Religious Marketplace of the Christian Second-Generation

What do second-generation Asian American religious choices in college have to do with multiracial church formation? Unlike other racialized groups in the United States, the college attendance rate of Asian Americans is well over the national average.[33] Given this pattern, it is fair to say that the college experience as it pertains to religion has a strong bearing on the understanding of faith for the second generation as they leave college. The first cohorts to graduate from college emerged from the late 1980s and continued through the 1990s. While we cannot estimate statistically the religious choices during their undergraduate careers, we do have evidence from several local studies that many of these young adults replicated the pattern of racial segregation.[34] Once they graduated their choices of religious participation were now informed not only by the ethnic immigrant church experience when they were growing up but also the multiracial or second-generation Asian American campus religious community in which they may have participated. They are, of course, also influenced by their religious options after they move from their alma mater. Generally, however, we can simplify these factors to five options in terms of their religious choices. A few returned to an ethnic immigrant community church; we know next to nothing about them. But what we do know is that they are not participating in multiracial congregations. A second option was to turn to pan-ethnic or same-ethnic dominant congregations. According to work by Russell Jeung and Sharon Kim, a good number of second-generation Asian Americans are participating in either exclusive second-generation or pan-ethnic English-preferred Christian churches.[35] Another group of the second-generation opted not to attend any religious organization. Whether they never cultivated or have abandoned their religious affiliations, they too are not participating in religious organizations. They might still be personally religious or they might exclude all religious practice, but what is most important is that they are not in a religious context in which they are participating in group life with other people.

Joining Predominantly White Congregations: The Perspective of Whites

We are now left us with options four and five which I describe as joining a predominantly white church or joining a multiracial church. In this section I unpack the fourth option as a way to think about option five. If second-generation Asian American Christians choose the latter, they become the single or relatively minor presence in a church that is dominated by another racial group (usually white). These individuals may arrive at these places of worship from the invitation of friends or through interracial marriage with a white Christian spouse. Regardless of the means by which they arrive at this place, one thing is certain: they are typically so small in number that two interconnecting dynamics emerge. On the one hand, their very presence makes cultural difference potentially significant. Whites in these congregations will likely welcome second-generation Asian Americans (or any minority group member) in part because they will be reminded of the kind of multicultural ethics that they were taught in school. Here white Christians have an opportunity to acknowledge racial difference but in a fairly light and perfunctory manner such as customs, food, dress, holidays, and the like. We can describe this interaction as a color-consciousness.

On the other hand, white Christians who participate in the same churches with a low percentage of minorities likely are meeting second-generation Asian Americans of similar class backgrounds. Recall that churches are drawn in part by the relative racial diversity of personal social networks of its members and the surrounding area of the church. Congregations that are largely white are likely more middle and upper class. By extension minorities like second-generation Asian Americans in these churches will likely have the same social status as most whites. Thus, while scholars like Emerson and Smith have shown that racial inequality is tied to class, whites in churches where there is a small presence of racial minorities will likely not be aware of the persistent systemic inequality that affects many (if not most) other minorities that never approach the doors of their congregation. Indeed, their immediate experience of token minorities in their congregation suggests as much. Structural inequalities, whether they exist, clearly have not hindered these minorities from achieving socioeconomic success. Therefore the burden of proof lies with those who have not been as successful and likely not a part of this church. This situation we might describe as a kind of structural blindness. Thus, whites in predominantly white congregations in which there is less than a critical mass of minorities will simultaneously be aware at a surface level of racial difference (i.e., color consciousness) while at the same time remain unaware of or reject persistent systemic structural racism (i.e., structural blindness).

Joining Predominantly White Congregations: The Perspective of Second-Generation Asian Americans

While the previous section affixes responsibility for ignorance over structural racial inequality on the part of whites who participate in these predominantly white congregations, there is another perspective that we should consider as well: that of racial minorities who participate in these congregations. Because discussion of this religious option is focused on second-generation Asian Americans, my argument centers largely on their experience, but much of this discussion may be relevant for any minorities in this same context. With regard to color consciousness, many second-generation Asian Americans in predominantly white congregations exist in tension as they try to find a home in these spiritual spaces. Their upbringing in immigrant Christian churches has largely been one where everyone looked like them and their parents. For those that retained their faith in college, the religious community was either Asian-specific, white-predominant, or racially diverse. In each of these contexts, to what extent did they retain their sense of ethnic heritage? As I noted earlier, American identity transformed in the 1960s as earlier models that paid little to no attention to the role of race were replaced by a new narrative of multiculturalism. This approach, which entered the curricula of public schools from elementary levels and beyond, emphasized a celebration of cultural difference by noting the ways in which ethnic and racial minority individuals and communities express civic engagement and identity. Often, however, this exercise is diluted into a kind of cultural tourism where difference is rendered symbolic and optional much in the way that third- and fourth-generation ethnic whites understand their particular backgrounds.[36] To the extent that multicultural education exemplifies this tourism, second-generation Asian Americans are also socialized to understand their ethnicity as having minimal effect in their lives.

In predominantly white congregations where cultural difference emerges in conversation, second-generation Asian Americans face the realization that their own relationship to the culture of their parents is a mixed bag and varies a great deal from person to person. Some recall and practice a great deal of their cultural traditions, and others bear hardly a trace of cultural practices that are different from whites. Thus, color consciousness from the perspective of middle-class second-generation Asian American Christians in these predominantly white environments reveals their own attachment (or lack thereof) to their familial backgrounds. Depending on the amount of reflection and experience on their cultural identity as both ethnic Asian and American, their articulations will suggest a range of ways that culture "matters" in their lives.

This outcome presumes that whites in these church circles will invoke opportunities in which these conversations might happen in the first place. Research on interracial marriages suggests that very often the solution to cultural difference is to not bring up the subject at all. Sociologist Robert Wuthnow, for example, demonstrated this solution in his analysis of interviews with interfaith couples. While one would think that interfaith couples would thoughtfully engage one another's beliefs to identify points of agreement, Wuthnow finds that the potential threat of significant disagreement is sufficient to deter many couples from this kind of dialogue. The end result is one of weaker religious attachment for both parties.[37] In similar fashion, the potential for disagreement may be significant enough in the minds of many white Christians that it discourages opportunities for conversation to occur. In terms of color consciousness then, second-generation Asian Americans may offer little to actual "consciousness raising" based on their own limited cultural fluency, And even if they were highly articulate about their cultural difference, the potential for disagreement may discourage them and their white counterparts from even bringing up these issues.

That said, the limited color-consciousness among second-generation Asian Americans is tied to structural blindness. Given the self-selective nature of church, the kinds of minorities that will likely participate in a predominantly white congregation would probably be someone who shares the class status of most of the congregant members. Social location often limits one's interactions across class lines, and because racial diversity is tied to class, second-generation Asian Americans likely have ethnic-specific ties and ties to middle- and upper-class whites. As such their awareness of structural racial inequality may be similar to that of middle and upper class whites with few ties to same-ethnics or other minorities who never had the same opportunities, lived in the same neighborhoods, nor attended the same schools as themselves. Without any lived experience of structural racism nor a network of minority friends who may have experienced unequal treatment or subtle (or blatant) exclusion from opportunities to advance, many second-generation Asian American Christians in predominantly white congregations may also suffer from the same structural blindness as their white peers.

Finally, we should also account for the group-percentage factor upon which much of the research on multiracial churches hinges. In predominantly white congregations, there is no critical mass of minorities for significant engagement to occur between the majority group and the minority group or groups. Only some whites in these environments will establish a tie with the minorities in the same pews, while the rest remain in their exclusively white networks. So by sheer group size alone, minorities in predominantly white congregations are not in a position to have the kind of influence needed to activate awareness of racial difference and inequality.[38] Group size dynamics bundled together with limited color consciousness and tacit structural blindness produces the makings of a sociological explanation for persistent ignorance over racial inequality even when racial minorities are present. Friendships with second-generation Asian Americans in these tokenized positions never pose a threat to the power and influence of whites in these religious organizations, can reinforce a defensive posture against claims of personal racist proclivities, and can justify previously held beliefs about unbiased structural opportunity in American society.

With reference to second-generation Asian Americans as society's "model minority," these dynamics have a particularly pernicious effect on how color-conscious structure blindness works. Recall that ethnic cultural identity varies a great deal for the second-generation, and it implicitly conveys the sense that cultural difference between minorities and mainstream society is not an obstacle for social advancement. By implication, racial minorities who place greater emphasis on their cultural background have only themselves to blame if they experience cultural discomfort in predominantly white congregations—after all, the thinking may go, other second-generation Asian Americans appear comfortable enough.

Alternatively, if culture is a matter of importance, according to the model minority stereotype, second-generation Asian Americans exhibit those cultural values that aid them in advancing in a predominantly white-privileged and white-controlled society. Their stellar educational credentials become proof that their cultural heritage (as opposed to the self-selection of higher skilled migrants from Asia) is the main influence that explains their particular position in society, which some have dubbed "honorary white."[39] Hence their entry into predominantly white congregations is only bolstered by this view that second-generation Asian Americans' cultures reflect the kind of values supported by middle-class whites. This understanding in turn justifies minimal exchange between non-Asian minorities and again reinforces the view that structural racism is nonexistent because evidently one racial minority has succeeded far beyond their expected proportions in society. For second-generation Asian American Christians in this fourth option of religious community, I suggest that many are hampered in their own racial awareness in part from their own socialization in a society that has minimized the significance of cultural values that emphasize collective communal identity along ethnic and racial lines. And when culture does matter, many happily acquiesce to the model minority stereotype. To the degree that such compliance is rewarded through acceptance in predominantly white congregations, both the congregation and these individual Asian Americans experience a mutually beneficial symbiotic relationship: the congregation enjoys symbolic diversity and the individual experiences access to the relationships and resources of the privileged.

Second-Generation Asian Americans and Multiracial Churches

We now finally come to the fifth option that second-generation Asian Americans have: the multiracial church. Consider the kind of Asian American that is likely part of this kind of congregation. Better still, consider the kind of Asian American that is likely *not* to be a part of this kind of congregation. They will most likely not include working-class immigrants who face language and economic barriers that keep them out of a church generally and keep them out of English-speaking congregations in particular. They will not include middle- and upper-class immigrants who might prefer, like many African American and Latino Christians, to be a part of a congregation that speaks their language of greatest familiarity and consists of a community of similar-ethnic or similar-race peers. They will also likely not include non-Christians of the second-generation whether they follow a different religion or no religion at all. They will likely not include working-class members of the second-generation who are probably economically disadvantaged enough to prevent them from participating in a congregation on a regular basis. They will also likely not include those middle- and upper-class second-generation Asian Americans who consciously or not have little attachment to their ethnic heritage and emulate the patterns of their white middle- and upper-class peers, many of whom have extended a warm welcome to their church.

Of the remaining Asian American Christians, largely second-generation at the time of this writing, some or perhaps many are part of same-ethnic, pan-ethnic, or predominantly white congregations. Without knowing precise prevalence rates, very few Asian American Christians remain who can participate in multiracial churches. They come from a variety of ethnic backgrounds, but Protestants will more often be Korean, Chinese, and Japanese, and Catholics more likely Filipino and Vietnamese. Most are familiar with the particularities of an ethnic immigrant church to which they will likely not return. They are likely aware of their marginal status and perhaps are also aware intuitively that culture matters not only in ways that suggest credibility to the model minority stereotype. Perhaps they too know that social structures are governed by culture, which often bears the memories of racism, marginality, and exclusion. However, once the motivations are discerned, we should not be surprised if only a small number appear at the door of the multiracial church. And the few who do arrive face a complex array of emotions given their particular social location. Many of them are empowered in some ways that are truly remarkable, but whether they can extend and share that empowerment to those with less power remains to be seen. Their task, I contend, is to give voice to their marginality within the context of other marginalities faced by fellow Christians and non-Asian racial minorities. In so doing they, with the aid and support of like-minded white, black, Latino, and Native American Christians, can identify structural racism and develop a structural color-conscious theology that fuels the identity and mission of a church that is truly united by faith.

Notes

1. Indeed variations of the phrase "Eleven o'clock Sunday morning is the most segregated hour in America" have been stated earlier by Billy Graham in a 1960 *Readers' Digest* article and by Dr. Kenneth Miller, executive secretary of the New York Mission Society during a conference in 1953. Notably, this phrase is preceded by the clause "It has been said that," which suggests that the phrase had reached wide audiences at this point making authorial attribution difficult.
2. This conclusion was drawn by the Dillingham Commission, which in turn led to the Immigration Act of 1924, also known as the Johnson–Reed Act. This act reduced immigration from all countries to minimize the flow of eastern and southern Europeans and to exclude immigrants from the Middle East and Asia. To accomplish the former, the act limited immigration to 3% of each immigrating group based on the 1890 census, over thirty years earlier. Because immigration

from eastern and southern European groups was high during the 1890s, the preceding census would show very low numbers of Hungarians, Poles, and Italians. This approach however favored northern and western European immigration considerably, and while the numbers of immigrants declined by more than 50% in a few short years, more of the new immigrants in the 1930s and 1940s were of English, Irish, and German descent.
3. Michael Omi and Howard Winant, *Racial Formation in the United States: From the 1960s to the 1990s* (New York: Routledge, 1994).
4. Gordon Allport, *The Nature of Prejudice* (Cambridge, MA: Addison Wesley, 1954).
5. As Curtiss DeYoung and his colleagues noted, historical examples of integrated religious communal life largely between black and white Christians date as far back as the 1700s. But most of these examples never grew, and most have not stood the test of time. See Curtiss Paul DeYoung, Michael O. Emerson, George Yancey, and Karen Chai Kim, *United by Faith: The Multiracial Congregation as an Answer to the Problem of Race* (New York: Oxford University Press, 2003).
6. A recent sampling of these studies continues to show that inequalities in wages and job opportunity remain linked strongly to race (e.g., minorities show little to no parity), and these differences are also associated with greater incarceration rates. See Arthur Sakamoto, Hyeyoung Woo, and ChangHwan Kim, "Does an Immigrant Background Ameliorate Racial Disadvantage? The Socioeconomic Attainments of Second-Generation African Americans," *Sociological Forum* 25 (2010): 123–146; Matthew C. Snipp and Charles Hirschman, "Assimilation in American Society: Occupational Achievement and Earnings for Ethnic Minorities in the United States, 1970 to 1990," *Research in Social Stratification and Mobility* 22 (2004): 93–117; and Bruce Western and Becky Pettit, "Black–White Wage Inequality, Employment Rates, and Incarceration," *American Journal of Sociology* 111 (2005): 553–578. Further, residential racial segregation remains significant, much more so for low socioeconomic neighborhoods. But across classes, black segregation from non-Hispanic whites is highest. See John Iceland and Rima Wilkes, "Does Socioeconomic Status Matter? Race, Class, and Residential Segregation," *Social Problems* 53 (2006): 248–273. These differences in residential quality affect school quality, which has also been shown to be one of the strongest predictors of the black–white achievement gap in primary education. See Gary L. Oates, "An Empirical Test of Five Prominent Explanations for the Black–White Academic Performance Gap," *Social Psychology of Education* 12 (2009): 415–441; and Salvatore Saporito and Deenesh Sohoni, "Mapping Educational Inequality: Concentrations of Poverty Among Poor and Minority Students in Public Schools," *Social Forces* 85 (2007): 1227–1253.
7. This Asian Exclusion Act was a component of the Immigration Act of 1924 mentioned earlier. In a recent study by Catherine Lee racial exclusion was legislated on the premise that both Japanese and Chinese immigrants were deemed similarly unassimilable (e.g., a racialized logic) and that Asian

immigrant women's sexuality was deemed a threat to the purity of white families. See Lee, "'Where the Danger Lies': Race, Gender, and Chinese and Japanese Exclusion in the United States, 1870–1924," *Sociological Forum* 25 (2010): 248–271.
8. Deenesh Sohoni, "Unsuitable Suitors: Anti-Miscegenation Laws, Naturalization Laws, and the Construction of Asian Identities," *Law and Society Review* 41 (2007): 587–618.
9. Alejandro Portes and Ruben Rumbaut, *Immigrant America: A Portrait.* 2nd ed. (Berkeley: University of California Press, 2006).
10. Census data indicates that all Asians groups in 1960 (prior to the new immigration law) constituted about 0.3% of the US population. See US Census Bureau data, September 13, 2002, accessed May 3, 2013. http://www.census.gov/population/www/documentation/twps0056/tabA-08.pdf.
11. Out of 980,000 Asian Americans, about 464,000 were of Japanese descent, 237,000 of Chinese descent, and 176,000 of Filipino descent (the remainder were listed as "Hawaiian" and "Part Hawaiian." See US Census Bureau data, September 13, 2002, accessed May 3, 2013, http://www.census.gov/population/www/documentation/twps0056/tabC-05.pdf.
12. This figure refers to all Americans who selected "Asian" in any combination of racial labels. For those who only selected an Asian background, the figure is about 15 million.

    The Asian American population is projected to increase such that by 2050, they will have a 9% share of the population or about 40 million. See "Asian/Pacific American Heritage Month: May 2011," April 29, 2011, accessed May 3, 2013, http://www.census.gov/newsroom/releases/archives/facts_for_features_special_editions/cb11-ff06.html.
13. As of this writing no official 2010 census reports are available on the Asian ethnic distributions, but the American Community Survey findings confirm that the top six groups have not changed since 2000. "America's Asian Population Patterns 2000–2010," accessed May 3, 2012, http://proximityone.com/cen2010_asian.htm.
14. Janelle S. Wong, S. Karthick Ramakrishnan, Taeku Lee, and Jane Junn, eds., *Asian American Political Participation: Emerging Constituents and Their Political Identities* (New York: Russell Sage Foundation, 2011).
15. Timothy P. Fong, *The Contemporary Asian American Experience: Beyond the Model Minority* (Upper Saddle River, NJ: Prentice Hall, 2001). Recently ChangHwan Kim and Arthur Sakamoto have also shown that immigrant and second-generation Asian American men's wages have still not reached parity with white men even when most of their education is obtained in the United States. See Kim and Sakamoto, "Have Asian American Men Achieved Labor Market Parity with White Men?" *American Sociological Review* 75 (2010): 934–957.
16. Timothy B. Smith, "Religion and Ethnicity in America," *American Historical Review* 83 (1978): 1155–1185.

17. The social functions of religion have been well noted by scholars Pyong Gap Min. See Min, "The Structure and Social Functions of Korean Immigrant Churches in the United States" *International Migration Review* 26 (1992): 1370–1394; and Helen Rose Ebaugh, "Religion and the New Immigrants," in *Handbook of the Sociology of Religion*, ed. Michele Dillon (New York: Cambridge University Press, 2003).
18. Frederic Cople Jaher, *A Scapegoat in the New Wilderness: The Origins and Rise of Anti-Semitism in America* (Cambridge, MA: Harvard University Press, 1994); Karen Brodkin, *How Jews Became White Folks and What That Says About Race in America* (New Brunswick, NJ: Rutgers University Press, 1998).
19. Some researchers have emphasized the growth of non-Christian religions in American society suggesting that a "new religious America" is emerging. Indeed with higher immigration from Asia and the Caribbean the United States has witnessed a greater presence of Buddhists, Hindus, Jains, Muslims, Rastafarians, and Sikhs, to name just a few. However, as a proportion of the population, these non-Christian religions together account for less than 10%. See Tom W. Smith and Seokho Kim, "The Vanishing Protestant Majority," *Scientific Study of Religion* 44 (2005): 211–223. Nevertheless more Americans are encountering non-Christians, many of whom are of Asian descent. See Robert Wuthnow, *America and the Challenges of Religious Diversity* (Princeton, NJ: Princeton University Press, 2005).
20. Readers should be cautious when reviewing survey findings of Asian Americans as many of them are specifically administered only in English and occasionally in Spanish.
21. The Pew Forum on Religion and Public Life, "Global Christianity: An Interactive Feature," December 18, 2011, accessed May 3, 2013, http://features.pewforum.org/global-christianity/map.php#/asia,ALL.
22. In a recent report by the Pew Research Center Forum on Religion and Public Life, of the estimated 214 million migrants around the world in 2010, nearly 49% were Christian, the largest share of all migrants. The United States remains the primary destination point of today's immigrants and remains the main receiving nation of the largest proportion of Christian migrants.
23. Prior to the public release of Pew Landscape Survey, I estimated that the actual Christian distribution would be somewhere between 45% and 50%. See Jerry Z. Park, "Assessing the Sociological Study of Asian American Christianity," *SANACS Journal* (2010): 59–94. But closer analysis of the survey method revealed that this survey was not administered in any Asian language. Thus Asian American responses in that survey are better defined as "English-preferred speaking Asian Americans."
24. The Pew Forum on Religion and Public Life, "Religious Affiliation and Demographics" in "A Religious Portrait of African-Americans," January 30, 2009, accessed May 3, 2013, http://www.pewforum.org/A-Religious-Portrait-of-African-Americans.aspx#1.
25. The Pew Forum on Religion and Public Life, "Religious Affiliations and Demographic Groups," in *U.S. Religious Landscape Survey*, February 2008, accessed

May 3, 2013, http://religions.pewforum.org/pdf/report-religious-landscape-study-chapter-3.pdf.

26. Lien and Carnes using the first national-level translated survey of Asian Americans administered in 2001also found that Korean Americans are predominantly Protestant (69%) and Filipino Americans are predominantly Catholic (68%). The Japanese come close at 43%, but Asian Indians, Chinese, and Vietnamese contain minority populations of Christians (3%, 23%, and 33%, respectively). See Pei-Te Lien and Tony Carnes, "The Religious Demography of Asian American Boundary Crossing," in *Asian American Religions: The Making and Remaking of Borders and Boundaries*, eds. Tony Carnes and Fenggang Yang (New York: New York University Press, 2004).

27. Roger Waldinger, *Strangers at the Gates: New Immigrants in Urban America* (Berkeley: University of California Press, 2001). For evidence of the effect of these bifurcated economic pathways on the lives of the children of immigrants, see William Haller, Alejandro Portes, and Scott M. Lynch, "Dreams Fulfilled, Dreams Shattered: Determinants of Segmented Assimilation in the Second Generation," *Social Forces* 89 (2011): 733–772; and the extensive work by Alejandro Portes and Ruben Rumbaut, *Legacies: The Story of the Immigrant Second Generation* (Berkeley: University of California Press, 2001); Min Zhou, "Segmented Assimilation: Issues, Controversies, and Recent Research on the New Second Generation," *International Migration Review* 31 (1997): 975–1008; and Alejandro Portes and Min Zhou, "The New Second Generation: Segmented Assimilation and Its Variants Among Post-1965 Immigrant Youth," *Annals of the American Academy of Political and Social Science* 530 (1993): 74–96.

28. Human capital refers to the specific skill sets of workers. The greater the abilities of a particular worker, the greater are his or her human capital. Workers with high human capital in post-industrial America are often distinguished by higher levels of educational attainment given the emphasis on information analysis, management, and application in most industries.

29. Shalini Shankar, *Desi Land: Teen Culture, Class, and Success in Silicon Valley* (Durham, NC: Duke University Press, 2008); Philip Kasinitz, "Becoming American, Becoming Minority, Getting Ahead: The Role of Racial and Ethnic Status in the Upward Mobility of the Children of Immigrants," *Annals of the American Academy of Political and Social Science* 620 (2008), 253–269.

30. Rebecca Y. Kim, *God's New Whiz Kids? Korean American Evangelicals on Campus* (New Brunswick, NJ: Rutgers University Press, 2006).

31. Asian American and religious studies scholar Rudy Busto first argued this very point from his observations on Asian American evangelicals on the campuses of the University of California schools. See Busto, "The Gospel According to the Model Minority? Hazarding an Interpretation of Asian American Evangelical College Students," *Amerasia Journal* 22 (1996): 133–147.

32. I reference some of these news items in a review of the research as of 2008 on Asian American Christianity. Jerry Z. Park, "Assessing the Sociological Study of Asian American Christianity."
33. Current college attendance for Asian Americans is slightly above their presence in the national population: 6%. This figure is surprisingly high because nearly all Asian American high school graduates (92%) enroll in college (compared to whites, 69%; blacks, 69%; and Latinos, 59%). So if Asian Americans went to college at a rate similar to that of their other race peers, their overall presence in college would be lower. "College Enrollment Rate at Record High," *New York Times*, August 28, 2010, accessed, January 17, 2013, http://economix.blogs.nytimes.com/2010/04/28/college-enrollment-rate-at-record-high/. The Census reports that Asian Americans in general have a much higher educational attainment level than other groups. See "Educational Attainment in the United States: 2009," February 2012, accessed May 3, 2012, http://www.census.gov/prod/2012pubs/p20-566.pdf.
34. Soyoung Park, "The Intersection of Religion, Race, Ethnicity, and Gender in the Identity Formation of Korean American Evangelical Women," in *Korean Americans and Their Religions: Pilgrims and Missionaries from a Different Shore*, eds. Ho-Youn Kwon, Kwang C. Kim, and R.S. Warner (University Park, PA: Pennsylvania State University Press, 2001); Kim, *God's New Whiz Kids?*; and Nancy Abelmann, *The Intimate University: Korean American Students and the Problems of Segregation* Durham, NC: Duke University Press, 2009).
35. Russell Jeung, *Faithful Generations: Race and New Asian American Churches* (New Brunswick, NJ: Rutgers University Press, 2005); Sharon Kim, *A Faith of Our Own: Second-Generation Spirituality in Korean American Churches* (New Brunswick, NJ: Rutgers University Press, 2010).
36. Mary C. Waters, *Ethnic Options: Choosing Identities in America* (Berkeley: University of California Press, 1990); Richard Alba, *Ethnic Identity: The Transformation of White America* (New Haven, CT: Yale University Press, 1990).
37. Wuthnow, *America and the Challenges of Religious Diversity*.
38. Research has shown that friendships with minorities that lack a minority network have little effect on racial prejudice attitudes and by extension resistance to structural solutions to solve systemic racial inequality. This finding is exemplified in oft-stated phrases such as "Some of my best friends are. . . ." whereby white non-Hispanics affirm their nonracism by offering their minority friendship as proof. See Mary R. Jackman and Marie Crane, "'Some of My Best Friends Are Black. . .': Interracial Friendship and Whites' Racial Attitudes," *Public Opinion Quarterly* 50 (1986): 459–486.
39. Bonilla-Silva, "From Bi-Racial to Tri-Racial: Towards a New System of Racial Stratification in the USA," *Ethnic and Racial Studies* 27 (2004): 931–950; Mia Tuan, *Forever Foreigners or Honorary Whites? The Asian Ethnic Experience Today* (New Brunswick, NJ: Rutgers University Press, 1998).

9

Knotted Together: Identity and Community in a Multiracial Church

Erica Ryu Wong

SINCE *DIVIDED BY Faith*'s appearance in 2000—and its indictment of evangelical Christianity's perpetuation of the racial divide—scholars have looked for ways that evangelical religion could solve the problem of race in America. A number of these scholars have suggested that multiracial churches might hold promise for addressing racial problems in society due to the potential for religion to bring different people together in meaningful ways. While this potential may very well exist, the degree to which multiracial churches can positively impact racial inequalities and prejudices in society at large remains to be seen. This uncertainty is in part due to the fact that multiracial congregations have the first-order challenge of addressing racial problems within their own walls.[1] That is, the presence of racial diversity does not necessarily mean different races are relationally integrated. The lack of such relational integration within a multiracial congregation can swiftly diminish the benefits of diversity. It is important that we understand how relational integration occurs within racially diverse churches. According to the National Congregations Study, the number of multiracial congregations is on the rise. The increase is not only a function of changing demographics in the United States. Instead, religious leaders are increasingly realizing and promoting the personal, social, organizational, and religious benefits of a racially diverse congregation. At the same time, congregants also report that racial diversity enriches their spiritual life. Indeed, the image of people of many colors worshipping together in unity is an idyllic one.² But to what extent is this multicolored image superficial? Is it possible to have mixed-race congregations that still maintain color lines? Do cross-race relationships actually undergird this picture of unity-in-diversity? These are the questions that need to be addressed before we can determine the efficacy of multiracial churches as a solution to the problem of race in America.

Individuals who lead or desire to lead multiracial organizations sometimes underestimate the problems associated with diversity, including the potential for greater conflict, less solidarity, and more dissatisfaction among its members. In other words, diversity, in many cases, promotes disunity. Further, racially diverse voluntary organizations such as churches tend to have unstable memberships, making retaining a multiracial membership a challenge in and of itself. As explained in *Divided by Faith*, because affiliation is voluntary, racial minorities, who often bear greater costs in racially diverse churches, are more likely to leave. Therefore, racially diverse churches can quite easily morph into racially homogenous congregations.³

Those who study diversity in organizations generally agree that, ultimately, diversity is better but that harnessing the positive aspects of diversity depends on how it is managed. This challenge is no less the case for multiracial churches. Certainly one critical aspect of "diversity management" within these churches is to facilitate not only a demographically integrated congregation, but a *relationally integrated* multiracial congregation that can mitigate many of the aforementioned challenges of a diverse membership, including the attrition of minority members. Close interracial friendships may have the greatest potential to improve intergroup relations and reduce prejudice, because they increase the likelihood of forming additional racially diverse ties and provide expanded opportunities for intercultural education. Having a network of interracial friendships is especially impactful in developing positive racial attitudes. Interracial friendship, although insufficient as a singular answer to racial inequality, clearly remains an important step toward racial progress as well as to the viability of multiracial congregations.⁴

Although good intentions are there, religious culture may work against such relationships. In *Divided by Faith*, Emerson and Smith find that white evangelicals in particular tend to hold a "color-blind" strategy not only as it concerns racial problems in general but also in regards to interpersonal relationships. Many white evangelicals believe that emphasizing a common religious identity among members alone should help overcome racial and ethnic divisions and thereby facilitate interracial friendship.

This color-blind strategy of overemphasizing common religious belief comes at the expense of recognizing racial differences and denies the reality that race matters. Inherent in these approaches is the troubling implication that only by doing away with race, ignoring race, or submerging race can racial problems be addressed. Yet, for many, race is a valued, God-given identity.[5]

Even if one were to accept the validity of interpersonal solutions to racial problems that are characteristic of the white evangelical response to racial inequality, it is important to be aware that interpersonal relations are in and of themselves structured by race and are thus hampered by race. That is, interpersonal relationships are set within and affected by the broader racial social context, the meanings that society assigns to race, and the racial inequalities that persist because of structural and individual prejudices. In other words, turning a blind eye to race does not mean that friendship across racial lines will organically occur; in fact, it can actually stymie such relationships.[6]

In fact, as numerous studies have documented, we are attracted to those who we perceive as similar. "Birds of a feather flock together" is an oft-cited adage when it comes to studies of friendship, and race is our society's strongest marker of who our "birds of a feather" are. Racial similarity characterizes friendship pairings more than any other demographic category, including gender, age, religion, and socioeconomic status (education, occupation, and social class). Because of the tendency toward same-race friendships, greater racial diversity can actually inhibit interracial ties. Paradoxically, greater diversity not only increases opportunities to befriend different race others, it also increases the likelihood that more same-race individuals are available—and thus chosen—as potential friends.[7]

Certainly one can think of particular contexts that defy these social tendencies. Interracial friendship appears normative, for instance, on sports teams, the military, or communes. These occurrences tell us that organizational context can affect the quality and incidence of interracial friendship. For multiracial churches it means that congregational leaders can affect the occurrence and quality of close interracial ties. But how?

To answer this question, I studied two multiracial churches in depth to assess how interracial friendship might be facilitated (see Appendix for a brief description of the methodology). The two churches, Mannington Church and Jackson Church, are similar in many ways. Both are located in the same large East Coast metropolitan area. Both are nondenominational and evangelical. And both were multiracial from their founding and are currently led by their founding pastors. Although the racial compositions differ, the congregations are similar on other demographic measures. Further, both churches' worship and organizational styles, although contrasting, typify the "new paradigm" cultural change in Christianity, marked by the appropriation of contemporary cultural forms and music styles, the restructuring of organizational forms, and an emphasis on lay leadership, that is, the priesthood of all believers.[8]

Despite these key similarities, Jackson Church and Mannington Church differ in their approaches to racial diversity and how they foster interrace relating among congregants. Correspondingly, their rates of interracial friendship also differ, with Mannington demonstrating higher rates of interracial friendship (see Appendix for interracial friendship statistics). I found that encouraging interracial friendship does not merely have to do with how the church talks about race but is rooted in the larger framework of how they define their evangelistic missions, the role of the Christian believer, and the "church." Mannington is able to give meaning and purpose to interracial friendship not as an end in and of itself but within the broader context of what it means to be a congregation.

Mannington and Jackson Church frame their religious purpose in ways that are as contrasting as a special forces military unit would be from a hospital. They differ in their identities as battle-ready, mission-oriented soldiers and as service-oriented, mercy-driven hospital workers and patients. These different approaches to evangelism have divergent implications for community. On one hand, for a special forces unit to succeed in a mission, the importance of the collective unit and the contribution of each member are emphasized. On the other hand, similar to a hospital, Jackson Church has a greater focus on individual healing and well-being. Indeed, differing conceptions of community are reflected in Mannington and Jackson Church, particularly in how they each define spiritual family, which, in turn, helps to form a basis for the kind of relationships that are perceived as important to cultivate.

Mannington Church
What's a Christian to Do? Evangelism as Mission

Mannington Church is explicit about their ultimate intention to convert people to Christianity particularly through being outspoken about their faith, a defining characteristic of evangelicals. Their stated mission is "to honor God and advance His Kingdom through church planting, campus ministry, and world missions to reach all nations," and their vision is "to win the city for Christ." Their mission and vision, invoking competitive or battle terminology ("advance" and "win"), are outwardly directed and require active recruitment of others to Christian faith.[9]

In Mannington, seeking opportunities for the verbal explanation of the gospel message is emphasized, with conversion as the goal. The head pastor, Bryce, shared numerous examples of how he participates in evangelism, for instance, praying with a woman that he met that she "falls in love" with God. He urged, "Touch somebody's life. It opens up all kinds of doors to then share the gospel and lead them to the Lord." At one service, members were brought up on stage to share how they had brought someone to the point of conversion. One member met someone at a health food store she frequented regularly and invited her to a small group where she eventually was "saved."[10]

This type of evangelism, sharing one's faith with the intent to convert, is expressed as the most important demonstration of faith and service to God. In the sermon excerpt that follows, the speaker interprets John 21:10, in light of Mark 1:17 where Jesus says to his disciples, "I will make you fishers of men":

> [God is saying,] "If you really love me, the sign of that is more than your [time], more than your worship. It's more than your attendance.... If you really love Me the greatest thing you can do for Me is take responsibility for the advance of My kingdom." ... I hear the Holy Spirit saying, "Where are the fish you have caught? It's the reason I left you on the planet."

"Catching fish" is used as a metaphor here for converting nonbelievers. Preceding this excerpt, the pastor noted that to "catch fish" is not only one of very few requests Jesus gives but is also Jesus' last earthly request, emphasizing its primary importance. He emphasized the high value of evangelism by contrasting it to "lesser" acts of devotion like church attendance and singing. Evangelism is expressed as the most authentic ("if you really love me") expression of believers' devotion to God. To further the military analogy, God is portrayed as an urgent commander who grants to God's people the singular mission of evangelism. In this sermon, God exhorts each believer to take part in "advancing" the kingdom.[11]

This mission mentality is furthered by a focused eye toward training and preparation. In a sermon, the head pastor Bryce expressed, "We want to equip all of our members to be the finest and most competent Christians they can be.... Our goal is to train you, to know what the Word of the Lord is and how you ought to respond in every situation." One congregant explained, "The church is for people to get together, get instructed, and then to go out again. They're not here to evangelize. *You* evangelize." Believers are expected to "respond" biblically, evangelize, and to be the "finest" and "most competent." Just like those serving in the special forces, believers are expected to be ready—they have a mission to accomplish.[12]

The notion of mission is not merely organizational rhetoric. One respondent compared the experience of church membership to being part of an elite military organization, like the "Delta Force or Navy Seals," who have the reputation of not only being the best but also of receiving the most intense and specialized training. He continued to say, "[Mannington Church] challenges people to live kingdom principles every day." The intent is that the mission orientation will carry over into all aspects of members' lives.[13]

Who Are We? Spiritual Family and the Congregation

Similar to the "band of brothers" effect that a special forces unit requires for accomplishing of its mission, Mannington's mission is enabled by a community of believers with a notion of a "spiritual family." The quality and depth of relationships between members is presented as a critical way in which people are drawn to Christian community and ultimately to Jesus Christ. Pastor Bryce likened the relationship between Christians to that of family members, with God as father, and with expectations that the same intimacy of relationship should be demonstrated. He explains:

> Church is . . . the joining of people's lives, the being interested in somebody's dreams, the preferring one another, the forgiving one another, the seeing how one another is doing, the praying for one another. . . . The sacrifice, one for another, is the way that we show something different than the world expects from a group of people. . . . This is where people are to notice our love and then, being then witnessed, they are to come to understand who God is.

The pastor described that the intimacy of relationships between believers should be qualitatively different than those among nonbelievers. They should exhibit characteristics such as forgiveness, prayer, and sacrifice. These relationships, however, do not exist for themselves. Rather, the quality of relationship is an important "witness" of who God is. In this way, even Christian community has evangelistic purpose.[14]

Not only should these relationships attract nonbelievers to Christianity but also the depth of the relationship between believers is described as the structural mechanism that enables evangelistic success:

> God ties the lives of His people together for harvest. The first great miracle catch broke the net. It was [because the disciples] were so immature and their relationships were shallow, it would never ever stand the test of harvest. . . . The knots that hold this church together—it's your relationships with one another.

Although each believer has a personal responsibility to participate in evangelistic activity, "catching fish" is also conceptualized as a corporate, collective endeavor for Mannington congregants. The speaker compared the fishing net to the network of relationships among congregation members. A large catch requires a strong net. In the same way, Pastor Larry suggested that the potential for a large "harvest," or conversions, depends on a tightly "knotted" congregation.[15]

Further, addressing this congregation is not idiosyncratic to this particular speaker or sermon. Mannington localizes the spiritual family concept and Christian community within congregational boundaries. Mannington speaks of one's Christian "brothers and sisters" as including other Christians at large. However, developing relationship is emphasized as beginning with one's fellow congregation members. These are the Christians to whom one is obligated. In the sermon excerpt below, Pastor Bryce defined the local congregation as the first level of spiritual family.

> Now being a part of the spiritual family of God requires that you fellowship with brothers and sisters. You can't be aloof and be practically a part. You can be in name a part, and you can be in theology a part but . . . I like to be with family members who want to sit down and have a meal and actually fellowship at a very deep level. That's the practices of knowing what it means to flush out the spiritual family concept in a local congregation.

Forming relationships within the local congregational body is the means by which Christians live out the concept of spiritual family and "deep level" fellowship as intended by God, because these are the Christians with whom you can actually interact. As expressed in an interview with Pastor David: "We're called together for a purpose," echoing the sentiment that who comprises one's local spiritual family is not accidental but providential.[16]

The metaphor of a "family" is further developed as Pastor Bryce compared the congregation to a household. Accordingly, each member must do his or her part in contributing to the development of the congregation as a whole. He said to his congregation, "You're not a renter here, you're an owner. Renters . . . do the minimal stuff . . . but owners take care of their house. . . . The only way we can build up our church is if every member is working." Pastor Bryce described commitment to and work within this congregational body as necessary to accomplishing its organizational goals. Each member must take responsibility for "building up" the congregation.[17]

As seen in the previous quote, leaders frequently refer to the congregation as a singular unit rather than a gathering of individuals. When referring to "the church," it almost always refers specifically to this congregation, not the Christian church at large. "This church" has an organizational identity that is more than the amalgamation of individuals. Pastor Bryce described the congregation as having a "corporate soul," and Pastor David characterized the congregation as having a "corporate call to do God's mission."[18]

Further, as a singular entity, the congregational body is described as having unique characteristics and a unique role within the evangelical mission that distinguish it from other congregations. Pastor Bryce explained:

> There are things that are specific to local congregations that allow families to be distinct from another within the larger family of God. . . . Every congregation has a specific emphasis [that] needs to be respected . . . God wants to reach certain kinds of people with certain kinds of congregations. God fashions congregations to be able to be a certain way and have a distinctive.[19]

Again, Pastor Bryce localized the spiritual family within the congregation by underscoring each congregation's distinctiveness in both its membership and purpose. As such, within the evangelical objective, each congregation is meant to attract a specific niche of people and fulfill a specific role. He thus developed an organizational identity by highlighting a sense of specialness and a purpose that few other congregations can fulfill.

Pastor Bryce defined its multiracial composition as part of this congregation's distinctiveness:

> So other congregations that are down in the inner city that are all black, bless 'em, happy, glad. Other congregations that are all white out in the suburbs, bless 'em, happy, glad. But if you want to a part of this particular clan of the family of God, this is how we roll . . . and we're not going to depart from it.

He clearly distinguished Mannington from other racially homogenous churches and firmly sets racial diversity as a nonnegotiable, defining aspect of the church. Immediately preceding this excerpt, Pastor Bryce explained that he does not mean to "demean" other churches that do not have the proper "skill sets" to have a racially diverse and unified congregation. By doing so, he portrayed Mannington's purpose as both different and inimitable from most others. He also reinforced organizational boundaries, for those who are not committed to racial diversity in the congregation cannot be part of "this particular clan of the family of God."[20]

Mannington Church is more than just an assembly of individual believers; it is a corporate entity with a specialized role in the greater world evangelistic mission of the Christian church. Mannington thereby mobilizes its congregants by conceptualizing the congregation as a familial network of relationships that comprises the organizational whole. It is within this context that interracial friendship must be understood.

The Role of Interracial Friendship

Mannington Church emphasizes that its dedicated congregational niche is in exhibiting not only a racially diverse community but also a racially integrated community. Logically, if those in this congregation comprise a spiritual family and this family is racially diverse, then one's relationships within the church should also be racially diverse. Indeed, Pastor Bryce explicitly stated that he does not think of family as "folk that look like me."

He continued by expositing the attitude that is necessary to establish a "family" that is multiracial:

> It takes a courageous people to say I'm not going to stop when I find a difference that I don't like. When I touch somebody's pain because of their experience and somehow somebody didn't like their difference, and it hurt them deeply, I'm not going to stop. When somebody misunderstands what I say, I'm not going to stop.

By using himself as a prototype, Pastor Bryce stressed that commitment and perseverance ("I'm not going to stop") should mark the approach to interracial relationships. Establishing such relationships involves making oneself vulnerable to misunderstanding and hurt. He acknowledged that differences, and specifically racial differences, involves addressing one's own prejudices as well as an awareness of a legacy of negative racial experiences another may bring to the table. It takes "courage," therefore, to make the relationship more important than one's personal preferences.[21] Pastor David, in a sermon entitled "Colorful Community," echoed the same sentiments:

> I know people who don't have [anything] against anybody but the reality is they don't have relationship either. God's standard is for you to press into something and to have relationship. . . . Jim Crow is gone, but you can't legislate love. . . . God says, "If you could see my family, then that means you wouldn't walk by three people to get to that person because they look like you. You could have seen the first person as the person God wanted you to interact with."

Similar to the previous sermon excerpt, there is recognition that interracial relationships require special effort. An attitude of tolerance is insufficient; one must "press in" to relationship. Such relationships are a matter of religious obedience, for it is that "first person" that "God wanted you to interact with," not just those that are racially similar. In essence, Pastor David expressed that to fail to establish interracial relationship is a failure to understand God's intent ("If you could see my family") and meet God's "standard."[22] It is a *religious* transgression.

The rewards, on the other hand, are also articulated. The fulfillment of its evangelistic mission as a multiracial congregation depends on deep-level relationships between different-race individuals. Because these relationships are difficult, they require spiritual intervention, thereby providing evidence of God:

> And Paul said, "I want you to know that a church of many colors is the church that can proclaim wisdom to every authority, every principality, every institution on the planet." Why? Because they know what it's like to go through barriers and come out reconciled on the other side . . . ; If He blesses us in such a way that we can take this thing to five and ten thousand with the same kind of diversity we've got without window dressing, with real substantive relationships, no hollowness, but depth—if we can do that, *we can change the world.*

Pastor David pointed out the role of this congregation—"if we can take this thing"—in making known God's intention of a family of "many colors" through the substantivity of cross-race relationships. This expression of God as seen in the church is said to give them the unique role of being able to "proclaim wisdom" to all. The experience of "going through barriers" effectively empowers the church to fulfill its evangelistic mission and have societal impact ("change the world"). That is, such friendship serves as a demonstration of God's power that would affect not only the church's ability to draw converts, but also its ability to be distinctive from other secular groups. In addition to its importance in realizing organizational goals, interracial relationships are also explained as beneficial to individual believers. Pastor David noted that having close interracial friendships will predict one's degree of personal influence: "The influence that God intends for you to have . . . will be limited to the people group that you are so narrowly focused on and the only ones you could see." Close interracial friendship is thus framed as a divine mandate. It unleashes both individual and organizational potential as an effective mechanism of evangelism by which God can be revealed.[23]

In sum, Mannington Church conceptualizes itself as a distinct, bounded organizational entity with a unique purpose in the context of an evangelistic mission. As such, it emphasizes spiritual family as embodied in the local congregation. More specific to its unique purpose, it emphasizes how the depth of relationships among different-race congregants can be demonstrative of God's power and meaningful as preparation for evangelism in other nations.

Jackson Church
What's a Christian to Do? Outreach in Love

Jackson Church's definition of evangelism, which they call "outreach" is defined expansively, with a focus on service. In his sermon, the Jackson Church outreach pastor explicitly stated, "Here's my definition for outreach: it's the activities that we involve ourselves in that show God's love in practical ways to people outside our Church community." He continued in his sermon to say that outreach involves (i) meeting people where they are, (ii) extending love and mercy, and (iii) patience. Outreach is not defined as leading to conversion but patiently "loving" nonbelievers practically. In addition, outreach is also defined in a later sermon as serving others and demonstrating upstanding character as representatives of Jesus: "We have to be people of integrity, people of moral purity.... Don't downgrade the importance of your unspoken witness in the work environment." Christians are described as actively demonstrating notable character traits, and the speaker urges them not to underestimate the power of "unspoken witness," but they are not described as needing to *lead* individuals to the conversion moment.[24]

Further, the verbal aspect of evangelism is not excluded but is included as one of many outreach behaviors.

> Christian outreach, the outreach that we're talking about this morning will shake that comfort zone at its very core.... You see there's nothing comfortable about washing a dirty little kid's feet in the poorest country in the western hemisphere, Nicaragua ... [or] sharing your faith with a coworker or speaking up for Christ at your school or giving out granola bars in Manhattan, [or] inviting people to try a new church or watching a single mom's rowdy kids because she needs a break.

Verbally leading someone to a conversion moment or even "sharing your faith" is not given primacy over other actions such as "washing feet" or "watching a single mom's rowdy kids." Jackson Church thus describes evangelism or outreach as a process that is much more broadly defined than the examples provided by Mannington Church, and it generally focuses on service and meeting community needs. Although Mannington does not exclude these other types of "practical loving" behaviors, there is greater discussion from the pulpit around "winning" converts and actively leading nonbelievers to a faith decision than there is at Jackson Church.[25]

Consistent with its definition of outreach, Jackson's conceptualization of God is that of a compassionate and patient gatherer of the hurting and lonely. In a sermon at Jackson Church, God's desire for "fish" is portrayed very differently:

> This is God thinking: Maybe there's someone there alone, alone with no prospects, alone with no hope and maybe he or she thinks that they'll never be a part of anything significant, never be a part of a community that loves them and that they'll never contribute anything in this world and maybe that person will be just desperate enough or hopeful enough or brave enough to trust me and jump in my truck and then I'll surprise them with joy, with grace and I'll lean back on my truck and watch 'em with a smile. That's our God. . . . He's always looking for one more and He'll go back and back and back again till He finds 'em.

God is described as waiting by his truck for nonbelievers to "jump in." He "leans back" with a smile. In striking contrast to Mannington's conceptualization of God as an urgent commander, Jackson Church's God waits, hopes, searches, and watches. He is the action agent, not the believer. Although the speaker expresses desiring the same "heart" as God for wanting people to be Christians and hopes that Jackson attendees would be "passionate" as well, the obligation of believers in this process is not emphasized. They are not urged to go and get people on the metaphorical truck.[26]

The excerpt below also paints a picture of how conversion might happen:

> I am convinced that there'll be thousands of people in heaven one day who when we ask them, "How did you get here? What was your journey?" They will say something like, "I worked with this woman or with this guy and I saw in him or in her that they were different; they were people of character. I saw something in them that I wanted in myself and I pursued it, I asked them, and I sought Christianity and this is how I got here."[27]

In this hypothetical example of a conversation in heaven, the nonbelievers were the ones that "pursued," "asked," and "sought" out Christianity. They are the ones that are given agency in the conversion process. The Christian's role of demonstrating "upstanding character" is a markedly more passive posture that the role Mannington assigns believers to "catch fish."

Who Are We? Relating to the Non-Christian

Similar to Mannington Church, relationships are considered to be important for evangelism. However, intrachurch relationships are not emphasized as being necessary for the fulfillment of evangelistic aims. Rather, it is friendship with nonbelievers that are highlighted:

> In spite of how busy our schedules are, like Jesus's was, we need to invest in authentic friendships with people outside these walls. [Most people in this county] don't go to church on Sunday morning. They don't have a personal relationship with Jesus Christ and many of them, I think, like [the Samaritan] woman, feel alienated and disconnected. They're probably not going to come to church because we send them a postcard. They might come to Christ because of a friendship and that's on us.

In this sermon, Pastor Darrell urged congregants to "invest in authentic friendships" with nonbelievers as a way to both meet a need for authentic friendships among those who may be disconnected and to proselytize. In addition, stating that "that's on us" implies a responsibility to establish those relationships.[28] As opposed to Mannington, where "church" is for training and equipping its members to do the work of evangelism, at Jackson, members are encouraged to invite non-Christian friends to church as part of the work of evangelism.

At Jackson, there is greater concern about its boundaries remaining permeable to nonmembers and non-Christians specifically. Thus, they avoid drawing organizational boundaries around its congregants. In Mannington Church it was unusual to find a sermon in which the congregation was not addressed corporately; in Jackson Church, it was rare to hear the congregation addressed as one body or as "the church." The concept of church community tended to be broadly defined. In one sermon, Mike, the head pastor, presented his definition of church: "God doesn't occupy buildings. . . . The church is a group of people that God's presence now takes up residence within."²⁹ The role of the congregation specifically is never explicitly delineated. Therefore, when the pronoun "we" is used or "church" is used, it refers to Christians generally, not Christians at Jackson.

Further, relationships with other Christians is spoken of broadly, without specific mention of intrachurch relationships. For example, Jackson Church also describes Christian relationships in the metaphor of "family," but the local congregation is not necessarily described as the place in which those relationships need occur.

> We are part of a family that is far deeper than any other relationship that you can have. The Bible says it's even stronger than a blood relationship. Our relationship in the kingdom is built around Jesus Christ and that's a deep commonality.

As expressed in Mannington, other believers are described as family. Here Pastor Mike spoke of those spiritual relationships being even deeper in commonality than blood relationships. Implied in the description of a commonality that is deeper than bloodlines is that race or other demographic differences should not be a barrier to Christian fellowship. However, unlike Mannington Church, it is not explicitly stated as such. Further, how these deep bonds affect the goals of the church is also not emphasized. Because Jackson Church as a bounded organizational entity is not clearly drawn, the purpose of intrachurch relationships is not as strongly linked to evangelism. At Jackson Church, there is encouragement to be in relationship with other church members, but it is not presented as necessary for the accomplishment of organizational goals.³⁰

Jackson Church tends to focus more on how relationships between Christians are important for spiritual growth generally, not just for help in time of need. For example,

> Weeds take spiritual health to the place where it's all about me. . . . We try to [grow] outside of the context of relationships and fellowship and that's not biblical at all, folks. We need one another to grow. We need one another to encourage and motivate and help. . . . [Spiritual growth] is often measured by the way you serve others. The level of serving and giving to others is a primary indicator of spiritual health.

The outcome of fellowship is not directly related to outreach or to any collective, congregational goal. Further, the Christian relationships mentioned in this sermon are not limited to those that take place among members of this particular church. This quote reveals a more individualistic orientation to and portrayal of Christian life in comparison to Mannington Church. The outcome of these relationships is described as one that pertains to the individual—the improvement of one's personal spiritual health—rather than to the group, such as the achievement of a collective mission.[31]

Another example of a more individualistic orientation is in this description of how to be different from non-Christians: "We want to be different and distinct and unique not just so that we draw attention to ourselves, but so that people can come to know God and praise Him for what He's doing in our lives. In the book of Philippians . . . Paul says . . . , 'You shine like stars in the universe.'" In this sermon, Pastor Darrell explained further that Christians need to be different in five ways: by being sacrificial, compassionate, faithful to God, demonstrating humility, and demonstrating servanthood. Therefore, Christians need to "stop whining," "quit fighting," "be holy," "love deeply," "work diligently," and "take risks." In this sermon, being different (exhibiting "star quality") is shown through individuals' upstanding character rather than through the Christian community's quality of relationships with each other.[32]

The Role of Diversity

At Jackson Church, racial diversity is indeed valued but is not given primacy as an organizational distinctive. For example, although faces of many colors appear on their website and printed materials, there is only one explicit mention of racial or ethnic diversity in all of Jackson Church's print or online materials. On a website page that extrapolates on the vision of the church appears the following: "It is a dream . . . of a church that mimics heaven in its diversity. We will welcome and celebrate people from all ethnic backgrounds. This will be evidenced by cultural inclusion and coloring of our crowd." As evidenced by the extent to which racial diversity is emphasized among the informational materials, its multiracial quality, though desired and welcome, does not appear as critical a component to its self-definition. Its primary identity is not that of a multiracial church; rather it is that of a "seeker" church. As such, Jackson tends to emphasize the relevance of its practices to the culture and their relationship to the secular community around them.[33]

Diversity, then, is important in and to the church because it demographically and culturally matches the make-up of the surrounding community. Pastor Mike expressed in an interview that "because we live in an area that is very integrated, it's absolutely critical to me to see that the church is the same." He explained, "It's not just diversity from a racial perspective that I'm interested in. I really want to become a church that values diversity on a larger scale because I really value creativity."[34]

Consistent with the emphasis on relationship with non-Christians and the importance of multiple dimensions of diversity, cross-race relationships are one of many kinds of relationships members are encouraged to establish with nonbelievers. Speaking specifically about outreach, Pastor Darrell discussed the commitment of the church to these kinds of relationships.

> We are committed at [Jackson Church] to reach across all kinds of diversity and all kinds of ethnic lines. If you're a Muslim or a Mormon, if you're a Buddhist or a Baptist, if you're Catholic or Charismatic, if you're Hispanic, Asian, African, white, Indian, a Dallas Cowboy fan, if you live in a trailer or in a townhouse, it really doesn't matter. We want to reach out. We want to show God's love to all people.

This statement points to Jackson Church's commitment to a generalized diversity, and one that is neither specific to nor limited to race. He mentioned the need to reach out to people who are different religiously, racially, in sports fandom, and in socioeconomic status. In addition, being a diverse church is described as predicated upon diversity in one's relational network, presumably by bringing different others in. The need for *intra*-church relationships between different individuals is not emphasized. The boundary between intrachurch and extrachurch ties is not clear in this sermon, except that extrachurch relationships can potentially become intrachurch relationships.[35]

In Mannington, reconciliation between members of different racial groups is significant because it demonstrates divine power overcoming social structural barriers. As such, cross-race relationships are an effective mechanism of evangelism by which God can be revealed to others. At Jackson Church, reconciliation is framed in terms of the resolution of interpersonal conflict. Reconciliation is described as an outcome of one's salvation rather than as a mandate for the purpose of drawing others into faith. In a sermon, Rick described changes that occur once someone has been "saved." Salvation can

> change our relationships. . . . Maybe there's someone in here today that you're just not getting along with. . . . But God is saying . . . , "I've already settled the relationship between you and me, now I want you to go out and I want you to settle the relationship between you and others."

Reconciliation, as described here, is about "settling the relationship" with someone "you're just not getting along with." Therefore, the meaning of reconciliation for one's faith has more narrow implications than that described in Mannington Church.[36]

In sum, Jackson Church demonstrates an approach to evangelism that is not only more broadly defined but also less aggressive than that of Mannington Church. Like a hospital, the focus is on compassionate acts and meeting needs as a means for evangelism but also on caring for their own members. In contrast to the goal-oriented agency of Mannington's Christian, Jackson's strategy is passive in comparison and more diffuse in its end goal, similar to that of a hospital, whose objective is to care for those around them, no matter what stage of spiritual "health."

Rather than promoting a religious identity rooted in congregational goals, religious identity at Jackson Church is much more individualized and personalized. Thus, the linkages between fellowship, diversity, and evangelism have less to do with intracongregational cohesion and more to do with relationships between Christians and non-Christians. Diversity is valued and encouraged without any particular focus on racial diversity.

Conclusion

Compared to Jackson's individualistic approach to church, Mannington's organizational orientation toward church mission has engendered higher rates of interracial friendship. As shown in Table 9.1 of the Appendix, 47% of the congregants at Mannington can name a close interracial friend, whereas at Jackson only 21.4% can name an interracial friend. The emphasis on corporate goals and actionable, cooperative tasks at Mannington is consistent with scholarly research that shows these to be important ingredients to the development of interracial friendship.

Indeed, an organization "knotted together" through interracial ties offers benefits that extend beyond the reduction of negative outcomes like racial conflict and prejudice and the attrition of minority members. An integrated congregation can also activate the resource richness from diverse social networks. Studies of diversity in organizations find that organizations reap benefits as their diversity grows: diverse perspectives increase problem solving and predictive abilities and stimulate creativity and innovation.

And to the extent that a church seeks to exhibit a different quality of community, consider this statistic: as of 2004, only 15% of Americans claimed to have a close cross-race friend. An integrated church community may be considered a microcosm of a greater call to reconciliation. Pastor James at Mannington expressed that bridging the racial gap "where we live" is necessary to "understanding the responsibility as believers to make disciples of all nations." Finally, a truly integrated environment offers greater opportunities for intercultural education within the safety of social relationship, an important part of the culture at Mannington. Douglas, a member at Mannington described what happened when someone made a racially prejudicial comment: another member responded with "I know you have a good heart, but you have no idea what that comment means to this group of people, and I don't think that's what you mean, but that's what's heard." In contrast, a member at Jackson wrote, "Will anyone challenge [attendees at Jackson] to examine their hearts for their true feelings? The race game is so deep, and I think most just like to pretend the elephant is not in the room," implying that discussion of racial issues are not part of normal discourse at Jackson.[37]

Notably, Jackson Church members have higher rates of extra-church interracial friendship than Mannington Church members (41.9% vs. 26.4%). Therefore, although they fall behind Mannington Church in their rates of intrachurch interracial friendship, they excel in establishing cross-race relationships with nonmembers, in their accommodation to different "levels" of religious faith, in their focus on acts of service to their community, and in their sensitivity to secular stereotypes about Christians and church.

Both of the churches in this study actively frame identities for their congregants and their relationship to religious community. They influence what it means to be a Christian person, they specify the obligations as a congregational member, they delineate the role of the church body, and they communicate the implications of intrachurch and extrachurch relationships, and the relationship of this religious identity with other relevant identities. It is in the context of the congregations' larger religious purposes and understandings that one must understand how intrachurch interracial friendship might be facilitated.

Mannington and Jackson Church frame their religious purpose in ways that are as contrasting as a special forces military unit would be from a hospital, and those who would be drawn to either organization would be vastly dissimilar. Both are specialized organizations, but they differ in their identities as battle-ready, mission-oriented soldiers and as service-oriented, mercy-driven hospital workers and patients. The content of religious identity as promoted by Mannington Church involves commitment to the specialized mission of the congregation, which necessitates depth of relationship between racial groups as a manifestation of their calling to evangelize the world. One the one hand, similar to that of a special forces unit, Mannington Church's version of evangelism requires directed, goal-oriented agency on the part of its believers. Jackson Church, on the other hand, operates more like a hospital than a military unit. Its version of evangelism is more diffuse in scope, with an emphasis on acts of compassion. Unlike Mannington's emphasis on its *collective* identity, Jackson Church tends to be geared around individual needs.

These different approaches to evangelism and identity have divergent implications for community. Differing conceptions of community are reflected in the Mannington and Jackson churches, particularly in how they each define spiritual family, which helps to form a basis for what kind of relationships are important to cultivate. Mannington Church emphasizes the responsibility to spiritual family as embodied in the well-circumscribed local congregation. Jackson Church lacks emphasis on cohesion within the local congregation because its boundaries are not delineated as such. Just as a hospital does not require community among its patients to function, relationships among its congregants—and by extension, intrachurch interracial relationships—are not emphasized to the degree seen at Mannington. Jackson Church has a greater interest in aligning themselves with the culture and community around them to make the boundaries between church and secular society more permeable, thereby allowing church to be more accessible to nonbelievers.

At Mannington, interracial relationships are given high religious and congregational significance; it is the manifestation of God's power and the expression of difference with the secular world. At Jackson, diversity is valued in a general sense. Interracial relationships among members are not given priority over relationships with dissimilar others. Whereas Jackson Church may be minimizing the impact of race because of this broad interest in diversity of all forms, at Mannington Church racial identity is made salient due to the recognition that overcoming racial barriers can be difficult. Race is construed as intertwined with and indispensible to religious faith, and racially integrated community is an indication of congregational calling. Therefore, Mannington Church provides of an example of a context in which minimizing or submerging race need not be a strategy for facilitating interracial friendship.

What, then, are some of the practical implications of this discussion? Particularly for those who may be religious practitioners who desire or are in multiracial congregations, there are several lessons that may be drawn from this study. First, racial diversity in and of itself cannot be the end goal, and racial integration is not an automatic outcome of diversity, even when there is religious commonality. Second, racial relational integration in the congregation derives from the organization's broader framework of what it means to be a believer and a congregation, and what *meaning* interracial friendship has in that context. Moreover, the question of how interracial friendship can be facilitated within one's church needs to be answered with an awareness of the congregation's *religious* purposes and strategies. Finally, race need not be diminished or ignored as an identity to create a racially integrated community. Likewise, acknowledging the importance of race does not necessitate diminishing the salience of religious faith.

Appendix
Methodology

I employed a mixed-methods design, using both quantitative and qualitative sources of data. I selected two multiracial Protestant churches to study in-depth as case studies. I administered a Web survey to congregants, which included several open-ended questions. An analysis of a national data set (Portrait of American Life Survey) also provided a context with which to compare these congregants. I also collected a variety of qualitative data sources, including semistructured interviews with pastoral and lay leadership and full-time staff (27 in total), online and printed materials, sermons (73 in total, ranging from 35 to 75 minutes each), and participant observation at services and other church-sponsored activities.

Interracial Friendship Rates

As shown in Table 9.1, about 21% of Jackson congregants have a close church friend of a different race. The expected rate of interracial friendship based on racial composition alone is 39.14%. Mannington Church is more racially diverse, and, correspondingly, a higher proportion (47%) of the congregation has a close friend of a different race in the congregation. The expected rate of interracial friendship at Mannington is 58.76%. Both fall short of what may be expected by the opportunity structure, but there is a greater difference between the actual and expected rates for Jackson Church. To confirm the statistical significance of the difference in interracial friendship rates between Mannington and Jackson churches, I conducted a sample selection analysis (unreported) that accounted for the propensity to make close friends in church as well as other demographic attributes. This analysis revealed Mannington attenders to be more likely to have close interracial church friends.

Table 9.1. Cross-Tabulations of Race, Gender, Education, Household Income, and Cross-Race Friendship by Church Site, Including National Data from the Portrait of American Life Survey

	Mannington		Jackson		
	%	n	%	N	National (%)
Close church friends					
Zero church friends	25.6	43	50.7	71	
Only same-race friends	27.4	46	27.9	39	
At least 1 interracial friend	47.0	79	21.4	30	
Total	100	168	100	140	
Race					
Whites	49.2	87	76.7	112	
Blacks	40.8	72	10.3	15	
Other race	10.2	18	13.0	19	
Total	100	177	100	146	
Gender					
Female	61.1	121	68.3	112	
Male	38.9	77	31.7	52	
Total	100	198	100	164	

(continued)

Table 9.1 (continued)

	Mannington		Jackson		National (%)
	%	n	%	N	
Education					
High school or less	20.2	36	21.2	31	55.92[b]
Trade certificate/ associates'	15.2	27	17.8	26	22.91[b]
Bachelors degree	40.5	72	31.5	46	14.03[b]
Graduate degree	24.2	43	29.5	43	7.14[b]
Total	100	178	100	146	
Household income					
<$25,000	2.4	4	8.8	12	21.89[c]
$25,000–$49,999	10.6	18	19.7	27	30.89[c]
$50,000–$74,999	17.1	29	20.4	28	23.20[c]
$75,000–$99,999	22.4	38	17.5	24	11.37[c]
>$100,000	47.7	81	33.6	46	12.83[c]
Total	100	170	100	137	
Marital status					
Married	72.9	129	57.9	84	57.37[d]
Unmarried	27.1	48	42.1	61	42.63[d]
Total	100	177	100	145	
Median age in years	41	191	39	162	46[d]
Mean number of church friends[a] (s.d.)	2.15 (1.79)	169	1.13 (1.46)	141	1.12[e,f,g]

[a]Of 5 possible. [b]$N = 232.50$. [c]$N = 205.62$. [d]$N = 236.49$. [e]Of 4 possible. [f]Standard deviation = 1.29. [g]$N = 182.50$.

Furthermore, assessing the number of church friends who are not known through any other contexts provides even greater insight into the likelihood of interracial friendship in these two churches. Among those who have interracial church friends, 78.35% of Mannington's respondents know them exclusively through the church context, compared to 56.41% of Jackson's respondents. This difference cannot be attributed to higher rates of cross-race friendmaking on the part of Mannington attenders—the number of attenders in both churches who have nonchurch friends of a different race are comparable: 36.4% of Mannington attenders and 41.9% of Jackson attenders have nonchurch friends of a different race.

Therefore, it is clear that Mannington Church is an organizational context in which one is more likely to develop close cross-race friendships.

Notes

1. Curtiss DeYoung Michael O. Emerson, George Yancey, and Karen Chai Kim, *United by Faith: The Multiracial Congregation as an Answer to the Problem of Race* (New York: Oxford University Press, 2003); Michael O. Emerson, *People of the Dream: Multiracial Congregations in the United States* (Princeton, NJ: Princeton University Press, 2006), 171. George Yancey, "An Examination of the Effects of Residential and Church Integration on Racial Attitudes of Whites," *Sociological Perspectives* 42, no. 2 (1999): 304.
2. Emerson, *People of the Dream*, 45, 105–130; DeYoung et al., *United by Faith*; Kevin D. Dougherty and Kimberly R. Huyser, "Racially Diverse Congregations: Organizational Identity and the Accommodation of Differences," *Journal for the Scientific Study of Religion* 47, no. 1 (2008): 23.
3. Brad Christerson and Michael O. Emerson, "The Costs of Diversity in Religious Organizations: An In-Depth Case Study," *Sociology of Religion* 64, no. 2 (2003): 163. Michael Emerson and Christian Smith, *Divided by Faith: Evangelical Religion and the Problem of Race in America* (New York: Oxford University Press, 2000), 69–82; Miles Hewstone and Rupert Brown, *Contact and Conflict in Intergroup Encounters* (New York: Blackwell, 1986); F. J. Milliken and L. L. Martins, "Searching for Common Threads: Understanding the Multiple Effects of Diversity in Organizational Groups," *Academy of Management Review* 21, no. 2 (1996); J. Miller McPherson, Pamela A. Popielarz, and Sonja Drobnic, "Social Networks and Organizational Dynamics," *American Sociological Review* 57, no. 2 (1991); Pamela A. Popielarz and Miller McPherson, "On the Edge or In Between: Niche Position, Niche Overlap, and the Duration of Voluntary Association Memberships," *The American Journal of Sociology* 101, no. 3 (1995): 157–170; George Yancey and Michael Emerson, "Intracongregational Church Conflict: A Comparison of Monoracial and Multiracial Churches," *Research in the Social Scientific Study of Religion* 14 (2003): 113–128.
4. Gordon Allport, *The Nature of Prejudice* (Cambridge, MA: Addison-Wesley, 1954); Anthony Antonio, "The Role of Interracial Interaction in the Development of Leadership Skills and Cultural Knowledge and Understanding," *Research in Higher Education* 42, no. 5 (2001): 593–617; Jeffrey Dixon, "The Ties that Bind and Those That Don't: Toward Reconciling Group Threat and Contact Theories of Prejudice," *Social Forces* 84, no. 4 (2006), 2203; Emerson and Smith, *Divided by Faith*, 115–133; Michael Emerson, Rachel Timbro, and George Yancey, "Contact Theory Extended: The Effects of Prior Racial Contact on Current Social Ties," *Social Science Quarterly* 83, no. 3 (2002): 745–861. Mary Jackman and Marie

Crane, "'Some of My Best Friends Are Black . . . ': Interracial Friendship and Whites' Racial Attitudes," *Public Opinion Quarterly* 50, no. 4 (1986): 459–486; Scott Page, *The Difference: How the Power of Diversity Creates Better Groups, Firms, Schools, and Societies* (Princeton, NJ: Princeton University Press, 2007); Thomas Pettigrew, "Intergroup Contact Theory," *Annual Review of Psychology* 49 (1998): 65–85. D. A. Thomas and R. J. Ely, "Making Differences Matter: A New Paradigm for Managing Diversity," *Harvard Business Review* 74, no. 5 (1996): 79–90.

5. Korie Edwards, "Bring Race to the Center: The Importance of Race in Racially Diverse Religious Organizations," *Journal for the Scientific Study of Religion* 47, no. 1 (2008), 6; Emerson and Smith, *Divided by Faith*, 128; Samuel Gaertner and John F. Dovidio, *Reducing Intergroup Bias* (Philadelphia: Psychology Press, 2000); Gerardo Marti, *A Mosaic of Believers: Diversity and Innovation in a Multiethnic Church* (Bloomington: Indiana University Press, 2005), 173.

6. Emerson and Smith, *Divided by Faith*, 131–132; J. Nicole Shelton, Jennifer A. Richeson, Jessica A. Salvatore, and Sophie Trawalter, "Ironic Effects of Racial Bias During Interracial Interactions," *Psychological Science* 16, no. 5 (2005): 397–402.

7. Maureen Hallinan and Richard Williams, "Interracial Friendship Choices in Secondary Schools," *American Sociological Review* 54, no. 1 (1989): 67–78; Peter Marsden, "Core Discussion Networks of Americans," *American Sociological Review* 52, no. 1 (1987): 122–131; Peter Marsden, "Homogeneity in Confiding Relations," *Social Networks* 10, no. 1 (1988): 57–76; Miller McPherson, Lynn Smith-Lovin, and James Cook, "Birds of a Feather: Homophily in Social Networks," *Annual Review of Sociology* 27 (2001): 415–444; James Moody, "Race, School Integration, and Friendship Segregation in America," *American Journal of Sociology* 107, no. 3 (2001): 679–716; Erica Wong, "Can Religion Trump Race? Interracial Friendship in Protestant Churches" (PhD diss., University of Michigan, 2009), 94.

8. Roger Finke and Rodney Stark, *Churching of America, 1776–2005* (New Brunswick, NJ: Rutgers University Press, 2005); R. Stephen Warner, "Work in Progress Toward a New Paradigm for the Sociological Study of Religion in the United States," *American Journal of Sociology* 98, no. 5 (1993): 1044–1093; Donald Miller, *Reinventing American Protestantism: Christianity in the New Millennium* (Berkeley: University of California Press, 1997).

9. Christian Smith, *American Evangelicalism: Embattled and Thriving* (Chicago: University of Chicago Press, 1998), 132–136.

10. Pastor Bryce, Mannington Church, sermon transcript, January 1, 2006.

11. Pastor Larry, Mannington Church, sermon transcript, January 15, 2006.

12. Pastor Bryce, interview with the author, January 16, 2006. Emphasis in original.

13. Ibid.

14. Charles Moskos and John Butler, *All That We Can Be: Black Leadership and Racial Integration the Army Way* (New York: Basic Books, 1996); Pastor Bryce, interview with the author, January 2, 2006. In addition to being emphasized from the

pulpit, a familial culture was evident among attendees. In open-ended survey responses, attendees often mentioned the feeling of "instant friendship and family-like bonds." Further, the small groups that I observed were marked by the sharing of personal struggles and problems.

15. Pastor Larry, sermon transcript, January 15, 2006.
16. Pastor Bryce, sermon transcript, January 29, 2006; Pastor David, Mannington Church, interview with the author, February 5, 2006.
17. Pastor Bryce, sermon transcript, January 16, 2006.
18. Ibid.; Pastor David, interview with the author, February 5, 2006.
19. Pastor Bryce, sermon transcript, January 29, 2006.
20. Pastor Bryce, sermon transcript, February 5, 2006.
21. Ibid.
22. Pastor David, sermon transcript, July 9, 2006.
23. Pastor Bryce, sermon transcript, February 5, 2006. Emphasis in the original; Pastor David, sermon transcript, July 9, 2006.
24. Pastor Darrell, Jackson Church, sermon transcript, April 9, 2006; September 17, 2006.
25. Pastor Darrell, sermon transcript, April 9, 2006.
26. Pastor Darrell, sermon transcript, July 9, 2006.
27. Pastor Darrell, sermon transcript, September 17, 2006.
28. Pastor Darrell, sermon transcript, April 9, 2006.
29. Pastor Mike, Jackson Church, sermon transcript, February 19, 2006.
30. Pastor Mike, sermon transcript, January 15, 2006.
31. Pastor Mike, sermon transcript, March 5, 2006.
32. Pastor Darrell, sermon transcript, January 22, 2006.
33. Kimon Howland Sargeant, *Seeker Churches: Promoting Traditional Religion in a Nontraditional Way* (New Brunswick, NJ: Rutgers University Press, 2000).
34. Pastor Mike, interview with the author.
35. Pastor Darrell, sermon transcript, April 9, 2006.
36. Rick, sermon transcript, April 16, 2006.
37. Antonio, "Interracial Interaction"; Miller McPherson, Lynn Smith-Lovin, and Matthew E. Brashears, "Social Isolation in America: Changes in Core Discussion Networks Over Two Decades," *American Sociological Review* 71, no. 3 (2006): 353–375; Page, *The Difference*.

10

Much Ado About Nothing? Rethinking the Efficacy of Multiracial Churches for Racial Reconciliation

Korie L. Edwards

BEGINNING IN THE 1990s, the Promise Keepers movement brought the idea of racial reconciliation to the forefront of religious discourse, particularly within evangelical circles. With its meetings across the country, many exceeding 25,000 men in attendance, Promise Keepers has had for more than a decade a captive audience of largely white men with whom to share their message of bridging racial and ethnic division. In many respects, we can credit the Promise Keepers movement for getting the contemporary white evangelical community to begin to engage the idea of racial reconciliation. Promise Keepers pricked the racial conscience of white evangelicals. For that, this organization and its leaders deserve to be heralded. No doubt, this achievement was not easy and took courage given the extent of racial isolation in this country.[1]

The form of racial reconciliation promoted by Promise Keepers has in many ways—as Michael Emerson and Christian Smith well document in *Divided by Faith*—privileged racial reconciliation among individuals, restoring relationships, forgiveness, moving beyond the past, and bonding with people from a different racial or ethnic group from your own. The emphasis on racialized social structures and racism, meanwhile, has been almost completely absent. In other words, there is little discussion about racial inequality in the workplace, education system, or the criminal justice system; the extensive racial segregation of America's neighborhoods;

or persistent racial discrimination. The main idea is that God works in individuals, giving them the strength to make changes within themselves and their immediate social world, thus producing racial and ethnic unity. Discussion of God's working through individuals, organizations or institutions to promote and make systemic changes that bring about racial justice is very limited if at all.

Alongside the recent wave of racial reconciliation initiatives church practitioners birthed a multiracial church movement that challenges the homogeneity principle of church growth. The homogeneity principle of church growth has dominated evangelicals' thinking about church discipleship and growth for decades. The principle simply says that churches that target and expend its resources to attract a particular group will experience greater growth than churches that do not. While not without controversy, there is support for the idea of homogeneity in voluntary organizations in general. The principle has been used by churches to increase congregation growth. Yet, since the emergence of the Promise Keeper-style racial reconciliation movement, religious leaders and parishioners have increasingly questioned the theological accuracy of the homogeneity principle of church growth and, subsequently, racially homogeneous congregations. One of the main Bible passages often quoted to support the multiracial church movement is found in the book of Revelation. Painted there is an image of a church where "all nations and tribes and peoples and tongues" are represented, standing among one another worshipping together. Proponents of multiracial churches say that congregations ought to represent this diversity whenever possible.[2]

At present the multiracial church movement seems to be gaining momentum. For instance, Michael Emerson's recent research shows that over the past decade there has been an impressive uptick in the proportion of megachurches that are racially diverse.[3] Aiming to get a sense of the breadth of this movement, I googled *multiracial church, interethnic church, multicultural church*, and so on. This method of surveying multiracial churches is not scientific. Still, the exercise is telling. What is clear is that there is an incredible amount of energy "out there" around the idea of congregational racial/ethnic/cultural diversity. Denominations are encouraging their congregations to be more racially and ethnically inclusive. The Evangelical Church of America and the Presbyterian Church (U.S.A.), for example, have Multicultural Ministries offices that are charged with the job of helping churches in their denominations become diverse. There are blogs dedicated to providing directories of multiracial churches, information on how to become a multiracial church, books on multiracial churches, and the latest media piece on the subject. Conferences on congregational diversity are popping up across the country in cities like Orlando, Florida, and Chicago, Illinois, and smaller communities like Walnut Creek, California, and Sheboygan, Wisconsin. Evidenced by their mission/vision/value statements, churches are making racial and ethnic diversity central to their identities. Here are just a few examples of statements that I found on churches' websites:

> [Our church] is a non-denominational church family of all colors, cultures and conditions. We launched [this church] in order to become a *congregation without segregation* . . . blacks, browns, whites, mixed couples and children, people of various social and economic conditions, worshiping together side by side under one roof every week. (Kentucky)
>
> We are an inter-ethnic church that embraces people of all races, colors, and ethnic groups. (New Hampshire)
>
> Intentional cultural and socioeconomic diversity is a necessity, not because it is politically correct or vogue, but because it is truly what God wants. . . . We actively train each member in cross-cultural skills and try our best to make corporate changes so our group becomes a place for all peoples. (California)

When we consider the historical and contemporary contexts of race in America, the contemporary multiracial church movement is quite notable. This country enslaved other humans, removed entire indigenous tribes from their lands, denied citizenship to Asian immigrants until 1954, and institutionalized black–white segregation. The legacy of these acts persists. For example, blacks and whites remain the most segregated of any racial and ethnic groups—in housing, education, and religion. Asian Americans are well underrepresented in nationally elected offices despite their disproportionately high levels of education and relatively high integration rates with whites. The average Native American poverty rate is the highest of all racial and ethnic groups at 27%—and is much higher at 36% for those who live on reservations. This rate is ten percentage points above the poverty rate of African Americans, who have the second-highest poverty rate in the country. People are coming together voluntarily in a country with this extensive and persistent history of excluding and oppressing people of color.[4]

Still, while the contemporary multiracial church movement challenges historical and contemporary patterns of segregation, can such a movement disrupt racialized social structures? In other words, to what extent does bringing people together across racial and ethnic lines for congregational worship improve, for instance, the political, economic, health, or educational statuses of people of color? How does it reduce racial inequality?

Divided by Faith got evangelicals talking about what it means for blacks and whites to be racially reconciled. As Emerson and Smith showed, the racial reconciliation message within white evangelical circles is about relationship building and individual actions. The concept of racialized structures, which is also central to the racial reconciliation message for black Christians, is overlooked or not recognized by white evangelicals. Dismantling institutionalized discrimination, for instance, is not presented as a primary solution to racial inequality. In this essay, I build on the discussion started by *Divided by Faith* by discussing the role of multiracial worship for addressing racial inequality. I propose that the multiracial church movement, especially within white evangelicalism, is an extension of Promise Keepers-style racial reconciliation. Building cross-racial relationships is now promoted within the walls of churches rather than on the arena floor. And issues related to racial justice are not central to the multiracial church movement just as they were neglected by Promise Keepers in previous decades. In the following pages, I briefly review the trajectory of multiracial churches in the United States, explore how racial reconciliation is done in contemporary multiracial churches, and end with a discussion of an alternative form of religious racial diversity that has the capacity to build cross-racial ties and address racialized social structures.

Trajectory of Multiracial Congregations

The prevalence of multiracial churches right now is likely the highest it has ever been in our history, making up about 8% of US congregations. But multiracial churches are not a recent phenomenon. Blacks and whites have worshipped together since before the Revolutionary War. However, denominations and churches actively affirmed the racial order providing it with moral validity and divine legitimacy. Black Christians were not treated as equals in these early racially diverse churches. They faced institutionalized discrimination. Some churches and denominations, for example, banned blacks from pastoral leadership and preaching. Blacks were also banned from sitting in certain areas of the churches. A particularly famous story that aptly reflects the level of racial exclusion in many antebellum churches is told in the autobiography of Richard Allen. Upon arriving to a very crowded service in Philadelphia, he and his friend Absalom Jones proceeded to find a place to sit in what they thought to be an appropriate place for blacks. Allen said:

> Meeting had begun, and they were nearly done singing, and just as we got to the seats, the elder said, 'Let us pray.' We had not been long upon our knees before I heard considerable scuffling and low talking. I raised my head up and saw one of the trustees having hold of the Rev. Absalom Jones, pulling him up off of his knees, and saying, "You must get up—you must not kneel here." Mr. Jones replied, "Wait until prayer is over, and I will get up and trouble you no more." With that he beckoned to one of the other trustees to come to his assistance. . . . By this time prayer was over, and we all went out of the church in a body, and they were no more plagued with us in the church.

Black Christians, recognizing that true freedom ultimately required independence from the white hegemonic religious structure, started their own churches and denominations, beginning with the African Methodist Episcopal Church, founded by Richard Allen, Absalom Jones, and other black believers in 1787.[5]

After the Revolutionary War, free blacks in the North and South largely worshipped in black churches. And whites generally worshipped with whites. But there continued to be instances of whites and free blacks worshipping together. Regrettably, however, the arrangements in the multiracial churches of this era were not racially equal. Multiracial churches continued to set aside certain pews for blacks. Sunday school classes were segregated by race. Even religious rituals were segregated. African Americans, for instance, were required to receive communion after whites. These practices communicated that blacks were inferior to and fundamentally different from whites. Differences in racial status were clearly more important than shared faith.[6]

Enslaved black Christians worshipped in clandestine black churches, headed by black pastors during the post-Revolutionary War, antebellum period. These black congregations worshipped in secret because it was illegal for blacks to organize publicly. Organization by enslaved blacks was considered a potential threat to the social order. Whites surmised that enslaved blacks could be planning slave rebellions if allowed to have their own churches. But convinced by missionaries that blacks should be allowed to worship, some white masters did make a way for enslaved black Christians to worship openly. The solution was multiracial churches, broadly defined. This organization occurred in two ways. Enslaved blacks attended the churches of their masters. In which case, the worship services were racially segregated. Enslaved blacks were required to sit in a separate area of the church, such as a gallery, so they were more spectators of the service than participants. In the other case of black–white worship, whites occupied pastoral roles and blacks were restricted to the role of parishioner. There were no white parishioners in this type of multiracial church.[7]

So both in the North and the South, the practices undergirding congregational racial diversity actually perpetuated racial inequality. Blacks were expected to "stay in their place." And services were structured in such a way that reinforced the racial hierarchy. The place of blacks was, of course, explicit and understood in the slave-holding South, but it was not so in the North, and northern free blacks were disheartened by the adamant maintenance of the color line by their white Christian brothers and sisters.

White evangelical abolitionists adamantly declared their abhorrence of slavery and called for its end. But they did not extend their fire for racial economic equality to other institutions, including the church. However, as the United States transitioned after the Civil War and into the twentieth century, Christians increasingly viewed the racial arrangements within churches as problematic. Christian leaders from a variety of traditions called for racial equality more broadly. For example, the Catholic Archbishop John Ireland, who served in the Union army during the Civil War as a chaplain, exclaimed in an 1890 address to St. Augustine's Church in Washington, DC, "My solution of the Negro problem is to declare that there is no problem to be solved since we are all equal as brothers should be and we will in consistency with our American and Christian principles treat alike black and white. I know no color line. I will acknowledge none." For Ireland, racial hatred invited the wrath of God upon those who held onto it. While the Southern Baptist Convention (SBC) supported the right of congregations to affirm (or not) racial segregation and inequality, other Protestant denominations, like the United Lutheran Church in America, the Congregational Christian Churches, and the Methodist Episcopal

Church explicitly affirmed their commitments to racial integration at the denominational level. Even in the South during the Reconstruction years, Gilbert Havens, the bishop of Methodist Episcopal Church in the region, steadfastly advocated for racial integration. He was particularly hopeful about the prospects for racial integration and equality in New Orleans, believing that New Orleans posed the best opportunity for making religious racial integration work because of its more liberal and inclusive culture relative to other southern cities. As James Bennett highlights, Havens and members of the Methodist Episcopal Church of New Orleans "believed their racially inclusive denomination would extend its influence to cool the 'fires burning in the furnace political' and thereby 'mold the State' toward a broad acceptance of racial equality." Bennett goes on to say that "black and white M. E. church members offered their own model of a shared religious affiliation that transcended racial differences as the best hope for the uncertainty of the 1880s. Racial inclusion stood at the very center of their M. E. religious identity." Congregational racial diversity was the answer to racial inequality. The Methodist Episcopal Church sustained its commitment to the role of congregational racial diversity in solving racial problems well into the twentieth century. Unfortunately, as history demonstrates, this multiracial church movement did not have the destabilizing effect on institutional racism and segregation for which Gaven and other Methodist Episcopal parishioners had hoped.[8]

By the 1930s, multiracial congregations, primarily in the North, were forming across the country. They were mainly in large cities such as Chicago, Philadelphia, and New York. These congregations were very intentional about getting blacks and whites to worship together. Recognizing the importance of a clergy's race for parishioners, the congregations often had two head pastors—one black and one white. The clergy alternated sermon responsibilities, one delivering the sermon one week and the other the next. In some cases, people who went to a multiracial church also had membership at another church. That is to say, they would be members of their black or white home church as well as the multiracial church.[9]

Multiracial churches of the "traditional" sort were also forming. The mass black migration from the South to the North in the 1930s was the primary impetus for the emergence of these multiracial churches. Churches located in neighborhoods experiencing racial transitions from all-white to increasingly black had a decision to make. They could remain in the community and attempt to draw white members from outside the neighborhood. They could move to a stable white neighborhood. Or they could welcome change and open their doors to blacks. Some remained and adapted to the demographics changes surrounding their churches. Often, these churches, too, were headed by both a white pastor and a black pastor who had equal levels of authority. Yet the South was not altogether removed from this slow steady change happening in churches. Religious interracial cooperation penetrated the South. Black and white churches conducted special joint programs together from time to time.[10]

California was a site of choice for pastors aspiring to start multiracial churches. In 1942, a recent graduate of University of Chicago's Divinity School, Daniel Genung, moved out to California to begin the All Peoples Christian Church and Community Center in Los Angeles. A study of the church published in 1945 proposes that key to the church's ability to sustain a racially diverse congregation was its variety of programs, involvement in children's and youth activities, strong clerical leadership, and community involvement and commitment. In 1946, *Ebony* magazine, a periodical that addresses issues relevant to the black community, did a feature story on a multiracial church—Fellowship Church of All Peoples—started by a young philosophy professor, Dr. Alfred Fisk, in San Francisco. Fisk's mission was to start a church that was not "run by whites 'for' negroes or one in which Negroes will merely be welcome to participate. We should establish a church which will be of and by and for both groups." Howard Thurman, a well-known black professor of religion and dean at Howard University, strongly believed in the mission of Fellowship Church. Thurman was a strong supporter of nonviolent activism, often giving speeches about Gandhi's approach to nonviolent protest and its reasons for success in ousting the British Empire from India. He is said to have been a pastor to the pastors leading the civil rights movement, including Dr. Martin Luther King, Jr. Yet he did not actively participate in the civil rights movement. He firmly believed that multiracial worship was the most important contribution Christians could make to undo racialized social structures. Thurman so believed in the social and religious significance of multiracial worship that he resigned from Howard University to co-pastor Fellowship Church with Fisk. Later in his biography Thurman explained that the basis of his belief was the transformative power of multiracial worship. Through multiracial churches, he believed that the gospel message of love and inclusion could be lived out, that through one's faith, personal transformation could take place, racial prejudice and fears could be overcome. Fellowship Church of All Peoples still exists today.[11]

In 1958, *Ebony* magazine did another feature article on multiracial churches. It tells the story of churches in every region of the country, in urban and rural areas. Near the beginning of the article, the author quoted the white pastor of an integrated church in Paragould, Arkansas, who said, "The members took the position that if we couldn't do something like this here, we'd look funny talking about foreign missions." To illustrate the point that the "quiet revolution" of multiracial churches was growing, the article presented photos of multiracial congregations in Houston, Louisville, Montgomery, St. Louis, New York, Chicago, Pittsburgh, San Francisco, Newark, and Milwaukee, among other locations. The threshold for racial integration in these churches is rather low by today's standards. For example, the article boasts that a once all-black congregation in Louisville, Kentucky, of more than 1,500 members had fourteen white members. But given the context in which these congregations integrated, even minimal integration was noteworthy. The integration of this Louisville church occurred in the 1950s Jim Crow South. Even today, it is rare to hear of white members joining a large, established black church.

Periodicals and scholarly literature on multiracial churches through the 1950s highlight the social importance of multiracial churches. Racial segregation was no longer seen as consistent with Christian principles. Congregational racial diversity was recognized as socially and theologically important. As the 1960s approached, discourse about multiracial worship assumed a slightly different, more socio-political tone. A sense of urgency about congregational racial diversity emerged. Racial diversity in religious organizations was explicitly framed as a civil rights issue, and multiracial churches were seen as part and parcel of the civil rights movement. It was believed that racial equality must penetrate churches as well if the goals of the civil rights movement were to be fully achieved. What was responsible for this sense of urgency? The "civil rights climate"—the nonviolent demonstrations and the violent retaliations in the form of church bombings and murders of children and youth volunteers—generated a context in which religious leaders already sympathetic to the movement felt emboldened to push for a "strong personal commitment to racial integration" in their denominations. One religious leader explained, "The Civil Rights Movement was demonstrating to the church what it ought to be doing." These leaders believed that it was the church's responsibility to be racially integrated. Congregational racial integration was in itself an act of social justice. Some Southern Baptists ministers too supported desegregation. And in response to the call for congregational racial diversity, many denominations began to invest resources into racial integration efforts. Several denominations even considered exacting financial penalties on congregations that did not racially integrate.[12]

Still, there was strong opposition to congregational racial diversity. Two white Baptists ministers from Lexington, Kentucky—Bob W. Brown and Henry A. Buchanan—painstakingly articulated the fierce opposition to racial integration by churches and religious leaders and called for the church to embrace integration in a 1966 article entitled "Integration: Great Dilemma of the Church: Nation's Foremost Moral Issue Forces Reappraisal of Racially Separate Worship." Buchanan and Brown's central question was "why . . . have church men not undertaken the task of integrating the churches with the same fervor they have shown for integrating all the other institutions of our society?" Buchanan and Brown went on to say, after highlighting the notable actions of several ministers who risked life and limb to participate in the civil rights movement:

> Ecclesiastical concern for integration of schools, motels, restaurants and swimming pools is understandable. Concern for employment, housing and voting rights is commendable. But the crux of the whole matter is in the segregated structure of the churches themselves. The minister's 'moment of truth' comes not when he takes a public position on the integration of public places, not when he marches for the Negro's right to vote in Alabama, but when he appears before his own congregation and asks for the complete integration of the church he serves. In addressing our attention to those areas which are affected by the law, and in neglecting the one sphere of influence where the principle of moral persuasion must operate, have we not forgotten our unique role in human society? The very integrity of the churches is at stake here.

For Buchanan and Brown, the church was a minister's primary sphere of influence. Ministers must, before they do anything else, be committed to affecting changes in their own churches. This commitment to the local church was necessary because at the heart of inequality was racial segregation of churches. Congregational racial integration must be foremost in the civil rights struggle. In their article, Buchanan and Brown, not unlike Emerson and Smith in 2000, recognized the very real retribution pastors faced for encouraging racial integration in their congregations. Clergy who pushed for racial integration of their congregations assumed the risk of losing members at best, losing their jobs, or at worst, being physically assaulted. Buchanan and Brown listed several examples of white pastors who lost their pulpits for pushing their congregations toward integration and others who sadly lost their lives for active participation in racial integration efforts. Buchanan himself was asked to leave his pastorate after he called for racial integration in his congregation. Yet they believed that the church has an imperative role to assume in race relations. Through the church, the moral issue of race must be addressed. Congregational racial diversity alone possesses the ability to bring about real racial reconciliation. They proclaimed at the end of the article, "[Cross-racial Christian brotherhood] the Churches must do, whatever the cost!"[13]

I have briefly reviewed the trajectory of multiracial worship in the United States through the 1970s. History shows that multiracial worship is not new. It dates back to at least the 1700s. In the early multiracial churches, blacks were not full, equal partners in ministry. However, during the twentieth century, churches and denominations became increasingly uncomfortable with the racial segregation and oppression that still pervaded American life and their own religious institutions. Race relations became more central to their agendas. Religious leaders were committed to racial diversity, so much so that they intentionally started multiracial churches. In other instances, pastors accepted the demographic changes of their communities and supported racial diversity in their congregations. Most of these changes happened in the North where still only a small minority of blacks lived. But, notably, there was some minimal support of cross-racial interaction and worship in the South. As the civil rights movement gained momentum, the civil rights narrative penetrated American discourse, which served to put pressure not only on government institutions but also religious bodies to deal with racial segregation and inequality. Denominations, churches, and religious leaders began linking congregational racial diversity to the ideals of the civil rights movement, albeit within a theological framework.

What we see then is a progression of views on multiracial worship. And by the time the civil rights movement began to take hold, multiracial worship was understood to be in itself a progressive act that would deteriorate racial prejudice and inequality. Leaders in the multiracial church movement like Gaven, Fisk, Thurman, Brown, and Buchanan firmly believed in the transformative power of multiracial worship for affecting change on the racialized and racist social landscape. They saw multiracial worship to be the single most important contribution that Christians could make in the struggle for racial equality. Still, while views on multiracial congregations became increasingly more progressive, the emphasis continued to be inward, focused on the congregation. Unlike black congregations and their leaders who, starting with the clandestine churches of the antebellum era to those of the 1960s, were actively engaged in a struggle outside of the church walls to dismantle a pervasive and oppressive racial structure, multiracial churches and their leaders focused on their very immediate context.[14]

Contemporary Multiracial Worship

Contemporary multiracial worship differs from the multiracial worship of most of the twentieth century in one important way. Congregations and denominations most active in congregational racial integration for most of the twentieth century were within the mainline Christian tradition, the more socially and theologically moderate or liberal wing of American Christianity. It was rarer for denominations or churches affiliated with white evangelicalism to promote or engage in multiracial worship. But in recent decades, white evangelical churches and denominations are more central to the multiracial church movement. Churches affiliated with white evangelical denominations are four times more likely to be racially diverse today than churches affiliated with mainline denominations.[15]

Where some leaders of mainline multiracial churches of the past at least acknowledged racism and racialized structures (such as Gilbert Gaven and Howard Thurman) Emerson and Smith's findings suggest that multiracial evangelical congregations are not inclined to even acknowledge racialized social structures and racial injustices. This inclination is exemplified in the following anecdotal examples of mission/vision/values statements that I came across during my Web surfing.

> Our vision is to build a multi-ethnic church in fulfillment of our part in the Lord's Great Commission. (Texas)
>
> Our prayer is to plant a church . . . that provides expository (one book at a time—chapter by chapter, verse by verse) preaching. This church will be non-denominational and consist of a congregation that reflects the complete ethnic and socio-economic makeup of the community. (South Carolina)

> [Multiracial worship] is a necessity, not because it is politically correct or vogue, but because it is truly what God wants. Many groups say that they would accept people of any and every background if the person walked through their doors. Reality is, though, many times groups are unaware to the many cultural barriers that exist and do nothing about them. We not only talk about it, we actively train each member in cross-cultural skills and try our best to make corporate changes so our group becomes a place for all peoples. (California)

These kinds of statements were typical of what I found on the Web. Again, given our racist and racialized structure, such commitments are notable particularly in religious circles. Nevertheless, what these statements seem to suggests is that multiracial churches are primarily about evangelism (live out the "Lord's Great Commission") and exemplifying the demographics of their surrounding communities ("reflects . . . ethnic and socioeconomic makeup of community"). The California congregation, which demonstrates a sounder grasp of the salience of racial and ethnic barriers, still emphasizes cultural differences, not structural patterns that divide racial groups and oppress people of color. The church's aim is to become a church in which people of all cultures feel welcome.

Although rarer, I did come across evangelical multiracial churches stating commitments to racial justice. Take for example this statement of a multiracial evangelical church in Massachusetts that according to its website is committed to both racial integration and racial justice:

> We seek to be a community that fully reflects the beautiful diversity of races, ethnicities, cultures, and nationalities in the Cambridge/Boston area. We are called to be a racially reconciled community, seeking racial justice in our relationships within the church and in the world.

It is unclear whether this congregation is connected to a broader civil rights agenda. Nor can I speak to how successful this congregation is at bringing about racial justice in its community. Moreover, it aims to bring about racial justice via relationships, not challenging social structures per se, which is quite consistent with the white evangelical strategy for racial reconciliation. Nevertheless, this congregation recognizes that racial reconciliation does not stop at racial integration. Racial justice is an important component as well.

Another anecdotal example that illustrates the ideological thrust of the multiracial church movement is a multiracial church plant guide published by the North American Mission Board of the SBC. *A Guide for Planting Multicultural Churches*[16] is not the only online publication connected to the SBC that highlights issues related to race and ethnicity. On the website of the Ethics and Religious Liberty Commission (erlc.com), which is a part of the SBC, there are several publications posted addressing topics such as racial and ethnic prejudice, the historical legacy of religious racial segregation, and multiracial congregations. I spend focused time on the multicultural church plant guide for three reasons. First, it is the only definitive position of the SBC on multiracial churches. Other online publications linked to websites of SBC-affiliated commissions or committees are opinion pieces or articles written by, for example, freelance writers, pastors, or editors.[17] Second, I focus on this guide is because it provides insight into how the SBC conceives of the purposes of congregational racial diversity and where and when this kind of diversity should occur. It is a blueprint for SBC congregations that express interest in becoming multicultural. Finally, I spend considerable focus on this guide is because it was published by the SBC, which has broad influence on American Christianity. The SBC is the largest evangelical denomination in the country. Thirty-eight percent of evangelical congregations are affiliated with the SBC.[18] The next largest denomination has 6% of all evangelical congregations. The SBC is also rooted in the South. It, therefore, has tremendous opportunity to live out racial reconciliation, not only because of its historical support of slavery and compliance with Jim Crow segregation but also because today one-half of blacks in the country live in this region, and the proportion of blacks in the region is increasing.[19] How this denomination addresses congregational racial diversity matters.

According to this guide, racially and ethnically diverse worship serves two main purposes: (i) it is symbolic, and (ii) it fills a niche in the religious marketplaces accommodating demographic changes in society. For instance, the guide begins saying that "the multicultural church matches a need in our society. . . . In a day of fear and mistrust the multiethnic (or multicultural) church is a sample of recomposition in Christ." The simple word *sample* in this phrase is important because it suggests that congregational racial and ethnic diversity *symbolizes* unity—a bringing together of people of different sometimes opposing cultural and ethnic backgrounds in the local congregation. It is a representation of the body of Christ in the local congregation. Congregational diversity is not as much about acting like the body of Christ as it is looking like the body of Christ. The guide continues to build upon this theme of symbolism. "The multicultural church," it says, "becomes an example of what can be done on earth and a foretaste of what will be in heaven." Heaven is culturally and ethnically diverse. Local congregations should demonstrate this diversity on earth. Presumably, however, all the consequences of historical racism and racial oppression have been erased in heaven, and justice has been done. Therefore, in symbolizing heaven on earth, the multiracial church should be working to do the same. It is unclear what and how the multicultural church will also work to right racial injustices.

The guide also defines a multicultural church as "a biblical community of believers: (1) who have as a current reality or hold as a core value the inclusion of culturally diverse people, and (2) who come together and serve as a single body to live out God's call to be a New Testament church." Even though congregational diversity symbolizes the body of Christ and heaven, racially and ethnically diverse worship is not for all congregations. It is for congregations with members who value this form of diversity and desire to worship together. The importance of the symbolic representation of Christ on earth extends only to congregations that find such symbolism important and relevant. This position is consistent with the SBC's earlier position on congregational racial integration. Churches have the right and freedom to make the decisions that they deem appropriate for their congregations.

Of course, the above anecdotal examples are not representative of all white evangelical perspectives on congregational racial diversity. And they are not reflective of what denominations or congregations actually do, only who they aim to be or what they believe about the topic. But the core sentiments of these ideas are consistent with contemporary research on multiracial churches.

Over the past couple of decades, there has been more written about multiracial churches than the whole century prior. The most prominent theme in this literature is that multiracial churches are biblical. God desires for churches to be multiracial. By coming together, the church will better fulfill its mission on earth. So to the best of their ability, churches ought to be racially diverse. By doing so, churches will exemplify the fullness of the body of Christ. Hence, much of the scholarly work on multiracial churches addresses how congregations can attract and retain a racially diverse membership. Similar to what Buchanan and Brown claimed, ministers are at the center of the strategy for creating multiracial worship.

Research shows that ministers articulate a vision for multiracial worship in their congregations. They also bind their parishioners together by emphasizing their shared human, if not Christian, identity, over members' racial identities. And similar to congregations of the 1930s and 1940s, changing neighborhood demographics are key factors that lead churches to become multiracial. Such changes require once predominately white congregations to assess how to respond to a steady migration of blacks into their local communities. Some decide to stay in their racially transitioning communities and encourage racial integration.[20]

Another thread of the contemporary literature on multiracial churches discusses the challenges of multiracial worship. Two foremost challenges exist for multiracial churches. One challenge is that multiracial churches run the risk of assuming a color-blind stance toward the structural realities of race. By supporting the idea that race does not have as much import in the church even though churches are embedded within a society that is highly racialized, multiracial churches can obscure the social structure of race—that is, that race has meaning for people's everyday lives such as the neighborhoods they live in, the types of jobs they occupy, the schools they attend, or who their friends are. A second challenge is similar to the first. Multiracial churches can ignore the privileges that their white members possess by virtue of being white in a society that valorizes whiteness. Whites rarely recognize their privilege because they have such little knowledge about or access to people of color. They only need to continue to live and believe as they normally do, and without any explicit intent they will reproduce a society that maintains the cultural and structural dominance of whites. For example, a white man who more than likely has always watched television that almost exclusively tells the stories of other whites, read books and media largely about other whites, lived in nearly all-white neighborhoods, and worked at companies that are nearly all-white and run mainly by whites has no sense that another way of thinking, living, and being in the world is possible that is different from his own and equally right at the same time. He is not a traditional racist who knowingly believes that whites are better than people of color and should stay clear of regularly interacting with them. But like for most whites, when he makes decisions about his life, his only reference is one located in a near totally white existence. Conversely, a black man is exposed to media and television that is largely about whites. As a child, he likely attended schools where he was taught by whites even if most of the other students were not white and where he learned about the important contributions of whites to society.

And as adult he works at companies where people who occupy the important positions are mostly white. Blacks, by necessity, are aware that whites are culturally and structurally dominant. The implication of color-blindness or ignoring white privilege for multiracial churches is that they, without any specific intent to do so, can reify white supremacy, a belief in the cultural and structural dominance of whites. As a consequence, they can communicate to members that the experiences, preferences, and beliefs of white members are more important and relevant than those of blacks. In my book, *The Elusive Dream*, I discuss the implications of this reality in greater detail for multiracial churches.[21]

Thus far I have provided a historical overview of multiracial worship in the United States. Blacks and whites have worshipped in the same religious space at the same time for the same reasons for hundreds of years. In many ways, contemporary multiracial churches and multiracial churches of the past are quite similar. Leaders of contemporary and past multiracial churches highlight the theological foundation for multiracial worship. Multiracial churches today—as well as those founded sixty or seventy year ago—emerge out local demographic changes. Leaders of contemporary multiracial churches are critical to congregational racial diversity. Buchanan and Brown fervently believed the same thing about congregational racial diversity of the civil rights era. Leaders in the contemporary multiracial church movements believe that congregational racial diversity is imperative for racial reconciliation. Religious leaders of past multiracial church movements shared this belief. Thus, in the face of remarkable changes in the broader social landscape—abolition of slavery, dismantling of Jim Crow, institutionalization of affirmative action policies, and so on—and a shift in the multiracial church movement from moderate or liberal Christian traditions to white conservative ones, the impetus behind multiracial church movements has not changed all that much. Multiracial churches have been and remain almost exclusively about bringing people together to build relationships and worship within a Christian community.

Religious Racial Diversity and Racial Justice

To what extent has congregational racial diversity been integral to a broader racial justice agenda? How has or does it impact racial inequality? Multiracial worship was tangentially linked to the civil rights movement, particularly during the 1960s. But this relationship was unique. Actually, it was the movement that inspired congregations and denominations to take up the cause of racial injustice through racial integration, not the other way around. Other than this relatively brief period, there is no evidence of which I am aware where multiracial worship has been *integral* to a broader agenda that intends to dismantle racial inequality and injustice.[22]

This lack of evidence is curious, however, given the broader social context wherein congregational racial diversity has taken place. During the antebellum period, over 90% of blacks in this country were slaves. White-controlled racially diverse churches even reinforced the slave system. Many white Christians during this era were content with just worshipping with blacks. After slavery, racial oppression persisted. Nearly all blacks lived under Jim Crow segregation. Blacks experienced systematic disenfranchisement. They were locked out of the better jobs and relegated to the lowest paying and menial work. For instance, 50% of black women in the labor force were domestics. This statistic is compared to less that 1% of white women. Seventy-five percent of black men worked in low-skilled jobs such as janitors, cooks, machine operators, and common laborers. This statistic is compared to 25% of white men. Overall, black family incomes were only about 55% of that of white families. If that wasn't enough, terrorism of blacks through public brutal beatings, burnings, and lynchings was at a fever pitch. The perpetrators of these terrorist acts were not held accountable, and sadly in many self-proclaimed God fearing communities, they were praised. These terrorist acts were often conducted on Sundays, suggesting an ironic, bizarre integration of faith and white supremacy.[23]

In contexts of blatant racial injustice and oppression during the antebellum and Jim Crow eras, multiracial worship was offered as the Christian answer for race problems. This response suggests a kind of disconnect from the "rest" of society. Black congregations could not afford this disconnect and responded to the injustices of these eras. It is as if multiracial churches were immune to the forces of racism in which their members live out their everyday lives. It is as if the social, psychological, economic, and physiological implications of race stopped at the front door of churches. It is as if race, as a broader structure, was inconsequential for religious life.[24]

There were Christians, however, who actively pursued true racial reconciliation. In the face of extreme racial oppression and entrenched racism, many black and white Christians had such deep spiritual convictions about the social injustices that they personally experienced or observed that they sacrificed nearly everything and worked together to right them. The comfort of their families, their opportunities for personal advancement, their livelihood, their lives, and the lives of their children, all of these things were put on the line and willingly sacrificed in the name of social justice and racial equality. These Christians were radical, especially for the antebellum and Jim Crow eras. For sure, the most important social movements in this country's history, ones that had a profound effect on how our society is structured, were multiracial movements led and mostly comprised of Christians with intense religious fervor and commitment to racial justice. These were participants in the Underground Railroad movement, the abolitionist movement, and the civil rights movement.[25] As a result of these movements, the racial status quo was destabilized, and real, positive changes in the social condition of blacks in this country occurred. Slavery ended. Jim Crow ended. Barriers to blacks voting were removed. Affirmative action policies were established.

One might argue that race does not matter for people's lives today as it did during America's antebellum or Jim Crow eras. And therefore, contemporary multiracial churches do not have to be concerned about racial inequality and injustice. This statement is partly true. Important barriers to blacks' freedom have tumbled. But let us consider the broader social context wherein the contemporary multiracial movement is taking place. Racial inequality and segregation persists. Whites and blacks live in separate places. Whites dominate more stable, quality jobs and those with better pay and benefits and greater opportunities for advancement, while blacks are more likely to hold jobs with limited authority, limited prestige, lower pay, and less benefits. The median household income in 2009 for whites was $54,461, compared to $32,584 for blacks. Racial discrimination is still commonplace in a variety of institutions. Landlords and real estate agents are still shown to discriminate systematically against blacks. Employers too are still shown to discriminate against black job applicants even when the only difference is an applicant's perceived race. Blacks are nearly twice as likely to be without healthcare coverage than whites. So, while racialization looks different than it did during the antebellum and Jim Crow eras and blacks are freer than they were in the past, the gulf between the life of the average white American and the average black American remains broad and deep.[26]

Are interracial churches "much ado about nothing?" Not exactly. Symbolism can affect how people see themselves and others. Evangelism can bring more people into a faith. Building cross-racial relationships might reduce racial misunderstandings and prejudice. Yet symbolism, evangelism, and interracial relationships are not what changed our country. None of the major changes to the racialized social structure resulted from multiracial worship.

It was rather social movements led by black and white Christians committed to something much bigger and much more audacious than congregational racial diversity working together to achieve that larger goal. There are calls for evangelicals to be committed to racial justice right now. Sojourners, for instance, is an evangelical organization committed to diversity and racial justice. Its mission is "to articulate the biblical call to social justice, inspiring hope and building a movement to transform individuals, communities, the church, and the world." And it is committed to supporting the inclusion and empowerment of people of color.[27] Still, this voice for a truer racial reconciliation is muffled by the multiracial church movement that affirms and enacts the white evangelical brand of racial reconciliation.

If indeed the goal of multiracial churches is racial reconciliation—including the sharing of power and dispensing of justice that true reconciliation entails—rather than merely acheiving congregational diversity, multiracial churches can follow the example of their more audacious predecessors. Through the cross-racial relationships that multiracial worship can foster, these congregrations can gather their diverse and rich human, social, cultural and financial resources and join together to continue the cause of racial justice.

Notes

1. Andres Tapia and Rodolpho Carrasco, "The Racial Promise: Could the Promise Keepers Be the Beacon of Civil Rights?" *Salon*, October 8, 1997, accessed May 3, 2013, http://www.salon.com/1997/10/09/news_388/; Ted Olsen, "Promise Keepers: Racial Reconciliation Emphasis Intensified" *Christianity Today*, January 6, 1997, accessed May 3, 2013, http://www.christianitytoday.com/ct/1997/january6/7t1067.html; David G. Hackett, "Promise Keepers and the Culture wars," *Religion in the News* 1, no. 1 (1998), http://www.trincoll.edu/depts/csrpl/RIN%20Vol.1No.1/promise_keepers.htm; Michael O. Emerson and Christian Smith, *Divided by Faith: Evangelical Religion and the Problem of Race in America* (New York: Oxford University Press, 2000); John Bartkowski, *The Promise Keepers: Servants, Soldiers and Godly Men* (New Brunswick, NJ: Rutgers University

Press, 2004); Barry Hankins, *Evangelicalism and Fundamentalism: A Documentary Reader*, (New York: New York University Press, 2008).

2. Donald McGavran, *Bridges of God: A Study in the Strategy of Missions* (Eugene, OR: Wipf and Stock, 2005); Ibid., *Understanding Church Growth* (Grand Rapids, MI: Eerdmans, 1990); C. Peter Wagner, *Our Kind of People: The Ethical Dimensions of Church Growth in America* (Atlanta: John Knox Press, 1979); Ibid., *Your Church Can Grow: Seven Vital Signs of a Healthy Church* (Glendale, CA: Regal Books 1983); Charles H. Kraft, "Anthropological Apologetic for the Homogenous Unit Principle in Missiology," *Occasional Bulletin of Missionary Research* 2, no. 4 (1978): 121–126; René C. Padilla, "The Unity of the Church and the Homogeneous Unit Principle," *International Bulletin of Missionary Research* 6, no. 1 (1982): 23–30; David Smith, "The Church Growth Principles of Donald McGavran," *Transformation* 2, no. 2 (1985): 25–30; Peter M. Blau and Joseph E. Schwartz, *Crosscutting Social Circles: Testing a Macrostructural Theory of Intergroup Relations* (Piscataway, NJ: Transaction Publishers, 1997); Peter M. Blau, *Inequality and Heterogeneity: A Primitive Theory of Social Structure* (New York: Free Press, 1977); J. Miller McPherson and Lynn Smith-Lovin, "Homophily in Voluntary Organizations: Status Distance and the Composition of Face-to-Face Groups," *American Sociological Review* 52, no. 3 (1987): 370–379; Pamela Popielarz and J. Miller McPherson, "On the Edge or In Between: Niche Position, Niche Overlap, and the Duration of Voluntary Association Memberships," *American Journal of Sociology* 101, no. 3 (1995): 698–720.

3. Michael O. Emerson, "Managing Racial Diversity: A Movement Toward Multiracial Congregations," paper presented at the annual meeting of the American Sociological Association (San Francisco, California, August 2009).

4. Domenico Parisi, Daniel T.Lichter, and Michael C.Taquino, "Multi-Scale Residential Segregation: Black Exceptionalism and America's Changing Color Line," *Social Forces* 89, no. 3 (2011): 829–852; James S. Lai, Wendy K. Tam Cho, Thomas P. Kim, and Okiyoshi Takeda, "Asian Pacific-American Campaigns, Elections, and Elected Officials," *Political Science and Politics* 34, no. 3 (2001): 611–617; www.census.gov.

5. Milton C. Sernett, ed., *Afro-American Religious History: A Documentary Witness* (Durham, NC: Duke University Press, 1985); W. E. B. Du Bois, *The Negro Church* (reprint, New York: Altamira Press, 2003); Carter Woodson, *The History of the Negro Church* (Washington, DC: Associated Publishers, 1921); James Melvin Washington, *Frustrated Fellowship: The Black Baptist Quest for Social Power* (Macon, GA: Mercer University, 1985); William E. Montgomery, *Under Their Own Vine and Fig Tree: The African American Church in the South 1865–1900* (Baton Rouge: Louisiana State University Press, 1993).; Eric C. Lincoln and Lawrence H. Mamiya, *The Black Church in the African American Experience* (Durham, NC: Duke University Press, 1990); David M. Reimers, *White Protestantism and the Negro* (New York: Oxford University Press, 1965).

6. Reimer, *White Protestantism*.
7. E. Franklin Frazier, *The Negro Church in America* (New York: Schocken, 1964); Peter Randolph, "Plantation Churches: Visible and Invisible," in *Afro-American Religious History*, ed. Sernett, 63–68; Du Bois, *The Negro Church*; Alfred J. Raboteau, *Slave Religion: The "Invisible Institution" in the Antebellum South* (New York: Oxford University Press, 1978); Frazier, *The Negro Church*.
8. Frederick Douglas, *Narrative of the Life of Frederick Douglass* reprint (New York: Penguin Books, 1997); Reimers, *White Protestantism*; Ralph E. Luker, *The Social Gospel in Black and White: American Racial Reform, 1885–1912* (Chapel Hill: University of North Carolina Press, 1991); David L. Chappell, *A Stone of Hope: Prophetic Religion and the Death of Jim Crow* (Chapel Hill: University of North Carolina Press, 2004); James Wood, "Personal Commitment and Organizational Constraint: Church Officials and Racial Integration," *Sociological Analysis* 33, no. 3 (1972) 142–151; James B. Bennett, *Religion and the Rise of Jim Crow in New Orleans* (Princeton, NJ: Princeton University Press, 2005).
9. Reimers, *White Protestantism*.
10. Ibid.
11. "History," accessed January 15, 2013, http://www.allpeoplescc.org/index.php/about/history; Riley Herman Pittman, "Building an Interracial Church," *Sociology and Social Research* 29(1945): 297–303; "Church of All Races," *Ebony Magazine* 3 (1946): 4–5; William Crain, "Editorial: Howard Thurman," *ENCOUNTER: Educating for Meaning and Social Justice* 1(2006): 2–5; Howard Thurman, *Meditations of the Heart* (Boston: Beacon Press, 1953); Howard Thurman, *With Head and Heart: The Autobiography of Howard Thurman* (San Diego, CA: Harvest, Press 1979).
12. Wood, "Personal Commitment," 143; Chappell, *A Stone of Hope*.
13. Chappell, *A Stone of Hope*; Martin Luther King, Jr., *Why We Can't Wait* (Boston: Beacon Press, 1986).
14. Raboteau, *Slave Religion*; Aldon Morris, *The Origins of the Civil Rights Movement: Black Communities Organizing for Change* (New York: Free Press, 1984).
15. 2000 National Congregations Study. This statement is not to say that mainline denominations are not committed to racial diversity in their congregations. At the denominational level, the larger mainline denominations explicitly state support for diversity in their congregations and provide resources to do so. Moreover, some state explicit commitments to racial justice (United Church of Christ is one example). Rather, I imagine, the theology and liturgical culture of mainline denominations are less attractive to people of color who tend to be more theological and socially conservative than most mainline Christians and prefer a less liturgical worship culture.
16. The guide specifically deals with congregational multiculturalism. However, the people featured in photos on the cover and first pages of the guide are of different racial backgrounds. I surmise that the guide also intends to address multi*racial* worship.

17. I had to do some online digging to find *A Guide for Planting Multicultural Churches*. The guide, which is fifteen pages long and was published in 1999, is not currently linked to the SBC main webpage. I could find no indication from the SBC main website that the denomination is committed to multiracial/cultural/ethnic worship. I finally found the guide on a linked website called Church Planting Village (churchplantingvillage.net) that is developed by the North American Missions Board of the SBC. The location of the guide was not immediately obvious on this website.
18. 2000 National Congregations Study.
19. www.census.gov.
20. Manuel Ortiz, "Bruce W. Fong, *Racial Equality in the Church: A Critique of the Homogeneous Unit Principle in Light of a Practical Theology Perspective*," *Christian Scholar's Review* 28, no. 1 (1998): 201–203; Charles R. Foster, *Embracing Diversity: Leadership in Interracial Churches* (Herndon, VA: Alban Institute, 1997); Michael O. Emerson and Karen Chai Kim, "Interracial Congregations: An Analysis of Their Development and a Typology," *Journal for the Scientific Study of Religion* 42, no. 2 (2003): 217–227; George Yancey and Michael Emerson, "Integrated Sundays: An Exploratory Study into the Formation of Multiracial Churches," *Sociological Focus* 36, no. 2 (2003): 111–127; Rodney M. Woo, *The Color of Church: A Biblical and Practical Paradigm for Multiracial Churches* (Nashville, TN: B&H Publishing Group, 2009); Gregory Stanczak, "Strategic Ethnicity: The Construction of Multi-Racial/Multi-Ethnic Religious Community," *Ethnic and Racial Studies* 29, no. 5 (2006): 856–881; Gerardo Marti, *A Mosaic of Believers: Diversity and Innovation in a Multiethnic Church* (Bloomington: Indiana University Press, 2005); Michael O. Emerson and Rodney Woo, *People of the Dream: Multiracial Congregations in the United States* (Princeton, NJ: Princeton University Press, 2006); Pittman, "Building an Interracial Church"; Penny Edgell Becker, "Making Inclusive Communities: Congregations and the 'Problem' of Race," *Social Problems* 45, no. 4 (1998): 451–472; Gladys Ganiel, "Is the Multiracial Congregation an Answer to the Problem of Race? Comparative Perspectives from South Africa and the USA," *Journal of Religion in Africa* 38, no. 3 (2008): 263–283; Elfriede Wedam, "Ethno-Racial Diversity within Indianapolis Congregations," *Research Notes* 2, no. 4 (1999): 4.
21. Becker, "Making Inclusive Communities"; Kathleen E. Jenkins, "Intimate Diversity: The Presentation of Multiculturalism and Multiracialism in a High-Boundary Religious Movement," *Journal for the Scientific Study of Religion* 42, no. 3 (2003): 393–409; Korie L. Edwards, *The Elusive Dream: The Power of Race in Interracial Churches* (New York: Oxford University Press, 2008); Barbara Flagg, "'Was Blind, But Now I See': White Race Consciousness and the Requirement of Discriminatory Intent," *Michigan Law Review* 91 (1993): 953; Ashley W. Doane, "Rethinking Whiteness Studies," in *White Out: The Continuing Significance of Racism*, eds. Ashley W. Doane and Eduardo Bonilla-Silva (New York: Routledge Press, 2003).

22. Wood, "Personal Commitment."
23. Sernett, *Afro-American Religious History*; Frazier, *The Negro Church in America*; Lincoln and Mamiya, *The Black Church*; Morris, *The Origins of the Civil Rights Movement*; Amy Louise Wood, *Lynching and Spectacle: Witnessing Racial Violence in the Jim Crow South 1890–1940* (Chapel Hill: University of North Carolina Press, 2009).
24. Chappell, *A Stone of Hope*; Morris, *The Origins of the Civil Rights Movement*.
25. For an exemplar book on the history of the Underground Railroad, see Fergus M. Bordewich, *Bound for Canaan: The Epic Story of the Underground Railroad, America's First Civil Rights Movement* (New York: Amidstad Publishers, 2006). For an exemplar book on the personal experience of a primary abolitionist movement leader, see Douglas, *The Narrative Life of Frederick Douglas*. For an exemplar book on the civil rights movement, see Harvard Sitkoff, *The Struggle for Black Equality* (New York: Hill and Wang, 2008).
26. Parisi et al., "Multi-Scale Residential Segregation"; Ryan A. Smith, "Race, Gender, and Authority in the Workplace: Theory and Research," *Annual Review of Sociology* 28 (2002): 509–542; "Income, Poverty, and Health Insurance Coverage in the United States: 2009," September 2010, accessed January 15, 2013, http://www.census.gov/prod/2010pubs/p60-238.pdf; Devah Pager and Hana Shepherd, "The Sociology of Discrimination: Racial Discrimination in Employment, Housing, Credit, and Consumer Markets," *Annual Review of Sociology* 34 (2008): 181–209.; Margery Austin Turner, Erin B. Godfrey, and Urban Institute, *Discrimination in Metropolitan Housing Markets: National Results from Phase 1 HDS 2000* Washington, DC: Urban Institute, Department of Housing and Urban Development, http://www.huduser.org/portal/Publications/pdf/Phase1_Report.pdf; Margery Austin Turner and Stephen L. Ross, "How Racial Discrimination Affects the Search for Housing," in *The Geography of Opportunity: Race and Housing Choice in Metropolitan America*, ed. Xavier De Souza Briggs (Washington, DC: Brookings Institution Press, 2005) 81–100; Vincent J. Roscigno, *The Face of Discrimination: How Race and Gender Impact Work and Home Lives* (Lanham, MD: Rowman and Littlefield, 2007); Philip Moss and Chris Tilly, *Stories Employers Tell: Race, Skill and Hiring in America* (New York: Russell Sage Foundation, 2001); Marianne Bertrand and Sendhil Mullainathan, "'Are Emily and Greg More Employable than Lakisha and Jamal?' A Field Experiment on Labor Market Discrimination," *American Economics Review* 94, no. 4 (2004): 991–1013; "Income, Poverty, and Health Insurance Coverage: 2009—Tables and Figures," accessed January 15, 2013, http://www.census.gov/hhes/www/hlthins/data/incpovhlth/2009/tables.html.
27. See Sojourners's website at www.sojo.net.

Theological Afterword

The Call to Blackness in American Christianity

Darryl Scriven

THE EXERCISE OF benevolence is necessary but not sufficient to solve the racial quagmire in which America and its Church find themselves. For too long we have engaged in the abstraction of spiritual and social; accepting the Church as a spiritual institution that might, but need not, surprise us with occasional social activism or pleas for justice. Embarrassingly, this behavior has become normative in many American congregations. But rarely do we annihilate this abstraction by demanding that the Church fulfill its social and biblical responsibility to speak for the voiceless and engage in self-critique to ensure that it does not succumb to the seduction of power. In fact, beyond conceptions of evangelism and benevolence, we are largely unaccustomed to speaking about the "responsibilities" of the Church at all.

In contrast, Jesus's message of solidarity with "the least" in society surpasses benevolence and crosses into the realm of *identification*. In other words, Christ's example through the circumstances of his incarnation suggests that part of what it means to be like Christ is to identify with the most downtrodden, despised, and mistreated in a given society. In the American saga of race, African Americans, while overwhelmingly Christian, remain the least in terms of socioeconomic status, excess deaths, health disparities, infant mortality rates, and ongoing violence against their personhood that intersects the physical, political, psychological, and even theological. Given the reciprocity and empathy demanded by the Golden Rule, I claim that to be aware of the vicious disparities reflected racially within America and to walk simultaneously as a Christian in that context means to identify with "blackness."

What I mean by blackness is that which represents a shared experience of uplift and redemption, marked by unrelenting struggle for equity, justice, dignity, and freedom against the backdrop of racism, segregation, and political violence. Alternatively, "whiteness" functions in American society as a construct of domination and exclusion that only benefits those who consent to its legitimacy. The intent here is not to romanticize, demonize, or essentialize any particular group or faith tradition. Rather the task is to provoke the kind of love that considers the other to the degree that divisive racial advantages would be surrendered as healing sacrifices at the foot of the cross.

It is my contention that Christian discussions of bridging the racial divide in America occur while many evangelicals jointly try to maintain white privilege, much like the young ruler's attempt in the Gospel of Luke to serve God in a setting of abject poverty without relinquishing his riches. Taking a cue from that narrative, I argue that the appropriate Christian response to make meaningful racial progress in America is for evangelicals to move beyond benevolence, surrender the construct of whiteness, and empathetically pursue social justice through the lens of blackness.

Evangelicalism and Whiteness

Evangelicalism is a Protestant Christian tradition with four key commitments: (i) the need for personal conversion or being born again, (ii) the active expression and sharing of the Gospel with non-Christians, (iii) a high regard for biblical authority and (in most cases) biblical inerrancy, and (iv) a primary emphasis on teachings that proclaim the death, burial, and resurrection of Jesus Christ. In this vein, evangelicalism primarily focuses on actively promoting and facilitating the salvific encounter of the individual with divine grace. Still, evangelical theology does have a theoretical framework that lends itself to building community and to social action. Michael Emerson and Christian Smith argued in *Divided by Faith*, "Evangelicals believe in engaged orthodoxy," which they define as "taking the conservative faith beyond the boundaries of the evangelical subculture, and engaging the larger culture and society." This belief then creates space for evangelicals to have dual emphases that combine the spiritual and the social. Accordingly, evangelicalism can be seen as a middle ground between strict, fundamentalist Christian traditions and mainline, liberal

Christian traditions. So, in some sense, evangelicalism is an attempt to reconcile two extremes.[1]

This mediation between traditions may be ideal if the populations concerned are relatively homogenous; that is, they share enough cultural, historical, and social commonality to make their relevant differences trivial. However, in America the notion of race is inescapable when discussing any cultural phenomenon, including religion. The black church and the white church (evangelical or otherwise) are viewed in many quarters as disparate traditions that were created to meet the spiritual needs of their respective congregants. Race is a marker of American society, and one would be hard pressed to find an instance of something that has not been racialized in America to some degree. Therefore, if evangelicals seek reconciliation along racial lines, it is appropriate that we have a discussion of what it has meant to racialize things in the American context, particularly in terms of whiteness, before attempting to understand what must be done to bridge the divide between whites and blacks in the Church and in society.[2]

Whiteness is not a skin color. Whiteness is an idea, a political construct, a notion that grants privilege and power through the imagery of purity, originality, and simply being considered normative. Nevertheless, whiteness is associated with ethnicity and is bestowed upon certain groups while it is withheld from others. In the early twentieth century the term *WASP*— white Anglo-Saxon Protestant—denoted that to be authentically American meant that one had to be caucasian, of Anglo-Saxon ancestry, and possess Protestant Christian membership such that, if one were lacking in any of those characteristics, American identity could be withheld from that person. Even though it is clear that the presumption of being white was an essential feature of being WASP, over time in a racialized environment, what it meant to be WASP was conflated with what it essentially meant to be white.[3]

It is clear from a survey of the American historical landscape that many European immigrant communities displaying epidermal whiteness were, nevertheless, barred from experiencing the status. For instance Irish, Polish, Czechoslovakian, Italian, Jewish, and Catholic immigrants all began their sojourn in America with nonwhite standing. Yet each of these groups gradually became white as they were exposed to, accepted, and participated in whiteness as a point of solidarity and dehumanization of nonwhite people. Whiteness functions as a dominating force that instills privilege upon some while denying it to others. It demands loyalty and even requires that one stand against nonwhites as a sign of membership. So some groups that were once outsiders became white, thus attaining new privilege and power. These groups need not have understood whiteness as primarily an economic construction, with the original function of justifying imperialism, race-based slavery, and mercantile opportunism upon the darker-skinned peoples of the world. But they definitely saw contemporary manifestations of the inner workings of the concept.[4]

In relation to the American church, whiteness is not something divorced from theological underpinnings. Instead, whiteness becomes amalgamated with the orientation and framework in which Christianity is practiced. In that context, Christianity is acculturated and mixed with whiteness but presented in the society as meta-cultural and imperceptibly free from racialized entrapments. In fact, some of the epistemic beauty of whiteness is how it seamlessly blends into its surroundings as if it does not exist. And what is presented is presumed to be, borrowing from C. S. Lewis, "mere" Christianity. Still, such a racialized notion of religion reflects the history and ongoing currents of race in American society. Jesus may be able to save a black soul, but Jesus may be less effective at saving a black body or protecting black rights in an atmosphere of whiteness. While contemporary whiteness in America is more institutionalized and less individually perpetrated through physical acts of violence, it is nevertheless a privileging concept that insulates some and exposes others to dangerous social currents.[5]

As it relates to the Church in America, even the preaching of Jesus is susceptible to the infiltration of whiteness given the historical conduits of xenophobia, chattel slavery, the Civil War, and Jim Crow segregation. This situation explains why some of the most heinous acts of antiblack racism and violence were perpetrated by white Christians of varying denominational stripes. Frederick Douglass powerfully conveys in his autobiography how, before escaping the chains of slavery, his slave master would come home to beat his slaves between Sunday School and morning worship service. Or how professing Christians formed organizations like the Ku Klux Klan, the Army of God, Christian Patriots, and Lambs of Christ to execute those who they deemed undesirable, who engaged in objectionable behavior, or who were considered nonwhite.[6]

To understand the magnitude of these acts is to grasp the breadth of whiteness in America and the amplifying power that Christianity lends to the pernicious practice of exclusion, bias, and even murder of nonwhite Christian Americans. The usual method for a vassal nation to be proselytized as a member of the conquering nation's society was to accept the religion of the captor. David Walker, a nineteenth-century abolitionist and Christian, held biblical Christianity to advocate this practice as a basic derivation of principle. At the very least, he minimally understood Christianity to stipulate fair and equitable relations among its practitioners. Cornel West suggested that social privilege was one of the three main reasons that many blacks embraced Christianity in the eighteenth and nineteenth centuries. In the modern era, groups like the Nation of Islam and the Black Panther Party have argued that whiteness has always co-opted and defined American Christianity to the degree that it is both irrational and self-deprecating for blacks to associate with the Christian Church.[7]

Why Evangelical Attempts at Racial Reconciliation Have Failed

Given the basic tenets of evangelical theology, it makes sense that evangelicals would attempt to resolve racial strife by promoting Christian unity as a renewed proclamation of the Gospel. To do so, evangelicals began wooing African Americans and other persons of color to form mixed race congregations in hopes of modeling the spiritual accord sought in society. Some groups were successful in attracting a substantial increase in multicultural and multiethnic membership such as Lakewood Church in Houston, Texas (Joel Osteen) and Saddleback Church in Lake Forest, California (Rick Warren). Yet on the whole, many evangelical congregations have not been able to achieve a measurable degree of diversity within their flocks. Thus, the question found in the minds of sincere evangelical racial reconcilers is why has the effort to create mixed congregations and tear down racial walls failed?

On the one hand, it is an incredible project for evangelicals to even attempt to overcome racial division and show tangible, corporate fruit of repentance. Further, if there was no historical consciousness driving these moments, the racial reconciliation project would be organic in that it naturally emerges from practical biblical theology when the disposition of Jesus in the Gospels and Paul in certain epistles is considered. Recall the Galatian episode where Peter refuses to eat with Gentile Christians in the presence of Jewish Christians. Paul rebuked Peter's prejudicial behavior as improper, thereby laying the groundwork for an understanding of Christianity as free from cultural, racialized, or ethnic hierarchies. Therefore, no culture group holds more power than any other within the faith and privileging or respecting of persons is forbidden both as a practice and as a mindset.[8]

But on the other hand, one might question what is meant by Christian unity in the face of the monstrous and the atrocious, particularly in light of the systemic and pervasive violence enacted upon people of African descent. So then the question becomes, what counts as Christian unity in an American context for black and white people? The answer seems to be from the evangelical context: the fact that we go to church together. A preference for this definition of unity is borne out in many of the evangelical interviews recorded in *Divided by Faith*. And while I would argue that multicultural churches are measurable indicators of Christian attempts at unity (for sociological purposes they are, in fact, observables that can be statistically documented), it does not strike at the heart of the robust, theological intention that unification be predicated upon principles of cooperative work and responsibility with an understanding of the Divine as calling us to love one another as ourselves. But if going to church together is the farthest that most white evangelicals are willing to go on the Christian unity/racial reconciliation front, then it is not hard to imagine why this approach has not gotten very far when other societal factors remain unchanged.

So why else has the project thus failed? Emerson and Smith provide an answer by relaying white evangelicals' understanding of the cause of economic inequality between races. In their interviews with conservative Protestants, the two sociologists sought to capture evangelical opinion as to why black people, on average, were worse off economically than white people in America. The answers conveyed the following sentiments: (i) everyone has the same opportunities; (ii) if blacks desired the same level as whites, they could achieve it; (iii) many blacks are apathetic and lack industry; and (iv) whites assume laziness and entitlement on the part of African Americans. If these assumptions are the starting point and guttural perspective that characterizes the essence of white evangelical sentiment regarding black people, Christian or otherwise, there is no wonder why such a project labeled as racial reconciliation would fail. Reciprocity of intent and mutuality of understanding are necessary for any historically victimized group to trust the sincerity of their penitent victimizer under any circumstances. Wrapping the request for reconciliation in the name of Jesus does not fundamentally alter the underlying social perception and black feeling of distrust. So the lack of regard for black people as honest, hard-working, and serious about their faith all-the-while having no legitimate political complaints against the prevailing social order is a formidable barrier to healing.[9]

In addition, black folks are not overly impressed by a reconciliation plan interpreted as a call for them to surrender autonomy in the freest place they have known as a group in America. Black people experience too much absence of authority in most workspaces to voluntarily surrender the power they have in the Black church. I recall being connected with a black congregation that was approached by a white congregation within the same denomination about a possible merger. The churches had previously visited each other's services and thoroughly enjoyed the fellowship. Being less than three miles apart, the merger made sense on many levels; including financial prudence, Christian unity, and modeling racial reconciliation. However, when the time came to vote on the merger, questions arose regarding the worship style of the blended fellowship. Being a southern black congregation, one of the congregation's worship style was spirited, high energy, and expressive. The other congregation was also southern but had a more serene and pensive worship-style, marked by periods of silent reflection instead of encores of hearty *amens*. But, by far, the most prolific and persistent query was: "Who will lead?" The hesitation on the black congregation's part was a healthy suspicion that they would be enlarging the flock of our white brethren as members only, not as leaders. Sure enough, the proposal came to appoint the black church's pastor to the leadership council while keeping the white church's pastor, and all other leaders unchanged. No other minister from the black congregation was considered for a leadership position. Needless to say that bill died in chambers and was never revived.[10]

Place in religious spheres is sacred. But to think of place as sacred is committing to think of it as both public and private in a way that sometimes shuts out uncomfortable, social encroachment. Yet the overarching call within the white evangelical notion of church unification is for all of us, white and black, to overcome our proclivities to self-segregate and make the Church into a microcosm of what the world should be. This construction would illustrate, at least in the Church, that racial harmony and reconciliation can be achieved. Still, I would argue that black folks are looking for assurances that ecclesial reconciliation is not the only game plan. From the black church perspective, Sunday morning interracial worship is mostly a symbolic gesture if not combined with mutual cooperation in the face of injustice. Social structures and power differentials that disproportionately bear down upon African Americans are well-documented and still persist today: for instance, unbridled police power, racial profiling, and unjust and uneven sentencing practices as it regards violent crimes and possession of controlled substances that are found in the black community as opposed to those that are largely found in white suburbs.[11]

So we must recognize that this is the lived experience of a people who have a memory that neither cognitively nor emotionally recalls substantive assistance from white evangelicals to ameliorate unjust conditions. Still, without the sacrifices of countless white brothers and sisters, many of the gains and strides for freedom that have been made in the racial context of America would not have been accomplished. So it is not the case that black folks don't understand that white people have been instrumental in bringing about positive social and racial change. But as an organized entity, the black church's understanding of vital, white participation in the struggle for justice and racial equality is not that this participation was ever an outgrowth of white evangelical theology. Further, it is not readily assumed in black church circles that the activity or actors who have personally participated in the struggle for justice and racial equality have come from the white evangelical context. So the pressing question in the reconciliation enterprise from the black church perspective is, "Why should we trust white evangelicals now, since the vast majority have not helped us in the past?" In fact, given the history that Emerson and Smith rehearsed, the white evangelical church has embodied some of the most vicious racial hatred ever to be perpetrated on the American landscape. Moreover, in the modern era, when measures designed to counterbalance some of the injustices that evangelicals had a hand in perpetrating are proposed, the white evangelical church is often one of the staunchest opponents of such measures, touting the mantra of reverse racism.[12]

This situation leads into the third reason that the racial reconciliation project has failed thus far: the notion of Christian unity that white evangelicals hold was not accepted by the African American Christian population and, therefore, not acted upon in the way evangelicals desired. Theological investigation on this point is necessary for greater understanding and would include a survey of the history, activity, construction, methodology, and praxis of the black church. Further, we must access how the black church understands itself, how its congregants broadly understand Christian theology, and what it means to live as a Christian. Many black Christians do not understand themselves as having the need to belong to a mixed or interracial congregation as a display of Christian love and unity. In fact, given the racial climate of America, it has historically been the case that African Americans understand church as a safe space, free from a white-supremacist gaze. If whites are present, it is very clear that they are visiting, in a minority status, not wielding determinative power, and not mirroring the larger society in which blacks have been abused by social hierarchies and antiblack, hegemonic structures. So, for many black Christians, interracial churches do not count as unified churches, at least not until America is more reflective of cooperation between ethnic groups outside of the church walls first—not the other way around.[13]

Thus, in a real sense, Christian theology for African Americans is firmly rooted in the socio-spiritual as opposed to what seems to be the prevailing evangelical idea that the theological precedes, overshadows, and therefore reduces the social to irrelevance. The evangelical claim is that conversion experiences fundamentally transcend barriers of race and class. This notion comes from a certain theological vantage point with hidden class and racial presumptions. Yet unearned privileges of whiteness can both insulate and bar groups from seriously considering racial discrimination. It also leads to opinions that racism, even discussions of race and class, have no place in theological contexts and that all social problems would be eradicated if everyone would humbly place all issues at the feet of Jesus. But here is the rub: black folks already have Jesus and have had Jesus for quite some time. Further, the Jesus that they have advocates liberation, social justice, identifying with the least among us, is sensitive to the plight of women in abusive/patriarchal contexts, and cares deeply for the poor while not stigmatizing them as lazy or shiftless. The Jesus of the black church is a progressive Jesus. Whereas the Jesus of the white evangelical church is a conservative Jesus that is primarily concerned biblical inerrancy, pietistic conduct, and culture war issues.[14]

Still the black church has its own Jesus that it thinks reflects the best of Christianity and the human struggle for liberation. It believes this Jesus, walking in blackness, should be the Jesus that white Christians see in Scripture. This black Jesus would not blame poor people for being poor without interrogating economic structures. Even a cursory scan of the historical record reveals the dehumanizing strategy inflicted upon blacks in America that has led to the current state of affairs. Hegemonic biblical hermeneutics will not work to explain away the complicity of whiteness and white Christians in the plight of black Americans. The bootstrapper Jesus proclaimed by white evangelicals directly contrasts with not only the

Jesus of the black church but also the Jesus who was anointed to preach liberty to the captives and glad tidings to the poor. Not to understand this Jesus is to iterate a different Jesus to a group that is already churched, promoting a "happy amnesia" that suggests we simply forget about the past, let bygones be bygones, and move on from here with a fresh slate in the name of Jesus. But which Jesus would advocate that?[15]

When Michael Emerson and Christian Smith claimed that black and white Christians are "divided by faith," we must ask whether they are actually divided by their idea of "the Faith" and its implications. Perhaps, if the Black church and white evangelicals are generally divided by the idea of what Christian faith is, they are further divided on what actions Christian faith demands as a response. It is clear that the white evangelical notion of the Christian faith is one that calls for conversion, salvation from sin, making disciples, and conquering the world for Jesus. But "winning the world for Christ" in a way that reflects the Christian faith as dominant and Christian language as correct could give some black Christians pause. It is not that many black Christians would at first blush disagree with these claims. In many ways, the black church is as conservative as the white evangelical church. But because black Americans have been exposed to both political and theological domination, renaming, and forced subjugation and compliance, black Christians have come to embrace God as a God of social justice *here and now*. In that light, the idea of reciprocity, toleration, mutual respect, and aid in the face of injustice become tantamount to being a Christian in the black tradition. With that backdrop, barring theological discussions of eternal security, one cannot claim to live as a Christian merely on the name of Jesus alone. Rather one's faith, as stated in James' epistle, is manifested by one's works.[16]

This alternate understanding of faith is what Jacqueline Grant captured in her work, *White Women's Christ and Black Women's Jesus*, in which she argued that there are radically different theological and social notions of who Christ is and what it means to live as a Christian that are informed by racial and gender vantage points. At stake here is a Jesus as protector and sustainer in the face of vicious assaults on black personhood and dignity in contrast to a multicolored, rainbow Jesus who does not focus on black folks in their particularity. The evangelical retort could be that blackness itself is a racialized notion that needs to be surrendered under the ubiquitous shadow of the cross. No doubt some black Christians would and do agree. Nevertheless, the difficult work will be to convince the majority of the black church that this idea is not merely clever speech but a true commitment by white evangelicals to share the lived experience with which black folks grapple on a daily basis. Translation: Unless you can assure me of some solidarity outside the walls of the church—no deal.[17]

The black church position amounts to a call for solidarity externalized and enacted. This imminent demand emerges from the empirical data of the past. It is easy to chastise black people for holding onto the pain of history but appeals for blacks to merely release this pain will not do. Black Christians understand this well. So, first, the rhetorical black questions to white evangelicals are: Where were you? Where were you when Emmett Till was killed? Where were you when Martin Luther King was slain? Where were you when Sixteenth St. Baptist Church was bombed and four baby girls were killed in the blast? Where were you when Amadou Diallo was shot forty-one times and murdered at the hands of a brutal abuse of police power? Where were you when it was proven through DNA evidence that scores of innocent black inmates have been falsely accused and sent to death row or life in prison? Where were you when Klan activity led to lynchings, and vituperative speech in white conservative circles targeting poor black and brown people as lazy, shiftless, and immoral? Where were your bodies and where were your voices crying against the demonic being perpetrated on your black brothers and sisters? Where were you, where are you now, and where will you be in the future?

Such existential questions looming in the mind of black folks create deep suspicion of any evangelical project that appears to be peddling a Jesus that they already have. Second, without allies to weather the storms that black and brown people face daily in America, the frank question becomes: "Why should we trust you?" If the answer is simply that "we share Jesus," then the message rings hollow because we've been sharing Jesus for quite a while now. I am aware that this position sounds cynical and contrary but, unless the starting point is honesty, no meaningful progress can be made. In the same vein, I further contend that the offending party bears most of the obligation to engage and persist in open-handed, conciliatory gestures to pursue reconciliation. In other words, white Christians don't get to say that black Christians seem resistant to reconciliation and that this resistance absolves whites of all Christian duties in the matter. Just as the breach took time, so will the repair. But in the face of that time of wall rebuilding, what will the white evangelical response be? How long will you persist and endure? How long will you pursue reconciliation? How long will you desire for the breach to be repaired? Will you hunger for justice and truth? These are fundamental questions that must be answered as conditions for the possibility of racial reconciliation; especially if white evangelicals are as "well-intentioned" as Emerson and Smith suggested in *Divided by Faith*.[18]

But as is often the case, we find the soliciting congregations to be almost entirely white and invoking the supposition that African Americans bear the burden of coming to evangelicals as an act of coming to Jesus. The invitation is typically for African Americans to come to the white church, which is what makes Emerson's post-*Divided By Faith* work revolutionary. In works such as *United by Faith* and *People of the Dream* Emerson contended that for the reconciliation/multiethnic church project to work, minorities must be heavily represented in key leadership positions and make up a substantial portion of the congregation. This argument is a radical departure from the previous model and constitutes the road less traveled and wrought with weighty, but joyful, sacrifices. Emerson's bold and innovative proposals to accomplish racial reconciliation and bring about meaningful, systemic change defy suppositions of whiteness as the only model to repair black/white relations. Whereas this knowledge is colloquial in the black community, it is rarely externalized by white brothers and sisters. Emerson's personal commitments to the project of racial justice in evangelicalism bolster his scholarship. (See the foreword to this volume.) I am persuaded that he possesses more than a clinical understanding of white-skin privilege and white supremacy because he has taken on the work of bearing in his body the marks of a Christian. There is much social capital invested in the concept of whiteness, and Emerson has divested himself of a portion by speaking plainly against racialized religion, making him one of the blackest white men I know.[19]

Blackness and Reconciliation

Blackness is not a racial designation. Although race can sometimes be a marker of blackness, it need not be. The plight of black people and their collective experience illustrates the framework of blackness. Anyone of any race or nationality can engage in blackness, yet the most vested individuals are always those who have a personal interest in the outcome of racial, class, gender, and spiritual struggle. Blackness is a construction that presupposes solidarity with the downtrodden, the emiserated, the least in society, the dispossessed, the disenfranchised, and those who understand the world from the underside. Quite often these are the poorest among us. They are those who are powerless and have experienced generational subjugation in ways that do not allow them to easily emerge from the cycle. Blackness reflects those whom Jesus said that he came to set free. As such, blackness is the frontier for American Christians because it is a call that reflects what it means to deny oneself, take up one's cross, and follow Christ in a market economy. Consequently, when evangelical efforts toward integration and multiracial churches fail, the unrecognized truth is that in a consumerist culture one cannot simultaneously repair the racial breach among Christians while retaining unearned privilege and embodying a faith that is complicit in the oppression of the population with whom one intends to reconcile. Either one denies him- or herself, or he or she does not. It cannot be both ways.[20]

Then what could it mean to reconcile black and white Christians in a racialized, religious context? One thing that would characterize reconciliation is an overt admission of the kind of privileges gained by participating in whiteness to varying degrees. Again whiteness is more than a biological notion of race. It is a presumption of higher class standing, capacity for intellection, moral high ground, and desirable social ranking in relation to nonwhites. Whiteness is an amalgam of these things and, as a comprehensive concept, has tentacles in every area of life. Church is no exception. So to engage in the project of repentance and reconciliation against whiteness is to form solidarity with the very people that whiteness has victimized. This solidarity is what I call embracing blackness.

In one way, to embrace blackness means to admit the advantages that accompany whiteness. It further means to stand outside the church walls with those persons one is trying to reach, such as in moments of social injustice and social unrest. If it is the case that white evangelicals are serious about substantive fellowship with black people, the black community must be able to trust that evangelicals are really who they present themselves to be. Nothing confirms solidarity like standing with blacks in moments of controversy. This commitment means standing in solidarity to challenge a racialized criminal justice system and staggering healthcare disparities between whites and blacks. Until such double standards among ethnic groups are addressed as a matter of justice and Christian love, trust will continue to be a barrier to reconciliation. Blackness demands that white Christians see themselves consistently in solidarity with black people, refusing to cloak themselves in whiteness or reframe heart issues in terms of politics.

One has to choose an orientation. If the orientation is Christian, then the objectives of Christian unity must be primary. Political conservatism cannot be primary, particularly since Christianity is a revolutionary strain of Judaism that seeks to change or amplify many things about conservative Judaic Orthodoxy. It does not fit with the spirit of biblical tradition for evangelicals to hold a scriptural interpretation that leads them to be conservative concerning direct violations of Scripture to behave justly with one's neighbor as an act of neighbor-self love. I understand that there will be limitations, considering what evangelicals see as foundational tenets of Christianity. But I am not asking evangelicals to condone something immoral. I am asking them to substantively challenge racism and white supremacy in a meaningful way. Neither is this a commitment to valorize all things African American as laudable or praiseworthy. The test of blackness for any construct is whether it seeks to uplift the downtrodden. What it will mean for evangelicals to embrace blackness is to surrender white privilege, which will have political, social, religious, and economic ramifications. These are the costs that need to be counted. Once the decision is made to seek this kind of justice and show this kind of neighbor-self love, a higher understanding is certain and will prevent evangelicals from falling back into the dark waters of ignorance and apathy concerning race relations and religion.

Because of the emphasis on personal salvation, individualism permeates evangelical theology. The notion that one is responsible only for one's own actions is an idea rooted in separateness. In the American context, it reflects a conspicuous selfishness that suggests I am neither responsible for nor accountable to those in my community for actions that I did not personally commit but from which I personally benefit. In other words, I may know that a particular practice, action, or policy is unjust and gives me an unfair advantage over another person or group, but if I did not personally bring about the state of affairs, then I should not be held responsible for either that unjust occurrence or any benefit to me that ensues from the occurrence. This individualism reflects an idea of community defined in a way that is deeply clannish and much like the parochial and bigoted conception of community that Jesus critiques with the parable of the Good Samaritan.[21]

The tenth chapter of Luke is arguably about unusual and untraditional formations of community. As it opens, Jesus sends seventy-two disciples on a journey to find persons who would receive them, as strangers, into their homes. While living off the hospitality of their hosts and eating whatever food is placed before them, the disciples performed miracles and blessed their dwelling with peace. Considering that the orientation of these disciples was Jewish and that they probably observed strict dietary and social association rules, this narrative enlarges the accepted version of religious community to such a degree that the writer employs another parable about community to elucidate the point further. In the next episode, a Pharisee asks Jesus how he can inherit eternal life. Jesus asks what the Mosaic Law says and the man roughly replies, "Love God with everything and love your neighbor as yourself." Jesus agrees but the man retorts, "And who is my neighbor?" This inquiry launched a parable about a Samaritan who has been degraded and treated as a lesser by the very people represented in the wounded person who he helps. The construction and moral of the narrative suggest that our neighbor is the person who needs us the most, one who will likely differ from us by class, race, gender, or geography. This transformative idea of community is instructive when we consider the demands of neighbor-self love to which the embrace of blackness calls us.[22]

When I consider some of the tangible ways that this neighbor-self love can be demonstrated, I think of universal healthcare as an end to the needless suffering and excess deaths of the least among us. I think of a moratorium on the death penalty until we, as a society, can figure out how to stop disproportionately sentencing poor people and minorities to death for similar offenses that receive much more lenient punishments when committed by whites and wealthy defendants. I think of foreign wars in which thousands of poor people are killed as civilian casualties, used as pawns, and sacrificed in an international chess game. I think of domestic violence, human trafficking in the Sudan, and the general mistreatment of women worldwide. I think of civil rights, particularly the vituperative discrimination against gay and lesbian brothers and sisters in the name of pure religion. A stalwart commitment to ameliorating any of these issues will affirm the character traits and spiritual fruit necessary for black Christians to consider seriously white evangelical reconciliation proposals.

I realize evangelicals are willing to go only so far because they see certain issues as antithetical to their understanding of the Christian faith. I also realize that some are not interested in racial reconciliation if it means deep and abiding sacrifice. But love and sacrifice are the joint foundation upon which the justification, reconciliation, and the entire Christian theological revelation is premised. To regard theology as culturally neutral is to misunderstand theology. To regard it as objective or context free is also to misunderstand theology. We cannot pretend to talk about God as if we have access to pure and objective knowledge categories. Rather, we can convey our understanding as an approximation of the Divine as we have come to know it from our evolving perspective. Sincere humility must envelope the project of racial reconciliation, realizing that often a major obstacle preventing racial unity in the Church is an unwillingness to surrender the benefits of whiteness.

I am reminded of that rich young ruler who also asked Jesus what he must do to inherit eternal life. Jesus recounted a few of the Ten Commandments to which the man replied, "I've been keeping those since I was a boy." Jesus rejoined that the man needed only to do one more thing: "Sell everything you have, give it to the poor, and then follow me." The young man's countenance fell and he walked away full of sadness. The subject of that sadness has always puzzled me. It is clear that the young man did not want to relinquish his fortune. But why? Why when faced with a simple directive to achieve ultimate gain would he walk away from it? Why, when he heard that role reversal and identifying with the victimized is a condition to following Jesus, would he resist? Did he not want eternal life? Unlikely. Did he feel that it was not within his power to dispose of what belonged to him? Doubtful. So why, after finding the answer to his question, did he immediately turn his back on the answer and walk away? Why indeed?[23]

Whiteness is intoxicating in the sense that it affects the central nervous system and, consequently, the emotions. To surrender whiteness in a racialized context is to become socially vulnerable in the way that nonwhite persons are. Money can mitigate racism, but it cannot provide absolute protection from its tentacles. Many white people want to play basketball and be *like* Michael Jordan. They don't want to *be* Michael Jordan. Many white people may want to sing *like* Aretha Franklin. But I haven't met any that actually want to *be* Aretha Franklin. Being penniless is frightening but possibly surmountable. Being black in an antiblack context feels both frightening and insurmountable. In a market economy, relinquishing the security of wealth would be unthinkable to a person of means. The young ruler, in hearing Jesus' directive, may have been seized more so by fear than greed or deliberate sin. The sorrow he experienced on his journey home may have been from a lack of courage to reconcile his being with his professed, ultimate concern of eternal life. To frame his dilemma in terms of greed is to oversimplify the motivations of an obviously religious but privileged individual. Notwithstanding, the claim of following Christ and being religious while surrounded by, but unwilling to engage, abject poverty is not only absurd, it is tragic.[24]

By application, the elimination of social ills takes a collective divesting of excess at the individual level. The racial divide in the Church could be overcome in time if whiteness is sacrificed on the altar of Christian discipleship. This sacrifice constitutes denial of the self in a racialized environment. The cross to be taken up is living continually in a state of blackness that trades social entitlement for social justice. Seeking eternal life means to ask what is required by God of the individual in his or her particularity. The answer always involves a form of surrender. For the rich person confronted with this question from the perspective of wealth, the surrender concerns wealth. For men confronted with this question from the perspective of patriarchy, the surrender concerns patriarchy. And for whites confronted with this question from the perspective of whiteness, the surrender concerns whiteness. Whereas the fear that gripped the rich young ruler was an understandable kneejerk reaction to the call of Christ, persisting in disobedience after having discovered what must be done as a minister of reconciliation is social sin. Persisting in whiteness is social sin. Living in blackness through solidarity, identification, collective work, and responsibility with black people to demonstrate seriousness of purpose and commitment to social justice is the practical way to bridge the gulf of Christian disunity. Without trust none of this works, and the initial effort to build trust falls to white evangelicals. This moment calls for courage and decisiveness. "Then he said to all of them: If anyone would come after me, they must deny themselves, and take up their cross daily, and follow me."[25]

Notes

1. Larry Eskridge, "Defining Evangelicalism," 1996, revised 2011, accessed July 10, 2011, http://www.wheaton.edu/isae/defining-evangelicalism; Michael O. Emerson and Christian Smith, *Divided By Faith: Evangelical Religion and the Problem of Race in America* (New York: Oxford University Press, 2000), 3.
2. James Cone, *For My People: Black Theology and the Black Church* (Maryknoll, NY: Orbis Books, 1984).
3. David Roediger, *The Wages of Whiteness: Race and the Making of the American Working Class* (San Francisco: Verso, 1991); Toni Morrison, *Playing in the Dark: Whiteness and the Literary Imagination* (New York: Vintage, 1992); Ruth Frakenberg, *White Women, Race Matters: The Social Construction of Whiteness* (Minneapolis: University of Minnesota Press, 1993).

4. Noel Ignatiev, *How the Irish Became White* (New York: Routledge, 1995); Karen Brodkin, *How Jews Became White Folks: And What That Says About Race in America* (New Brunswick, NJ: Rutgers University Press, 1998).
5. Colin Kidd, *The Forging of Races: Race and Scripture in the Protestant Atlantic World, 1600–2000* (Cambridge: Cambridge University Press, 2006); J.Kameron Carter, *Race: A Theological Account* (New York: Oxford University Press, 2008); Willie James Jennings, *The Christian Imagination: Theology and the Origins of Race* (New Haven, CT: Yale University Press, 2010).
6. Frederick Douglass, *Life and Times of Frederick Douglass* (reprint, Mineola, NY: Dover Publications, 2003).
7. Darryl Scriven, *A Dealer of Old Clothes* (Lanham, MD: Lexington Books, 2007); Cornel West, *Prophesy Deliverance! An Afro-American Revolutionary Christianity* (Philadelphia: Westminster Press, 1982); Elijah Muhammad, *Message to the Blackman in America* (Phoenix, AZ: Secretarius MEMPS Publications, 2009).
8. Galatians 2:11–14 (NIV); Curtiss Paul DeYoung, *Coming Together in the 21st Century: The Bible's Message in an Age of Diversity* (Valley Forge, PA: Judson Press, 2009); Love Sechrest, *Former Jew: Paul and the Dialectics of Race* (New York: T&T Clark International, 2010).
9. Michael O. Emerson and Christian Smith, *Divided By Faith*, 98–102.
10. Kersten Priest and Robert Priest, "Divergent Worship Practices in the Sunday Morning Hour: Analysis of an 'Interracial' Church Merger Attempt," in *This Side of Heaven: Race, Ethnicity, and Christian Faith*, eds. Robert J. Priest and Alvero L. Nieves (New York: Oxford University Press, 2007), 275–292.
11. To this point, in late 2010, evangelical televangelist Pat Robertson critiqued the hypercriminalization of marijuana possession and harsh and mandatory minimum sentencing guidelines imposed upon offenders. He approached the issue from both an intervention and fiscal angle as both an ineffective and costly national expenditure. Robertson also acknowledged that the policy is ruining the lives of many young people. His network, Christian Broadcasting Network felt the need to redact his statement and clarify his stance against illegal drug use. However, they could not edit away the fact that Pat Robertson, a leading spokesman and advocate for whiteness in the ultra-conservative Christian arena, irretrievably displayed a flash of blackness in challenging an unjust power differential. From some of his comments over the years, I never thought I would say this but, "Way to go, Pat!" "Pat Robertson tells '700 Club' Viewers Current Marijuana Laws Should Be Changed," December 23, 2010, accessed December 25, 2010, http://latimesblogs.latimes.com/washington/2010/12/pat-robertson-marijuana.html.
12. Emerson and Smith, *Divided By Faith*, 21–50, 69–92.
13. Korie Edwards, *The Elusive Dream: The Power of Race in Interracial Churches* (New York: Oxford University Press, 2008).
14. Emerson and Smith, *Divided By Faith*, 116.

15. Luke 4:18 (NIV); Stephanie Smallwood, *Saltwater Slavery: A Middle Passage from Africa to American Diaspora* (Cambridge, MA: Harvard University Press, 2008).
16. James 2:14–17 (NIV).
17. Jacquelyn Grant, *White Women's Christ and Black Women's Jesus: Feminist Christology And Womanist Response* (Atlanta: Scholars Press, 1989).
18. Emerson and Smith *Divided By Faith*, 1.
19. See Curtiss Paul DeYoung, Michael Emerson, George Yancey, and Karen Chai Kim, *United by Faith: The Multiracial Congregation as an Answer to the Problem of Race* (New York: Oxford University Press, 2003); and Michael O. Emerson, *People of the Dream: Multiracial Congregations in the United States* (Princeton, NJ: Princeton University Press, 2006). These sentiments on racial reconciliation were also echoed in Emerson's closing remarks at the conference, "Divided by Faith: A Decade Retrospective," Indiana Wesleyan University, October 16, 2010.
20. Luke 9:23 (NIV).
21. Luke 10:25–37 (NIV).
22. Luke 10:1–37 (NIV); Mark 12:30–31 (NIV).
23. Matthew 19:16–30 (NIV); Mark 10:17–31 (NIV); Luke 18:18–30 (NIV).
24. John Francis Kavanaugh, *Following Christ in a Consumer Culture: The Spirituality of Cultural Resistance* (Maryknoll, NY: Orbis Books, 1981).
25. Luke 9:23 (NIV).

Index

African Americans, 4–5, 7, 15–20, 23–24, 26–27, 33, 45–53, 55, 59, 61–65, 72, 74, 77, 82, 101, 107, 109–110, 116, 118–119, 130, 161–162, 167, 169, 172, 180–184, 189, 233, 235, 255, 259–260, 262–263, 266
African Methodist Episcopal Church, 235
Afro-American, 19
Alexander, Fred, 75, 91
Alexander, John, 75, 90
Allen, Richard, 235
American Indian Movement, 84
Amsterdam News, 56
Anabaptist, 103
Argue, Don, 87
Asian Americans, 179, 182, 189
Assemblies of God, 102

Baker, Ray Stannard, 161–165, 168–170
Barnhouse, Donald Gray, 25
Bell, L. Nelson, 28
Bentley, William, 78
Bethel College, 111
Biko, Steve, 82
Bible Institute of Los Angeles (BIOLA), 24
Bill of Rights, 186
Black Belt (Chicago), 48
Black Power, 110

Brown, Bob W., 240–241
Brown v. Board of Education, 22, 33, 72, 171, 174
Buchanan, Henry A., 240–241
Burgmer, J. A., 50

California v. Bakke, 90
Calvin, John, 165
Campus Crusade for Christ, 192
Carnell, E. J., 16
Carroll, Charles, 170–171
Carter, Jimmy, 79
Catholic Worker, 54
"Chicago Declaration of Social Concern," 76, 89
Chicago Defender, 19
Chicago Sun, 56
"Christ in the Negro," 45–46, 61–62
Christian Century, 24
Christian Life (CL), 23, 33
Christian Life & Times (CL&T), 18
Christianity Today (CT), 3, 27–28
Civil Rights Act of 1964, 79, 181
Civil Rights Movement, 3, 24, 59, 75, 85, 180, 238–241, 247, 249
Civil War, 165, 236
Clapp, Rodney, 86
Clinton, Bill, 87

Cold War, 83
Collum, Danny, 80, 93
Committee Against the Extension of Race Prejudice, 55 (see also Federated Colored Catholics)
Communist Party, 54
Cone, James, 81, 93
Cullen, Countee, 59
Curse of Canaan, 172 (see also Curse of Ham)
Curse of Ham, 29–30, 172

de Hueck, Catherine, 45, 56, 58–59, 61, 63–65
Daily Worker, 54
Day, Dorothy, 54
Diallo, Amadou, 265
Durkheim, Emile, 158

Ebony, 238–239
Emerson, Michael, xii, 72, 88, 91, 94, 101, 128, 130, 136–137, 143–144, 166, 168–169, 178, 181–182, 193, 240, 242, 256, 264
  and *Divided by Faith*, 2–5, 47, 72, 88, 100–102, 115, 119, 129, 143, 162–163, 168–169, 178, 181–182, 205–206, 232, 234, 256, 260
  and *People of the Dream*, xii, 266
  and *United by Faith*, xii, 266
Eternity, 25
Evangelicalism, 128
  and accountable freewill individualism, 130, 137, 179
  and antistructuralism, 130, 179, 221
  and evangelism, 208–216, 218, 221
  and individualism, 164
  and relationalism, 130, 133, 221
  and white evangelical toolkit, 128–129, 136

Evangelicals for Social Action (ESA), 73–74, 76, 83–85, 90, 93
Evans, Tony, 128–129

Falls, Arthur, 55
Falwell, Jerry, 80
Federal Bureau of Investigation, 84
Federated Colored Catholics, 55
Fellowship Church of All Peoples, 238
Finney, Charles, 102
Fisk, Dr. Alfred, 238, 241
Foreman, James, 110
Frazier, E. Franklin, 167
Freedom Now, 74–94
Friendship House, 46–47, 57, 59–60, 62–66
Fuller Theological Seminary, 104

Gandhi, 238
General Social Survey (GSS), 130–132, 139
Genung, Daniel, 238
Graham, Billy, 17, 20, 30, 33, 102, 104
Great Depression, 47, 54, 77
Great Migration, 48

Harding, Rosemarie, 81, 105
Harding, Vincent, 81, 93, 100, 105, 107–108, 116
Harlem Renaissance, 59
Harrigan, Ann, 45, 56–57, 60–61, 63–65
Henry, Carl F. H., 16, 18, 28
HIS, 18, 31
Horner, George, 18
Howard University, 238
Hybels, Bill, 1, 3

Immigration, 185, 195–199
Immigration Act of 1924, 48, 181

Interracialism, 113
  and evangelicalism, 165
  and friendships, 207–216, 221, 224
  and heterosexual marriage, 171–172
  and ministry, 113
  and Roman Catholic Church, 46–47, 59
  and worship, 170
Intervarsity Christian Fellowship, 18, 192
Ireland, John, 236

Jim Crow, 24–25, 66, 182, 214, 239, 244, 247–249
Johnson, James Weldon, 59
Johnson, Lyndon, 77
Jones, Absalom, 235

King, Coretta Scott, 81
King, Rodney, 85
King, Jr., Martin Luther, 74, 88, 92, 110, 178, 238, 265
Krehbiel, Ron, 100, 104–106, 116
Ku Klux Klan, 165, 258

LaFarge, John, 55
Latinos, 182, 189
Lewis, C. S., 258
Liberty, 56
Life, 18, 25
Lindsell, Harold, 26
Loving v. Virginia, 174
Luce, Henry, 18
Luter, Fred, 2

Malcolm X, 81
Markoe, William, 55
McGreevy, John, 48
McKay, Claude, 59
Megachurches, 232
Moody Church, ix
Moody Monthly, 18

Moral Majority, 80
Multiracial congregations, 179, 181, 184, 189, 193, 198–199, 206, 213–214, 232, 235, 239, 243, 247–248
Mundelein, George, 50–53, 66
Myrdal, Gunnar, 120
Mystical Body, 57–60, 66

National Asian American Survey (NAAS), 187, 189
National Association for the Advancement of Colored People (NAACP), 16, 22
National Association of Evangelicals (NAE), 16, 18, 20, 23, 33, 87, 104
  and Social Action Committee, 21
National Black Evangelical Association, 78
National Congregations Study, 205
Native Americans, 84, 182
New Deal, 57
Nottage, B. M., 26

Ockenga, Harold, 16
Olson, Mark, 78
Osteen, Joel, 259

Pannell, Bill, 78, 81
Parks, Rosa, 22
Perkins, John, 1–2, 72, 78, 81, 128–129
Pew Research Center, 187
Piper, John, 1
Pittsburgh Courier, 19
Plymouth Brethren, 92
Pope Leo XIII, 54
Portrait of American Life Survey, 225
Post-American, 74–94
Potter, Ron, 77
Presbyterian Church, United States of America, 146

Prism, 91
Promise Keepers, x, 34, 87, 128–129, 231–232, 234

Racial reconciliation, 221, 232
Reagan, Ronald, 73, 79–80, 82–83
Reconstruction, 165
Relationalism, 120
Religious Right, 73, 86
Rerum Novarum, 54
Rivers, Eugene, 87
Roosevelt, Franklin, 20

Sankey, Ira, 166
Selma March, 16
Sider, Ron, 73, 92
Simons, Menno, 103–104
Simpson, Nicole Brown, 86
Simpson, O. J., 86
Singer, C. Gregg, 20
Skinner, Tom, 73, 78
Smalley, William A, 18
Smith, Christian, 2, 72–73, 88, 91, 94, 101, 128, 130, 136–137, 143–144, 166, 168–169, 178, 193, 240, 242, 256, 264
    conversion to Roman Catholicism, 11 n. 7
Social Gospel, 16
Sojourners, 72–94 (*see also* *Post-American*)
South Africa, 82–83

Southern Baptist Convention (SBC), 2, 23, 146, 236, 244–245

Tarry, Ellen, 46, 61, 63–65
The King's Business (TKB), 24–25, 33
The Other Side, 74–94 (*see also* *Freedom Now*)
Thurman, Howard, 238, 241–242
Till, Emmett, 22, 24–25
Trinity Evangelical Divinity School, 76
Trulear, Harold Dean, 88
Truman, Harry, 20, 171

United Evangelical Action (UEA), 20, 30
University of Chicago, 105
University of Chicago Divinity School, 236

Vatican II, 57
Vietnam War, 76
Voting Rights Act of 1965, 79

Walker, David, 259
Wallis, Jim, 73, 76, 78, 80–82, 89–91, 94
Warren, Rick, 259
Washington, Booker T., 25
Wheaton College, 15, 104
Whiteness, 167, 246, 256–271
Wilson, William Julius, 77
Woodson, Carter G., 168
World War II, 47, 50
Wright, Richard, 59